The World, the Work, and the West
of W.H.D. Koerner

THE WORLD
THE WORK
AND
THE WEST
OF
W.H.D.KOERNER

BY W. H. HUTCHINSON

UNIVERSITY OF OKLAHOMA PRESS

Books by W. H. Hutchinson

The Little World Waddies, editor (Carl Hertzog, El Paso, 1946)
Songs of the University Club, editor (San Francisco, 1947)
A Notebook of the Old West (Chico, California, 1948)
One Man's West (Chico, California, 1949)
Another Notebook of the Old West (Chico, California, 1951)
A Bar Cross Man: The Life and Personal Writings of Eugene Manlove Rhodes (Norman, 1956)
The Rhodes Reader, editor (Norman, 1957; revised edition, 1975)
A Bar Cross Liar: A Bibliography of Eugene Manlove Rhodes . . . (Stillwater, Oklahoma, 1958)
Pacific Panorama (Chico, California, 1958)
California Heritage, A History of Northern California Lumbering (Chico, California, 1958; revised edition, Forest History Society, Santa Cruz, California, 1974)
Oil, Land, and Politics (Norman, 1965)
Another Verdict for Oliver Lee (Clarendon, Texas, 1965)
Whiskey Jim and a Kid Named Billie, with R. N. Mullin (Clarendon, Texas, 1967)
California: Two Centuries of Man, Land, and Growth in the Golden State (Palo Alto, California, 1969)

Library of Congress Cataloging in Publication Data

Hutchinson, William Henry, 1910–
   The world, the work, and the West of W. H. D. Koerner

   Bibliography: p. 234
   Includes index.
   1. Koerner, William Henry Dethlef.   2. Illustrators
—United States—Biography.   3. The West in art.
I. Title.
NC975.5.K63H87   741'.092'4 [B]   78-58125
ISBN 0-8061-1471-1

For Clarence F. McIntosh
whose integrity, dedication, kindness and demand for excellence in the teaching of history have enhanced my satisfaction at spending some latter years of a not uninteresting life as a leaf raker in the Sacred Groves he tends so well.

ACKNOWLEDGMENTS

THROUGHOUT the long gestation period of this book, many kindly souls have soothed my anxieties and gratified my pickle-craving whims. Many of my debts and my borrowings have been noted in end-of-chapter notes and bibliography, but there are those whose kindnesses are not to be acknowledged in such wise.

Without the whole-souled cooperation of the descendants of W.H.D. Koerner, and the freedom of interpretation they afforded, this book would not have been possible. For gracious hospitality long extended, I owe a debt not to be whittled at with words to Fallis L. and Ruth Koerner Oliver, Santa Barbara, California.

A Chancellor's Creative Leave from the California State University and Colleges system as well as a one-semester sabbatical from my own school were of major assistance, as were the support services provided by the Department of History. I have especial obligations to Gene M. Gressley, University of Wyoming, and to Michael Harrison, Fair Oaks, California, for permitting me to forage at will in the warehouses of their knowledge, and Robert M. Utley, National Park Service, provided essential background to the Wright Brothers Memorial at Kitty Hawk, North Carolina. My colleague, Joanna Cowden, did me the service of reading the manuscript, which benefitted accordingly, while Al-bert H. Bowers and the Clinton County Historical Society provided background on the community wherein "Will" Koerner spent his youthful years.

Noelle Jackson of the Henry E. Huntington Library and Charlotte Harriss of the California State Library were pillars of research strength, while I was fortunate again to have the advice and assistance of John Barr Tompkins before his retirement from the Bancroft Library at Berkeley. Harold W. Ryan foraged in the Library of Congress on my behalf and Frances Orkin did the same in the New York Public Library. Without the help of Jacqueline Hall, Leatrice Yonker, and Michael Wilson, all former students of mine, certain foundations of this book would have been laid upon sand. Ellen Rockwell, Rosemary Augustine, Mary Bock, and Christine Spencer did yeoman service in transforming my hentracked drafts into manuscript copy.

As has been so for more than thirty years, *La Colorada Brava* made the writing possible. The omissions, commissions, and infelicities herein are mine own.

W. H. HUTCHINSON

California State University, Chico
13 August, 1977

CONTENTS

ILLUSTRATIONS

Unless indicated by legend, caption, text, or otherwise, all the photographs and illustrations herein are from the Koerner family collection and all reproductions of W.H.D. Koerner art are from the Koerner Studio Collection, which has retained reproduction rights to works sold from it into private collections.

The World, the Work, and the West
of W.H.D. Koerner

Chapter I
"EET EES WEETH REASON TO DO THEES"

AMONG "BIG BILL" KOERNER's more than 2,400 illustrations were those that illumined Eugene M. Rhodes's classic of the cow country, *Pasó Por Aquí*, later one of the most anthologized of all western stories.[1] In this novella, Rhodes entrusted the task of explaining the continuity of the generations in New Mexico to Rosalio Marquez, a professional gambler called Monte from his speciality.

". . . *Well, eet ees good camp ground, El Morro* [Inscription Rock], *wood and water, and thees gr-reat cleef for shade and for shelter een estr-rong winds. And here some fellow he come and he cry out, 'Adiós, el mundo! What lar-rge weel-dernees ees thees! And me, I go now eento thees beeg lonesome, and perhaps I shall not to r-return! Bueno, pues, I mek now for me a gravestone!' and so he mek on that beeg rock weeth hees dagger, 'Pasó por aquí, Don Fulano de Tal'—passed by here, Meester So-and-So—weeth the year of eet.*

"*And after heem come others to El Morro—so few, so far from Spain. They see what he ees write there, and they say, 'Con Razón!'—eet ees weeth reason to do thees. An' they also mek eenscreepción, 'Pasó por aquí'"—and their names, and the year of eet.*"

Biographical and bibliographical research into Rhodes's life inevitably required initial attention to Koerner's illustrations, and now, many years later, "eet ees weeth reason" that this book on the world, the work, and the West of W.H.D. Koerner has come to pass. The approach has been that of a man who wished to know more

about what had informed and entertained him in his youth and abided with him thereafter. Thus this is one man's book about another man's influence in creating the images of our national experience, with special attention to that last brief spasm in our three centuries of restless westering that gave us the folk hero of *all* our westering, the cowboy and the West he rode.

Koerner was among the most versatile in story competence, possibly the most productive, and, from the evidence in his papers, the most dependable of the great magazine illustrators when the mass-circulation magazines were the television screens of their day and their advertisements were the commercials. For example, the writings and illustrations of Ernest Thompson Seton during the first decade of this century were the equivalent of television's "Wild Kingdom" today.

Koerner's most productive years, 1910–35, were part of a significant cultural era that included the close of the Golden Age of American Illustration, 1880–1914,[2] most of what Jeff C. Dykes has called the Golden Age of Western Illustrating, 1888–1938, and most of what I long ago termed the Golden Age of American Popular Fiction, 1910–41.

The first of these was a period, as J. C. Furnas has noted, ". . . when who did the illustrations for popular fiction was almost as important as who wrote it."[3] That this is not as illogical as it may seem today is attested by four articles on "The Great Southwest" by Ray S. Baker, later to win fame as a muckraking journalist, that were illustrated by Maxfield Parrish.[4] The landscapes glowed with color from the special Parrish palette but the cowboys and horses were wooden figures. The most famous illustrator of this period, Charles Dana Gibson, provided the illustrations for Rex Beach's serial "Heart of the Sunset," a Tex-Mex Border action-romance.[5] The heroine was suitably Gibson Girl-ish, even in a riding habit, while the Texas Ranger hero was given a Baden-Powell hat, leather puttees, and choke-bored riding breeches. But Gibson's name on the cover would sell copies which is what the editors intended it to do.

The Golden Age of Western Illustrating began with Frederic Remington, who dominated it until his death in 1909. It was Remington, first in the taste-making magazines such as *Harper's Monthly,* and then in *Collier's,* who gave the magazine-reading public its first dramatic images of the vanished West.[6] Charles M. Russell, despite his clique of cultists today, did not influence the popular images of the West to any such extent as did Remington, although it is considered that he did influence other artists in their depictions of it. Other than Remington in the years preceding America's entry into World War I, and contributing the most to western illustrating in the mass-circulation magazines, were such as George Gibbs, Jay Hambidge, Gayle Porter Hoskins, Martin Justice, J. N. Marchand, L. Maynard Dixon, P. R. Goodwin, in whom the Russell influence was evident, and W. H. "Buck" Dunton, who was closer to Remington. N. C. Wyeth contributed briefly to the western scene and its symbols after 1906, and Harvey T. Dunn hit his peak in western illustrating, following Wyeth, in these pre-World War I years and thereafter did more teaching than illustrating.

It was in the post-World War I years that western illustrating in the mass-circulation magazines, fertilizing and being cross-fertilized by Hollywood, bequeathed the imagery and iconography that have dominated the popular conceptions of the West-That-Was ever since. F. B. Hoffman, Douglas Duer, Mead Schaeffer, Clark Fay, J. Clinton Sheperd, Matt and Benton Clark, Albin Henning, H. M. Stoops, and Harold Von Schmidt were prolific illustrators of western material in this period. Will James hit the mass-circulation magazines with the impact of a primitive activist in the middle-twenties, while Ross Santee brought them his almost calligraphic brush work and his awareness of the immensity of space that was the West. Both men did their best work in illustrating their own material.

In this post-World War I period, appearing mainly in the *Saturday Evening Post* as its circulation climbed to 3,000,000 copies weekly, Koerner produced more than five hundred illustrations of western scenes and people in fifteen years. The authors he illustrated were among the best who wrote about the West: Emerson Hough, Stewart Edward White, Zane Grey, Eugene Manlove Rhodes, Oliver La Farge, Henry H. Knibbs, Will L. Comfort, Hal G. Evarts, C. E. Scoggins, Ben Ames Williams, and three outstanding novelists who dealt with the West in their own especial ways upon occasion: Martha Ostenso, Rose Wilder Lane, and Mary Roberts Rinehart. If it be true, as Henry Nash Smith has said about "Buffalo Bill," that "the *persona* created by the writers of popular fiction were so accurate an expression of demands of popular imagination that it proved powerful enough to shape an actual man in its own image," then must we give credit to the illustrators for enabling the readers to *see* what otherwise only could be imagined from the authors' words.

The collaboration between author and illustrator transcended the field of western illustrating to illuminate the entire spectrum of the Golden Age of American Popular Fiction. For most of Koerner's productive life, reading was the primary amusement of the American people, and nowhere else in the world were there so many magazines or so diverse a clientele of magazine buyers and readers. It can be suggested firmly that, in this period, the mass-circulation magazines, the so-called "slicks," were the central fixtures of American culture. This was a popular culture, the despair of all right-minded intellectuals and esthetes, but it was valid and the magazines, beginning with *Mc-Clure's* in 1893, virtually created it, certainly perpetuated it, and definitely expanded its appeals. These magazines brought better reading, more information, and finer visual appeal to more people at less cost than at any other time or place in the world's literary history.

Some simple arithmetical calculations are germane to the emphasis placed upon magazines rather than upon books. *The Virginian* sold upwards of 300,000 copies during its first two years of publication, 1902–1904. When Wister's two-part story "With Malice Aforethought," in which the Virginian's imminent marriage to Molly is delayed temporarily by his "walkdown" with Trampas, appeared in *Saturday Evening Post* (5/3–10/1902), that magazine had a circulation approaching 400,000 copies with an average of three readers per copy, thus reaching a weekly audience exceeding 1,000,000 readers. It is admitted cheerfully that the life of a hard-bound book is longer than that of a magazine, but the point to be remembered is that the visual impact of magazine illustrations carried over into the more durable medium. It should be noted, too, that one short story or serial installment in a magazine often carried more illustrations than did a whole book, and that the book illustrations were commonly those that had appeared previously in the magazine. This was especially true of the western story in its formative years, 1900–12. Even after book illustrations became little more than a frontispiece and a gaudy dust jacket, between 1912–15, this was no barrier to continuation of the visual imagery because the images had been established in the magazine for whatever other medium the story assumed.

Let us note that two illustrators, Sidney Paget in England and Frederick Dorr Steele in this country, forever fixed the visual image of Sherlock Holmes, with his fore-and-aft cap, curvilinear pipe, and other accoutrements. In like vein did Anton Otto Fischer and later Von Schmidt so depict Tugboat Annie in her innumerable magazine appearances that Marie Dressler could not depart from her on film. Those millions who listened avidly to "Amos and Andy" in the halcyon days of radio entertainment had their images of the various characters ready made in the illustrations that J. J. Gould had supplied over many years for the urban "darky" stories by Octavus Roy Cohen and Hugh Wiley.

In the collaboration between illustrator and author, never should the illustrator interpose his interpretation between the author and his readers. There were illustrators who did so; Remington most blatantly. In illustrating more than nine hundred articles, short stories, and serial installments, Koerner interpreted what the author meant and did it without giving away the story or detracting from it, but enhancing it. This is no small feat.

The question legitimately may be raised of why Koerner, until recently, has been so little

known and even less recognized. One answer is to be found in the peculiar canons by which artists, art critics, and art collectors, be they competent or self-anointed, distinguish between illustrators and those who do "easel painting." To such as these, the fact that Koerner did illustration, first, last, and all the time, with his easel painting being done for his own relaxation, education, and amusement, brands him as "impure" in their eyes. In this regard, it is apt to note the adjuration of Frank Luther Mott that "Art criticism is a field from which the dogmatist should be barred,"[7] and to note further that for Koerner, even as for Winslow Homer and Remington, illustration was a vivid form of art and he gave his best to it. In every sense, he fulfilled Pruett A. Carter's dictum that the illustrator "must know his characters—their emotions and desires—he must set the stage and direct the conflict of drama. He must do the scenery, design the costumes, and handle the lighting effects. . . . he must make his characters breathe and react as the author intended."[8] Koerner did. What is most relevant to this matter finally comes down to the question whether the illustrator was or was not a good artist? Koerner was.

Another reason for the neglect of Koerner stems from another foible in the realm of art with the capital A, which is an invidious distinction between those who illustrate books and those whose work is done primarily for magazines. It is impossible to find a serious discussion of magazine illustrators and their works, although it is comparatively easy to locate learned disquisitions on book illustrators and their works. Perhaps the greatest boost to N. C. Wyeth's distinguished career, and certainly a tremendous factor in his popular acclaim, was the steady procession of Christmas books, primarily for children, that he illustrated year after year for Scribner's and other major houses.

The classics of Robert Louis Stevenson,[9] plus Jules Verne, plus *Scottish Chiefs* and *Robinson Crusoe*, plus *The Last of the Mohicans*, guaranteed Wyeth a new audience every six to eight years as a new crop of youngsters made a new market for these books.[10] These books also used color plates and it was not often before 1920 that an illustrator had his work reproduced in such lavish color as was given to these publishers' equivalents of a best-selling cookbook in terms of steady sales. Koerner was not readily available to book publishers because, at the height of his career, he did not want to be; he was busy—tremendously engaged in doing what he wanted to do—without book work. While he did illustrate fifty books in his career, a number entitling him to canonization by the standards cultists apply to their favorite Artists, only fourteen of these contained original work done specifically for the books in which they appeared.

Worse possibly than the bar sinister of being a magazine illustrator was the fact that more than one-half of Koerner's total output was done for the *Saturday Evening Post*; for the last five years of his productive life, he illustrated for no other magazine. This was the ultimate damnation for both writers and artists in the eyes of the post–World War I cognoscenti and moved Bernard DeVoto to wry comment, paraphrasing Dr. Johnson, to the general effect that there were two classes of writers who did not write for the *Post:* those who could not and those who had a satisfactory income from other sources.[11] The same applies to the illustrators of this period, because George Horace Lorimer, the five-button mandarin of the *Post*, insisted on verisimilitude in his magazine's artwork as he did in its editorial content, and he permitted neither writers nor artists to load their dice when they appeared in its pages. Lorimer was a man of monumental integrity; so, too, was Koerner, who, in the words of Oscar Helmer Ericson, "never cheated himself."[12]

Almost three-quarters of Koerner's work was done for magazines that were not based in New York, which made him independent, especially in his latter years, of the New York literary and artistic cliques, almost incestuous in their intermingling, that believed that they and they alone were the glittering jewels in the very navel of the universe. While his outlets made him independent of New York, they also removed him from the possibility of acquiring fame by being obsequiously present in its centers, where success was regarded as a goal and not as a result. As John Fischer later would say about Mark Rothko,[13] Koerner had no ties to the world of art critics, museum curators, collectors, or fashionable painters. Where Rothko actively distrusted people of this ilk, Koerner did not need them. He was versatile, vigorous, productive, and dependable—as dependable as the due date

on an unpaid note—and his life was filled thereby. This makes another and a salient reason for his neglect both in his time and later, although it must be noted that counterfeit Koerner paintings have made their appearance in the little world he shunned by choice.

Had Koerner's ties with the *Post* not been so close, both professionally and personally, he might have been better known as an artist in his own time. Beginning in 1915, Koerner began to do many of his illustrations, even though they were for black-and-white reproduction, in full color—in oil, charcoal, watercolor, crayon, and the combinations of all he used so well. From 1922 until he could no longer paint, he used color exclusively unless specifically commissioned to provide pen-and-ink or charcoal work. Unfortunately, the *Post* used no color inside the magazine and only two-color covers, albeit the techniques of printing created the impression of three or more colors, until 1926. Then the *Post* went to four-color covers and some color inside, but never in such array as to do Koerner's palette justice until it was too late. Remembering the color treatment given Von Schmidt's *Post* work in the years after Koerner's death, it *is* unfortunate that he could not have had similar treatment. He would have been better known and his use of color recognized in his lifetime.

Koerner was never identified with specific types, as was Charles Dana Gibson with his famous Girl for classical example, or A. B. Frost with his Uncle Remus characters, or Henry J. Soulen with his opulent oriental illustrations. Neither was he identified with specific and popular characters, as Paul Meylan was identified with Clarence Budington Kelland's Scattergood Baines, a lineal descendant of Joseph Jefferson's stage character Rip Van Winkle—"honest, shrewd, sentimental, independent and possessed of a heart of gold"—and as Tony Sarg became identified with the interminable succession of "Earthworm Tractor" stories by William Hazlett Upson in the *Post*.[14]

Koerner was a working artist and he turned his hand and eye and heart and imagination to whatever came his way, from the works of Achmed Abdullah to I.A.R. Wylie, not forgetting Thomas Beer, William Faulkner, Joseph Hergesheimer, and J. P. Marquand in between.

He worked by choice in the outdoor-action school of American popular fiction; most of all, in its western genres. After 1915 he refused to accept "pink tea," or "pretty girl," or "society," or "urban" stories unless he had spare time or economic necessity absolutely demanded their acceptance. The stories he did by choice and the manner in which he illustrated them reflect a man of a quiet and a private competence; a simple man, perhaps, but simple only in the sense that he believed in the eternal verities of life as he knew them: truth, honor, valor and communion with God, fortitude and magnanim-ity. A man whose subtleties were in his paintings.

Ultimately, an artist must be judged on what he chose to do. Koerner chose to be an illustrator. Then, past middle years, he chose so far as the exigencies of his profession permitted, to concentrate upon the West. It is on these choices, and only these, that this book seeks to present the world, the work, and the West of "Big Bill" Koerner. The judgments, if such be needed, of both artist and writer must be yours.

1. Reprinted, University of Oklahoma Press, 1973, with the original illustrations.

2. Francis W. Browne said of the magazines of this period, ". . . much of their text appears to exist only for the sake of the pictures." *Dial*, 10/1/1892, 204.

3. J. C. Furnas, *The Americans: A Social History of the United States, 1587–1914*, 876.

4. *Century*, 5/1902 *et seq.*

5. *Hearst's International Magazine*, 5/1915 *et seq.*

6. Generally in this book the popular names, rather than the full and formal titles, of magazines are used.

7. Frank Luther Mott, *A History of American Magazines*, IV, 144; cited hereafter as Mott, *Magazines.*

8. Walt Reed (ed.), *The Artist in America*, 122.

9. N. C. Wyeth, *The Wyeths* (ed. Betsy James Wyeth), 389, states that he received $2,500 from Scribner's for the seventeen *Treasure Island* canvasses.

10. Unlike many illustrators, including the great Howard Pyle, Koerner did no work for the boy's magazines, *St. Nicholas, American Boy, Boy's Life,* and *Youth's Companion,* which was an excellent way to achieve early recognition by later adult readers.

11. "Writing for Money," *Saturday Review of Literature,* 10/9/1937.

12. Interview, Santa Barbara, California, 4/25/1970. Mr. Ericson, born in Sweden and trained there as a copyist, cleaned all of the Koerner work exhibited to date, and has cleaned and restored works by such as Van Gogh, Picasso, Remington, Russell, and Borein.

13. *Harper's,* 7/1970, 16.

14. Russell Nye, *The Unembarrassed Muse: The Popular Arts in America,* 150.

Chapter II
AN IMMIGRANT IN IOWA

THE RECORDS of the Evangelical Lutheran Church in his birthplace show that he was born on November 19, 1878, in the village of Lunden, Holstein, and was baptized on December 16, 1878, as Detlev Heinrich Wilhelm Körner. He and his year-younger sister, Auguste Margaretha Wilhelmine, were the only ones of the at least seven children born to Hans Henning Wilhelm Körner and Anna Margaretha Wilhelms to survive infancy and accompany their parents to the New World. His father, who used tobacco but shunned alcohol, was then a thirty-one-year-old *schumacher meister* (master cobbler), who had served in the Franco-Prussian War as a cavalry officer; his decorations, including the Iron Cross of unknown class, were buried with him in his adopted land. His mother was two years his father's senior, a woman of limited education but indomitable will, who spoke her native tongue by choice until she died and invariably wrote her only surviving son in German, using the self-addressed envelopes with which he kept her supplied after he had gone out into the world on his own.

Why the family decided to leave their homeland remains unclear. Herr Körner's aversion to eventual enforced military service for his only surviving son appears to have been a factor. Another influence was one that prompted many another to shed the Old World's past: letters from Herr Körner's older sister, who with her husband, had settled somewhere in Indiana. Early in 1881, the family took passage at Hamburg for the Atlantic crossing, during which, by family tradition, the last child in the family, an infant daughter, died and was buried at sea.

What happened after their arrival in New York was reconstructed years later by their only daughter-in-law:

They took the train to Indiana where Father Koerner expected his sister to meet them at the station. He knew that she would come, even though they had been delayed by rough weather in reaching New York. All day they waited at the depot; standing together with their feather beds enclosing a wall clock, their clothes and a few blankets. Finally a man with milk cans in his wagon drove up. He recognized the sister's name and told Father Koerner that his sister had died two weeks before and that her husband and his family were in very poor circumstances. He said that he could not take them there but that they could sleep in an abandoned school house nearby. The next day Father Koerner got permission to live in the school house and got a few odd jobs mending shoes. Then, when he had earned enough money, the family pushed on to Clinton, Iowa, where other German immigrants had settled.[1] [In 1880, the German Society of Clinton numbered 85 members and owned its own gymnasium, theater, and schoolroom.]

The family's move to Clinton made them statistics in that city's growth from 9,052 in 1880 to 12,012 in 1885. Situated on the west bank of the Mississippi River opposite Fulton, Illinois, whence a ferry had transported argonauts bound for the California Gold Rush, it had been re-incorporated in the year of the Koerners' arrival and was the county seat of Clinton County. It was also either on its way to becoming or already

Raft boat and log rafts at Clinton, 1880s (Courtesy Clinton County Historical Society)

had become the largest lumber-manufacturing center on the river between Minneapolis and Saint Louis, a status it would hold intermittently for the years of Koerner's boyhood there. This civic eminence was due to the fact that the river narrowed appreciably as it made a sharp bend around the bluffs that bounded Clinton to the west, and thus made it a convenient landing place for the gigantic log rafts—275 feet wide by more than 1,000 feet in length—that came down from the white pine forests of Minnesota and Wisconsin. The sawmills had clustered at the river's edge and the town had grown up as best it could between the river and the bluffs, seven and one-half miles long and one and one-half miles wide after it merged with the adjacent community of Lyons; much of it built on sawdust both literally and financially.

The river's attractive width at Clinton had brought it the second railroad bridge across the Mississippi in 1865, and in 1881 it was a division point on the Chicago & North Western Rail Road

and boasted that system's largest shops beyond its Chicago headquarters. To the Protestant farmers of Iowa's hinterland, the river towns were anathema—sinks of iniquity and depravity and doubly damned by their Irish-Catholic inhabitants, who had a lamentable addiction to voting the Democratic ticket. An offset to this view is provided by the recollections of a lifelong resident of Clinton whose portrait as a child was painted by a teen-aged grammar school graduate called "Will" Koerner.[2]

Clinton wasn't a little of both, a lumber town and a railroad town. It was a lot of each! It is probably quite true that Clinton had more than an average number of Irish, and among them some hell-raising roughnecks. The town, however, had an antidote in the form of a number of Irish cops who knew how to handle them, and handle them they did. If you will bear with me, I would like to recollect the names of a few: Bill Desmond, whom President Grover Cleve-

The river steamer "J.S." nears a landing at Clinton, 1890s (Courtesy Clinton County Historical Society)

land called the handsomest United States Marshal he had ever seen; Ed Burke, Tome Burke, Joe Moran, John Donnelly, Bill Dougherty, Tom Hudson, and among the non-Irish, Pete Oster, Herb Knutzen, Jens Farum and Big Bill Lorenz. These men were either city police or sheriffs; they were big men physically and mentally; they commanded respect and got it. Where some of them carried their guns was a mystery to me as a kid. None of this present-day swashbuckling stuff, with a belt full of ammunition, loaded down with other equipment, jangling at every step. These river towns were not nearly so bad as some writers would have us believe some of your California mining camps were. Wherever you have rough labor, you are going to have rough men, and some of these men are bound to make trouble.

Father Koerner was a member of the craft that built shoes from the ground up. Later he opened a shoe store in the 400 block of North Second Street, just two blocks from his residence, and put in a stock of ready-made shoes as a sideline to his own hand-crafted wares. "He could have had a very good business," his son recalled in later years, "but he was easy-going, friendly, ready to loan money to good-for-nothing friends who never paid him back. That is why my folks never had anything but a mere honest living." His father became a naturalized citizen on September 9, 1884, and a respected member of the Knights of Pythias and of the Royal Workingmen. He appears to have prospered more than his son remembered, until ill health beset him in 1898.

By 1893, he was carrying considerable fire insurance on his stock of leather, lasts, machinery, furniture, and fixtures. He owned his own home at 504 North First Street and an adjoining dwelling which he rented and which became his widow's residence, free and clear, after his death

Father Koerner, about 1895

in 1902. This was a workingman's section of town, right by the tracks, but there was room for an ample garden, chicken pens, and a Jersey cow.[3] Will took the cow several miles out to pasture each morning, weather permitting, and brought her home each night, absorbing the tricks of morning and evening light in the process and learning bovine anatomy at first hand. He put this latter knowledge to immediate use in his first illustrating for pay by painting her head on local milk wagons at five dollars each. His father also was able to give him the money to join the Y.M.C.A. when he was seventeen and to enroll him in the Art School in Clinton conducted by a vivacious Bavarian, John M. Stich, who had settled in Clinton in 1875 and augmented his instructional income by painting portraits of the local lumbermen and their families. "He taught me to *see* things, to remember what I saw, and to draw well, and to have a photographic mind."

It was a good town for a boy to grow up in and Will Koerner grew up to six feet two. The river teemed with activity, not only with lumber rafts but with upwards of forty steamboats a day, many of which called at Clinton; there was fishing off "Sunfish Log" in Joyce's Slough in summer and ice skating on it in winter, and "Billie" Koerner, he became "Will" as the gram-

View of Clinton mills from the bridge across the Mississippi, late 1890s

Clamming near Clinton was a diversion as well as income

Raft and boat on the Mississippi near Davenport, Iowa, late 1890s

mar school grades were surmounted one by one, almost drowned one time from overconfidence in the thickness of the ice. There were lazy summer days spent with the family of his favorite teacher, Miss Julia Gordon, at the Gordon farm on Elk River—days of hunting and fishing—and there was, it appears, a compulsion to draw and

paint and sketch, even before coming under Herr Stich's tutelage.

It was this compulsion that made him cover any empty blackboard in the Clinton Grammar School with freehand sketches and these first brought him to the attention of Miss Gordon, who made him the unpaid and unofficial art instructor of the other pupils.[4] More than seventy years later, Carrie Maier would remember him being summoned into Miss Gordon's room to pass judgment on Carrie's sketch of George Washington; James N. Schenck upon seeing the illustrations for Stewart Edward White's "Ranchero" in 1932, would write a note of congratulation to his old "drawing teacher," and Schiller Sorensen would remind him by letter of the days when they both lived "down by the tracks" and he would come running over to have "Will" draw him "devils."

That his artistic progress was not without its setbacks was recalled by Koerner in one of the few anecdotes he told about himself:

I drew everything I saw; used house paint, crayons, pencils; made my own canvas and sketched along the river. One canvas I began in Spring; next I painted it over in Summer with heavy green foliage; then came Autumn and I was still working on it, only now in vivid reds and yellows. It was to be my masterpiece but

Mrs. Koerner and the Koerner residence in Clinton

Mother used it to stop a leak in the roof of our hen house.

Mrs. William Lorenzen of Clinton still owns a 33 × 24 inch oil canvas of Joyce's Slough, signed "W.H.K.—1896" which was given her husband as a wedding present by Will's mother, and the Clinton County Historical Society, at this writing, boasts a watercolor of a winter scene near Clinton by the same artist in the same period.

As he neared the end of his formal schooling, his books reflected his major interest. On the back flap of the heavy paper cover he made for a paper-bound volume of Whittier's poems he drew a laurel wreath enclosing the one word, Fame. He made his own pictorial cover for D. H. Montgomery's *Leading Facts of American History* (Ginn & Co., 1894) and on its inside front flap he wrote: "Sir John Millais, English artist, painted 300 pictures and received on an average $5,000 apiece. He is dead. An opening for the right kind of boy." On the blank reverse of a map page in this book, he sketched a fair damsel's head and shoulders, whether for practice or for the furtherance of an eighth-grade romance remains unknown. As early as 1895, he had begun a practice he would continue for the remainder of his career: collecting clippings that contained grist for his mill—ships, wild animals, slaughtering of buffalo on the Kansas Pacific

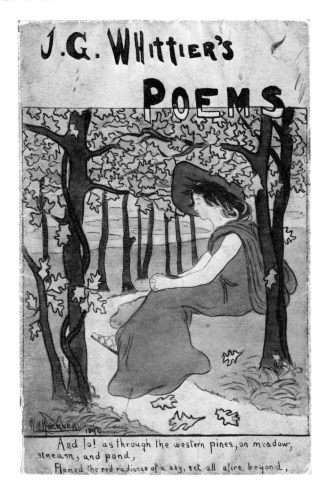

Koerner's own personal copy of an edition of Whittier's poems, with the art for one of Koerner's first cover designs; note the signature and date in lower left-hand corner

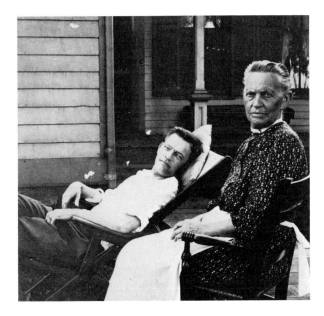

Bill and mother, in Clinton

Railway, Mexican *vaqueros,* "Buffalo Bill," Chief
Iron Tail, several muddy reproductions of Remington's western scenes, including three white
men in a dry wash, stripped naked and pierced
with arrows, and always and forever, it would
seem, horses of all shapes, sizes, and kinds. He
knew horses at first hand already—there were
no internal combustion engines in the Clinton
of his boyhood—and he never ceased to love
horses and study them. The results are clearly
evident in his later work, where each and all
of his horses, whether at rest or in motion, are
alive and individually distinct.

Rural free delivery of mail was inaugurated
in 1897, the year that Emerson Hough's *The
Story of the Cowboy* saw publication; the year
that *Munsey's* became the first general illustrated monthly magazine to reach 500,000 circulation, and the year that the Curtis Publishing
Company took over the virtually defunct *Saturday Evening Post.*

On June 4, 1897, the Clinton Grammar School
held its graduation exercises for a class of 131,
mostly English, German, and Scandanavian
names with a salty sprinkling of Irish. There was
an admission charge of fifteen cents for parents
and well-wishers, and there was an elaborate
program, as was common in the days when graduation from the eighth grade was the pinnacle
of most young people's education.[5] Harry Shadle
declaimed "A Tribute to Grant," Bessie Fallon
recited "Debit and Credit," Fred Hansen conducted a chemistry exhibit on "The Composition
of Air," and Edward Young and Flo Taylor,
autoharp and guitar respectively, rendered a
duet of "Whispering Pines." These were inter-
spersed with musical pieces and choral numbers, and the Clinton *Herald* reported that "Master Will Koerner's six charcoal sketches were
the outstanding display of talent by his class at
their graduation exercises." That these were
done freehand, on stage, to a musical accompaniment by Mae Howes, went unnoticed by the
paper.[6]

His sister recalled in later years that her
brother attended Stich's art classes for about one
year after his graduation from grammar school,
which jibes with the chronology established for
his life between 1898–1904. This year was a
time of economic trouble for Clinton and its
citizens, as the aftermath of the Panic of 1893
was compounded by a diminishing supply of logs

Self-portrait at age seventeen

from the depleted up-river forests whence they
came. Several thousand Clintonians moved
away, several savings-and-loan associations
failed, and over-extended merchants took the
bankruptcy route out of their difficulties. The
general economic climate affected his father's
shoe business and this may have contributed to
his father's declining health. Neither of these
factors seems to have affected his father's desire
to see his son better his condition in life, a gen-

erational attitude that marked the actions of so many immigrant parents, and it is certain that the yeasty ferment that stirs the blood of youth was working powerfully in Will Koerner.

Between mid-summer and early autumn of 1898, he became a member of the great internal migration of the closing years of the past century. He raffled off watercolors and oils, one of which was won by Anna Matzen who still possessed it in 1928, to gain funds for his great adventure. His father gave him a gold watch and what cash he could spare and his mother gave him her blessing. Thus armed, he bought an eastbound ticket at the C&NW depot, and the major portion of his scanty baggage con-sisted of his drawings and other artwork. When the Holstein-born youth from the river town of Clinton boarded the train that day, he began a career during which he would illustrate the top-ranked authors for the top-ranked magazines, top-ranked both in quality and circulation; a career that would bring him more than $350,000 in the money current down his years, before illness dulled his eye and stilled his hand. This was in the future. His immediate destination was Chicago. His goal was a job as staff artist on that city's prestigious, crusading, and tumultuous *Tribune*. The illustrated supplement in its Sunday edition had been a fertile source of clippings for his collection.

1. The Koerner Papers contain an unpublished and un-paged manuscript in several drafts prepared after his death by his widow. This is cited hereafter as Koerner, *Narrative*.

2. A. A. Hansen, Clinton, Iowa, to W.H.H., 8/10/1970.

3. This district was subject to flooding when the Mississippi River went on a rampage but there is no evidence that the Koerner family suffered therefrom.

4. Julia Gordon to Lillian Lusk Koerner, 1938, Koerner Papers.

5. On January 22, 1897, just two months past his eighteenth birthday, Will Koerner took home his report card from the second quarter of the eighth grade for his father's perusal and signature, as was the unenlightened custom of those times:

Days Absent: 0   Times Tardy: 0   Times Excused: 0
           Deportment and Effort: Both Excellent

Language:	Good	Algebra:	Very Good
Spelling:	Good	History:	Good
Literature:	Fair	Science:	Good
Latin:	Good	Penmanship:	Very Good

           /sgd/ Julia McCullough, Teacher

6. Clippings and other ephemera in the Koerner Papers.

Chapter III
CHICAGO AND LILLIAN

KOERNER's Chicago years marked the beginnings of political progressivism and of muckraking as a journalistic genre. They were years of challenge by the West to the East, "Europe stops at the Alleghenies!"; years of a convulsive reflex against the disappearance of the frontier, and the emergence of that claustrophobia which so grips and gripes the land today. The city to which he went was "an overgrown gawk of a village" in Lincoln Steffens's words.[1] To touch it was electricity and the young of its contiguous marches went there to live the juices that boiled within them.

It was a city where the skyscraper was emerging as a native art form, where William Rainey Harper was presiding over the adolescent years of the University of Chicago, and where Samuel Insull was serving his city well and efficiently with electricity and gas. It was the city, too, of Bertha Honoré Palmer, the beautiful and gracious wife of the famous tobacco-chewing hotelkeeper, who allied her personal charm to the hope of civilizing the city where Jane Addams had founded Hull House in a response to the challenge of unfamiliar urbanization's social problems. It was the city of such reform-minded gentry as William Kent, later a stalwart of the Progressive Era, and of the Municipal Voters League and its successful mayoralty candidate, Carter H. Harrison.

It was dirty, ill-smelling, and irreverent; lusty, gutsy, vital, and brawling; the "tough" among American cities and hog butcher to the world, but still a city where murder was a crime and not a diversion. It was a city of foreign-born and their first-generation descendants—400,000 Germans, 215,000 Irish, 50,000 Bohemians, 10,000 "Eyetalians," and seventeen other national groups—plus a substantial Negro population. Blocks of brothels stood on land owned by the city's oldest families, and Mont Tennes, "King of the North Side," was making gambling a "new" American business. Political corruption abounded, albeit petty by Saint Louis standards and unprofessional by those of Philadelphia. Elections were bought with whiskey and aldermen with boodle, while 2,500 police kept what peace they could in a population of 2,000,000 spread over almost two hundred square miles. Drifters and grifters found it open and fair by their standards and they flocked to it in droves, some 50,000 of them in 1901 alone.[2] Militant unions and equally militant employers combined for the protection of a mutual monopoly, attested by the ability of the Coal Teamsters and the Coal Team Owners Association to drive natural gas out of Marshall Field's great department store in 1902.[3]

Ventilating the doings of boodlers and reformers, pimps and prostitutes, traction magnates and militant unionists, probing every facet of the city's lust for life, was a vigorous and intensely competitive cluster of newspapers. It was an innovative group—the first color printing on a rotary newspaper press was done by the Chicago *Inter Ocean*, while Eugene Field began the by-lined newspaper column in the Chicago *Daily News*—and it produced some famous figures in the nation's journalistic and literary life. George Ade and Theodore Dreiser were Chicago trained, as were Franklin P. Adams, Ring Lardner, Burns Mantle, and Floyd Gibbons. So was Brand Whitlock, for whom newspaper experience was a springboard into novel writing and reform politics, as mayor of Toledo, and an ambassadorial career.[4] Ray S. Baker left the Chicago *Record* in 1898 to join *McClure's Magazine* and find fame as a muckraker. Peter Finley Dunne created a presence as real as Huckleberry Finn for the *Evening Post* in 1893—the year of the Columbian Exposition in Chicago, of the completion of Henry Ford's first automobile, and of the founding of the Anti-Saloon League—when he gave its pages Martin Dooley, an Irish-born saloonkeeper. Once a week, Dooley leaned his elbows on his bar and addressed a steady customer with these words: "I see be th' pa-a-pers, Hinnissy . . ."[5] It is worth noting that the enduring Chicago milieu and the equally durable habits of its "press gang," both accentuated by prohibition, provided the setting and inspiration for the famous play *The Front Page* by Ben Hecht and Charles MacArthur in 1928.

Four papers dominated the Chicago press in 1898: *Daily News, Inter Ocean, Times-Herald,* and the target of Will Koerner's quest, the *Tribune.* Three of these were Republican, only the *Daily News* professing political independence, and none more so than the *Tribune,* which had risen to eminence as the first and foremost booster of Abraham Lincoln in 1860. The afternoon *Daily News,* thanks to six editions daily, one of them a morning issue called the *Record* competing directly with the *Tribune,* boasted the largest total daily circulation, but it printed no Sunday edition. The *Tribune* bestrode the morning field with its sixteen pages, each 18 × 24 inches with seven broad columns, and its Sunday edition often comprised seventy-two pages, including an illustrated section; a magazine section, which used stories by Rudyard Kipling, Stephen Crane, and Will Levington Comfort; a book section; and a comic supplement. It also offered Sunday readers beautiful 14 × 20 inch reproductions of watercolors and oils by "famous" artists. The *Tribune* was not a full-fledged "yellow journal," although it used successfully some of the Pulitzer-Hearst techniques: "screamer" headlines, lavish illustrations, and ostentatious sympathy for the underdog, no matter where it found one. In 1902, "A Magnificent Colored Nature Study" came free with each daily issue and a two-page Literary Supplement accompanied the Saturday edition in 1903.

It gave ample coverage to high school sports and amateur athletics in general, while the annual football match between the universities of Wisconsin and Michigan got full-page treatment, including a play chart of the entire game. Hugh Fullerton, one of the great sports writers of his time, was its resident baseball eminence when the Cubs boasted an infield composed of Tinkers, Evers, Chance, and a third baseman, and carried a total of eighteen players on their roster. In 1898, the *Tribune* was the most prestigious and influential of its contemporaries and its presiding editorial genius, just elevated from city editor to managing editor, was James Keely, who promptly lured John T. McCutcheon, the Thomas Nast of the Middle West, away from the *Record* and daily splashed his arresting line work across the front page.

An emigrant from England, Keely had come to rest in Leavenworth, Kansas, in 1883, still short of his sixteenth birthday, where he got his first taste of newspaper work. After stints on papers in Kansas City, Memphis, and Louisville, he reached Chicago in the summer of 1889 and got a job with the *Tribune* on the "night police" beat. His rise was rapid and for good reasons. Short, dark, strongly built, with a massive jaw and a fierce flow of physical and nervous energy, he was "brutally conscientious," "brave as a lion, industrious as an ant, resourceful as a mongoose."[6] If it was news, Keely "would go to the west coast of Hell to get it,"[7] and he once trailed an absconding Chicago bank president clear to Morocco and persuaded him to return to face the music.

When the over-publicized Johnson County War erupted in Wyoming between large ranchers and those who wanted to be larger, Keely left Chicago on April 9, 1892, and filed his first story three days later from Buffalo, Wyoming, recounting the fighting at the KC Ranch where Nate Champion and Nick Ray were killed by the "cattle barons." This made the front page on April 16. After the cattlemen's minions had been rescued by a detachment of cavalry from the aroused settlers, small ranchers, and rustlers, Keely intercepted the cavalcade, got his story, cut the telegraph wire to keep Sam Clover of the Chicago *Times-Herald* from filing first, and sent his copy off to Douglas, Wyoming, by a hired rider, while he rode the train that took the captives and their protecting escort to Cheyenne. In all, he gave the *Tribune* eleven front-page stories on this imbroglio in two weeks.[8]

During the Spanish-American War, Keely personally advised President McKinley of Admiral Dewey's victory at Manila by telephone from Chicago.[9] When General Nelson A. Miles brought charges of "tainted beef" against Chicago packing houses for the products they furnished the Army, the hearing was held in Chicago where Miles was slated to be pilloried. That he was not came from Keely's front-page support of Miles, whom he had known when Miles commanded at Fort Leavenworth.[10] Keely resolutely refused to permit the *Tribune* to accept any patent-medicine or other advertising he considered disreputable, and he made it clear to Mandel Brothers when they contracted to run full-page advertisements for their store for a full year at a total cost of $100,000 that they had bought advertising only, not the *Tribune.*

Appearing before a committee of the United States Senate, he would say, "Over the Chicago *Tribune,* sir, my power is absolute in all departments." He paid his top reporters between forty and sixty dollars a week, legmen and the rewrite desk twenty to thirty dollars per week, and "cub" reporters less. He drove others as hard as he drove himself, and he did not leave his desk until the final edition came off the presses at three in the morning. Failure on assignment he would not tolerate, excuses did not interest him in the least, and he had no patience with drinking, on or off the job. He has been described as "the best *news-man* Chicago has had. He knew what was news and how to get it; not *make* it, he was not that kind of an editor; and how to present it and when to drop it. Perhaps he was not either a great publisher or a great editor, but as a newsman he was superb and supreme."[11] This was the man Will Koerner had determined to brace for a job, and he did his homework first.

Arriving in Chicago, he found quarters on the West Side's Washington Boulevard near Garfield Park, with "Mrs. Carroll," where he had a room and two meals a day for $4.50 a week. For additional sustenance, he daily purchased a dozen bananas for five cents and never relished them thereafter, and gorged himself on the free lunch that went with a nickel glass of beer at noon. For the next three weeks, he roamed the city, pursuing horse-drawn fire engines and am-bulances to get the kind of action drawings that embellished the *Tribune's* pages. When his portfolio seemed impressive, and his funds were perilously low, he walked the four miles from his boarding house to the *Tribune* office. In his own mind, he was attempting the Rubicon that had challenged Caesar and he possessed the necessary gall.

On being told that Mr. Keely had not yet come to work, he somehow slipped past the receptionist-stenographer, no mean feat for a broad shouldered, six-footer with a portfolio of sketches under his arm. Seating himself in Keely's chair, behind Keely's desk, he placed his hat and portfolio on a corner of the desk and waited. That there were inner tremors at his own temerity seems quite possible. Then Keely strode into the room, his head darting back and forth in the movements that had earned him the nickname "Bird" behind his back. Emitting one of the grunts that were another trademark, a burst of concentrated wrath and skepticism in equal parts, Keely barked, "What the Hell do you want!?" The reply came as steadily as Will Koerner could produce it, "A job as a staff artist."

Keely may have recalled his own efforts to find a job, a stranger in a strange land, at Leavenworth fifteen years earlier, or he may have been impressed by the sheer effrontery of the youth, who fumbled nervously to unwrap his sketches for inspection. Convinced that they were indeed freehand, as Koerner claimed they were, Keely took him to the head of the paper's Art Department, William L. Wells, then in his fiftieth year, for a tryout. Wells looked at his sketches, gave him a bunch of silver prints to do, said "Bring them back tomorrow," and went on with the day's work. Koerner did not know a silver print from the Chicago Board of Trade but luck was with him that day. Bob Campbell, one of the staff artists, was at work nearby and, noting the new chum's reaction to Wells's brusque instructions, beckoned with his head. Campbell was working on some silver prints at the time and gave Koerner rudimentary instruction.[12]

Essentially, the silver print was a specially prepared photographic print, using paper sensitized by a silver salt, of artwork designed for line reproduction. These prints could be made in a few minutes in any size and degree of strength, light prints being most desirable for most purposes. The artist then drew the photograph in pen-and-ink directly on the print, after which either he or the engraver bleached the print in bichloride of mercury, a dangerous compound, and washed it until nothing remained but the pen work on the bleached paper. The print then was ready for reproduction as a line cut.[13] Armed with this information, Koerner walked back to his boarding house and toiled all night. Next morning he took his handiwork to Wells for inspection and was hired at the munificent salary of $5.00 per week, which gave him a disposable income weekly of fifty cents.

His hours were from noon until ten o'clock or later, six days a week, and he often stayed on "after the other fellows left and observed their work and techniques." He walked both ways to work, and did his own washing and ironing. Within about a year, his salary had been increased to $9.00 weekly; he sported the six-pointed badge that identified him as a *Tribune* artist, and his colleagues in the Art Department knew him as "Big Bill" Koerner, a man touched with the romance of Mark Twain's Mississippi. As a staff artist, he accompanied reporters to do what today's cameramen do with sophisticated photographic equipment—provide the visual impact for the story. It was a pressure-packed apprenticeship and it placed a premium on the artist's ability to grasp the picture quickly, make his rough sketch notes, often on his shirt cuffs, hustle back to the office, do the final drawing, get it photographed, complete the silver print, bleach and wash it, and meet the deadline.

It was work that demanded an eye—a quick, accurate, unsentimental eye—and a hand that could record swiftly the highlights that the eye saw, and a memory that could re-capture what the eye had seen but the hand, under pressure, could develop only imperfectly on the spot. It was the beginning of Koerner's mastery of line, his post-primary education in what Jean Auguste Dominique Ingres meant when he said that "drawing is the probity of art." As another artist, muralist, and illustrator of medical texts has said, "You can fake a soft edge or a hard edge; you can fake color and composition, but you *cannot* fake draftsmanship. It is universal and international. . . . you cannot fake the lines."[14] By the same token, clean design was vital to the line reproduction, with which the *Tribune* displayed the run-of-the-news train wrecks, fires,

explosions, strikes, murders, embezzlements, lost children, stray pets, love-nest denouements, hangings, court trials, civic meetings, weddings, routs, soirees and balls, and the picnics of various ethnic groups. Two of Koerner's distinguished contemporaries in the field of magazine illustration, Frederick Rodrigo Gruger and Henry Raleigh, served their practical apprenticeships on newspapers, as did Everett Shinn, N.A.

Thirty years later, he recalled some incidents from his newspaper days:[15]

Once I got the cops to lock me in the cell with a particularly brutal murderer, for that was the only way I could get to see him. I didn't dare sketch him there or he would have had two murders to answer for instead of one. But I memorized his features and when the cops let me out after about ten minutes, pretending to take me to the Judge, I hustled back to the office and put his face down while it was fresh in my mind.

Once I was sent down to the morgue to get the likeness of a criminal who had been killed in a brawl. The boys at the morgue would not help me find the body, so I went down to the slabs to look for myself. I went from body to body, lifting each sheet just a little to see if it was my man, and just as I started to lift one more, it moved! and a man rose up saying, "What the Hell you doing here?" It was the night watchman.

The son of one of the prominent citizens was involved in a scrape and our reporters were given the bounce every time they went to his home. I learned that he had attended the University of Chicago and went there but could not find a picture of him. So I collected a group of his student friends and went through some old yearbooks, asking them to pick out characteristics in the pictures that resembled the man I was after. From these I did a composite that was good enough to impress Wells and Keely that it was the lad in question.

Then the [newspaper] boys set up a hectic chase for the picture of a University professor [Jacques Loeb] who had made himself famous overnight by some discovery or other.[16] He was as shy as an unbroken colt and didn't want his picture in the papers. He slammed his door in my face when I called on him but I got a glimpse and drew a portrait of him that was printed. He protested vigorously to Keely but the picture had

On these two pages are examples of Koerner's work as a staff artist for the Chicago Tribune, *1898–1903*

run and that's what counted. Then McClure's Magazine *wired me to send them the picture to be used with an article they were going to run on him. I didn't want to use the same old picture, so I went down to the University one morning and went in with the students as they entered his classroom. I sat in the very back row and was busy sketching when he called on me to recite. I excused myself by saying I was unprepared. "See that you are better prepared tomorrow," was his rejoinder, but there wasn't any tomorrow as far as I was concerned. I had gotten enough notes to do a fine portrait and* McClure's *paid me a small fortune for it* [Frontispiece, McClure's, 3/1902].

By early 1900, he had graduated to work for the Sunday illustrated section, in addition to his chores for the daily news editions, and his work appeared consistently on Sundays until his *Tribune* years were done in mid-1903. Sometimes his work was intermingled with "boilerplate" reproductions secured from other sources, and one of these placed him in distinguished company. The page contained drawings of "The Ideal American Woman" by such as A. B. Wenzell, Henry Hutt, Alice Barber Stephens, C. Allan Gilbert, and Albert Herter, better known as a muralist. Their pictures surrounded the central figure which was Koerner's conception of a page boy in court, kneeling on a cushion and offering an elaborate crown on a fluffy pillow to the lovely ladies all around him.

William Randolph Hearst invaded Chicago in 1900, with the first edition of his Chicago *American* rolling off the presses quite logically on July Fourth. It quickly built up a tremendous following, and the *Tribune* tried to keep the *American* off the streets by hiring strong-arm types to intimidate Hearst's drivers and newsboys. Hearst employed more and bigger protectors and vicious street warfare ensued until things simmered down. More important to Koerner's future career was what Hearst's advent did to some of his colleagues on the *Tribune,* including Emerson Hough who wrote feature stories and book reviews for the paper, in addition to his other writings and his position as western editor of *Forest and Stream.*

The Hearst organization made overtures to men in the *Tribune's* Art Department, including Koerner, and to the paper's top reporters, with the promise of doubling their *Tribune* salaries. Koerner refused, but at least five men left the Art Department to join the *American.* There they experienced heavier work loads than at the *Tribune* for about five months and then either were fired or given only special assignment work, whereby they were paid by the assignment. Keely not only refused to re-hire the erring sheep but blacklisted them, Hough included.[17] Koerner never forgot this Hearstian *modus operandi* and consistently refused to succumb in later years to Hearst's practice of signing top-ranking illustrators to exclusive long-term contracts.

Of Koerner's personal life in his early Chicago years but little has been exhumed. When his salary reached $9.00 a week, double his expenses for room and board, he began to send money home to assist his parents and continued this practice with his mother until her death in 1934. When his salary reached $15.00 a week, he was able to save some of it, building a nest egg to further his education in his profession, and he was affluent enough on November 18, 1901, to take out a life insurance policy. That he was lonely in Chicago is attested by the fact that he visited Clinton whenever possible and that he sent his sister money to visit him, finding her suitably chaperoned accommodations in his own boarding house. On one of these visits, Margaretha met a young man of Irish extraction, who later became more than successful in Chicago's business circles, and eventually married him, converting to the Catholic faith in the process. Apparently this troubled Koerner's Lutheran upbringing no more than did Robert Ingersoll's molten-silver fulminations against all orthodox religions. By the time his father died on August 29, 1902, Koerner was assistant art editor of the *Tribune* at $45.00 a week. He went home for the funeral and to put his mother's affairs in order, and his sense of loss was assuaged by the fact that he had found the woman in his life, a willowy miss with large blue eyes and hair that came alive with copper glints when the sun caught it. His pursuit of artistic training had brought them together.

It is known that he attended the Chicago Art Institute in 1901 and there is evidence that he lectured to classes at the Institute in 1902–1903, although he does not appear in its catalogs for this period. It was during this time that a powerfully built, raw-boned teen-ager from South Dakota began his formal art education at the Insti-

City room of the Chicago Tribune: *Koerner stands between the lady reporter in the big hat and the sign reading, "Gee, Ain't It Hell To Be Poor!"*

tute, before going on to advanced study under Howard Pyle at Wilmington, Delaware. Whether Harvey Dunn and Koerner met in Chicago has not been determined but later internal evidence indicates that they did. It was not at the Institute, however, that Lillian Lusk entered his life but at The Francis Smith Art Academy of Chicago, "three flights up on Wabash Avenue." She remembered it in this wise after his death:

There was the soft scratching of charcoal sticks on white charcoal paper snapped with clamps on black portfolios. The air was heavy with Chicago dust that drifted unseen, up and through the top-floor back windows which looked out over roofs and pigeons. In the skylighted studio, art students were working intent on drawing the nude model. The drone of the charcoal, and the air, still and stifling, was making the whole class a little dull [July, 1900].

Our easels were circled about the model stand. The best pupils were down in front to get the drawing foreshortened; the others graduated on an uneven line to the back of the room according to their ability. I was in the eighth row struggling to draw the feet of the female model and trying to get them on the paper. I had the head placed and the largest breasts I had ever seen all oblivious to the fact that the rest of her sitting position must get on the paper, too, when I heard a quick step on the long flight of stairs, then the classroom door opened and a tall man entered. He tossed his hat

Lillian as the camera saw her

on a horn of a bedraggled deer's head, grabbed a big black portfolio from the rack, and walked directly to the farthest side of the room and, to my surprise, to a front easel under the model. He went to work drawing and the whole class seemed to take on vibration and interest. The class monitor, Mack Ketcham, who timed the poses, drifted over to my easel and said under his breath, "That's Koerner of the Tribune."

I finished up the feet cockeyed; then, with that accomplished, I yawned, no hand over my mouth. A little embarrassed I looked over to "Koerner of the Tribune" *and his mouth was wide open, too, no hand over. We smiled.*

When the twenty-five minute pose was up and "rest" called, he stood beside me as we leaned against the back wall. "I did not get much sleep last night," he said, "I was on an assignment," and I returned, "I did not get much either, I was at the opera." We laughed together until Mack Ketcham, the monitor, called "pose."

As I took my place before my easel I looked over to see "Koerner of the Tribune" *but he was gone, portfolio gone too, his stool empty. I went back to my work to check up on my woman and her feet. The twenty-five minutes went fast and I was still at my easel when Mack drifted over again and said under his breath, "Did you see Koerner's portrait of You?"*

"No, where is it?"

"He's back and to the left of you and the whole class is around him."

I followed him over and Koerner came to me quickly and said, "Do you like it? Wish I could have done it in color."

He told me that he attended art school each morning from ten until noon when he must be back to the Chicago Tribune *at one o'clock, and from then on he made sketches of me. He drew me in his full-page Sunday Editions, and one Sunday a full page in colors appeared with a toast:*

"Here's to the grape and its sparkling wine,
I'll be your sweetheart if you'll be mine,
I will be faithful if you'll be true."
It was a full-length likeness of both of us, with a wine glass raised.

During the months that followed, he unfolded the story of family in Clinton, Iowa; of his own work and his own ambitions. His moods were unaccountable. His impulses were always fine and honest, at times terribly deep and sincere; other times he was like a boy. I called him "Boy." Noth-

*ing he said nor did bothered me. I would keep very
quiet and wait until he smiled again. Then, I'd
smile back. He called me "Dick." We were like
pals and sweethearts, too.*

*The Easter of 1902 my widowed mother, Eliza-
beth Stewart Lusk, came to Chicago to meet this
man, Koerner. I was her only child and she was
filled with anxiety and fear that my sweetheart,
being a newspaper artist, would not be good
enough for me. Then, too, she was not ready for
me to marry. Surely, I would not leave her, a kindergarten teacher in a Battle Creek [Michigan]
Public School. I was but a child to her. She called
me "Baby." [Lillian, born June 3, 1883, was
almost nineteen.]*

*In the Tribune, Monday, March 31, 1902, there
was a story headed: "Winter's Dying Gasp Works
Strange Transformation on Easter Morning." All
across the top of the page of printed photos were
eight sketches of William, Mother and me going
to church in the wind and slush, and all over the
margins of the clipping he sent me were messages.
In the center with the three of us, he wrote in
pencil, "The Trinity," and for years we called ourselves, "The Trinity." He had courted his prospective Mother-in-law and won! What won't a man do
when he is in love?*

*Our next goal was to visit my home in Battle
Creek. It must be accomplished between his leaving the Art Department, where now he was Assistant Art Editor, after ten at night on Friday, and
be back before one o'clock on Sunday. We spent
the trip there and back talking of his people and
of our next trip to visit them. He wanted me to
meet and know them. He wanted me to understand and like them. He wanted to be proud of
me before his friends and asked me if I would
try to remember to take the beautiful poses that
I naturally took. He wanted me to be beautiful!
That overwhelmed me! That almost queered the
whole trip! For the first time in my life I was self-
conscious and ill at ease, and I realized I was not
beautiful! It was he who saw and painted me time
after time as beautiful.*[18]

They were married on June 24, 1903, in her
mother's house at Twenty Rose Street in Battle
Creek. Reverend S. J. Stewart, pastor of the Independent Congregational Church and a mater-
nal kinsman of the bride, performed the services.
"Dick" was gowned in "a beautiful creation of
cream white Tabitu silk," while the groom wore

Lillian as Koerner saw her

Koerner's drawing of the couple, May 2, 1903

After a three-week honeymoon, part of which was spent in Clinton with his mother, they returned to Battle Creek and set up housekeeping in the downstairs portion of her mother's home, while she confined her residence to the upstairs section. This was a foretaste of what in time became a long and often aggravating *ménage à trois*, but they were newly married and Mrs. Lusk was younger then and still active in her kindergarten teaching. The primary reason for this arrangement was economy: the newlyweds felt that by renting from her mother they could save one-half of the $50.00 per week he would receive as art editor of the *Pilgrim: A Magazine for the Home*, for which he had begun to do story illustrations while still employed on the *Tribune*. He had realized that the improvements in photoengraving which gave it increasing use in photograph reproduction doomed the newspaper artist's usefulness. The opportunity to enter magazine work had been far more alluring than the slight increase in weekly compensation.

1. *McClure's,* 10/1903.

2. Josiah Flint, *McClure's,* 2/1901.

3. Ray S. Baker, *McClure's,* 9/1903.

4. Alfred Henry Lewis, of "Wolfville" fame, did an article on Whitlock, *Saturday Evening Post,* 11/17/1906.

5. Furnas, 877.

6. James Weber Linn, *James Keely: Newspaperman,* 13. See also *American Magazine* 12/1909, *Collier's* 6/28/1913, and *Saturday Evening Post* 10/3/1903 for material on Keely.

7. Linn, 14.

8. No writer on the Johnson County "war" has used Keely's material so far as is known, although that filed by Sam Clover has been cited extensively.

9. Linn, 78–79.

10. *Ibid.*

11. Linn, prefatory, pages not numbered.

12. There are several family versions of Koerner's first encounters with Keely and Wells, the latter having contributed illustrations to the second edition of Emerson Hough's *The Story of the Cowboy* together with Charles M. Russell.

13. Lawton Kennedy to W.H.H., 9/7/1972.

14. James Bodrero to W.H.H., 1/26/1971.

15. These have been assembled from fragments in his surviving papers and from Koerner, *Narrative.*

16. Loeb was professor of physiology and experimental biology at the University of Chicago. His thesis was that electrical, not thermal, energy was the basis of all muscular activity and vital processes.

17. Delbert E. Wylder, a Hough scholar, to W.H.H., 5/8/1970.

18. Koerner, *Narrative.*

the conventional black and signed his name as William Henry Dethlef Koerner. If they were members of an uncertain, restless society, they did not know it. They expected one another to be brave, handsome, and resourceful; beautiful and pure, and they expected their conjoined life to have a happy ending, although they did not demand that it be tranquil. The virtues they prized were familiar and simple, and from all that has been learned of their life together, they ended as they began.

Chapter IV
"PILGRIM," GRAPE-NUTS, AND NEW YORK

PILGRIM was part of that magazine era which began in 1893 when S. S. McClure, a voluble, eccentric Scots-Irish entrepreneur, whom Robert Louis Stevenson sought to portray in *The Wrecker,* started *McClure's Magazine* as a well-illustrated monthly using top-flight authors and selling for fifteen cents, soon reduced to ten. His success brought competition in the ten-cent field — *Cosmopolitan, Munsey's, Everybody's,* for examples — and these magazines and their price recruited millions of new readers from the middle segments of a populace in which universal public education had produced a level of literacy not far below that enjoyed by Japan and Germany. These "cheap" magazines — so the editors of such taste-makers as *Century, Harper's, Scribner's,* and *Atlantic* viewed them — quickly supplanted the book as the primary means of popular entertainment and as the primary means of disseminating information and enlightenment.

Perhaps the greatest outside stimulus to *Pilgrim's* founding was the success of *Ladies Home Journal,* which it imitated in part and which had scored such dramatic gains in circulation, first at five cents and then at ten, that in 1903 it became the *first* magazine in the world to reach one million copies per month. In this same year, *Red Book* was founded by a group of Chicago merchants,[1] attaining 300,000 copies per month within two years, and the *Saturday Evening Post,* appearing weekly at five cents a copy, went from 425,000 to 635,000 copies. Ida M. Tarbell, Lincoln Steffens, and Ray S. Baker began to ply their muckrakes in earnest for *McClure's,* and *Everybody's* was on the verge of jumping from 150,000 to more than 700,000 copies per month with Thomas W.

Lawson's twenty articles on "Frenzied Finance," in which he dealt with financial skullduggery of all kinds, shapes, sizes, and participants, particularly in high places.

More germane to *Pilgrim's* progress was the local potential of Battle Creek, population 22,000 give or take a few hundreds. It was a city with factories producing printing presses, threshing machines, and pianos; it had several large flouring mills, and it boasted a long-standing and growing health industry, capped by the nationally famous Battle Creek Sanitarium. Perhaps more relevant to today's breakfast tables and certainly more important to Koerner's later career, it had factories producing the cereals and other products of Dr. J. H. Kellogg and C. W. Post, and these meant advertising revenues then as now.

Pilgrim had been founded at Marshall, Michigan, on May 18, 1899, by its first editor, J. C. Bartholf, a Milwaukee Republican who had apostatized to Bryan and Free Silver in 1896; Dr. J. F. Campbell, Lansing; P. H. Gilkey, Rickland; C. S. Williams, Grand Rapids; and Abram C. Wisner, Marshall.[2] Shortly thereafter it moved to the more promising prospects of Battle Creek, where it built its own field-stone building, reorganized as a joint stock company, undercapitalized it appears, and established a graduate fellowship at the University of Michigan for "research in English composition and rhetoric." Selling for ten cents per copy, one dollar a year, it began its slow climb towards its peak circulation of about 103,000 copies per month, which it attained shortly before it moved to Detroit and expired early in 1907. Because it "stayed at home," so to speak, *Pilgrim* never gained the circulation that

The Pilgrim *staff, 1904: Hiram M. Greene, Business Manager, left; Karl E. Harriman, Editor, middle; and Koerner, Art Editor, right*

would attract the big national advertisers, and its expansion was circumscribed by the financial panics of 1903 and 1907. Additionally, its advocacy of Free Silver was passé even at its founding. Koerner's eighteen months on the magazine brought him some lasting and important friendships and contributed substantially to his education as artist and illustrator.

Pilgrim's titular editor during Koerner's stint was Willis John Abbott, a veteran of several Chicago papers and of long service with the Hearst organization.[3] He was the author of many "drum-and-trumpet" books for boys, had managed Henry George's bid for the mayoralty of New York in 1897, and remained a perfervid supporter of William Jennings Bryan for many years. That he actually handled the daily editorial chores of the magazine is open to question, as the only city directory of Battle Creek to list him is that for 1904–1905, which shows his residence as "boards at Post Tavern." His autobiography is notable for its failure to mention *Pilgrim* even once, but this may be explained by the fact that when it appeared, he was basking in the glory of having rescued the *Christian Science Monitor* from de-

suetude and restored its prestige. The best explanation of why his name, and generally his only, was carried on *Pilgrim's* masthead stems from the fact that its promoters first had offered W. J. Bryan $10,000 a year to permit his name to be used as its editor, with Bryan's only responsibility to be one signed article per month;[4] they probably got the use of Abbott's name and his editorials for much less.

The actual editor of *Pilgrim* was Karl Edwin Harriman, an 1895 graduate of the University of Michigan, who was writing a daily column of humor and verse for the Detroit *Free Press* when he succumbed to *Pilgrim's* blandishments in 1901. He was a writer in his own right, appearing frequently in *Lippincott's* between 1901–1904, with a circus article thereafter in *Cosmopolitan* (7/1906) and an article on "Graft and Trolleys" in *Saturday Evening Post* (3/25/1905) for which N. C. Wyeth supplied two unexceptional illustrations. The story was told of him that his New York agent had been unable to place one of Harriman's offerings in that city and sent it off on a tour of the hinterlands where it eventually came to *Pilgrim* "over the transom" and Harriman rejected it as not being up to the magazine's standards.

He also published five novels during his *Pilgrim* stint, one of which, *The Girl and The Deal*, was Koerner's first book illustration. He did twelve line drawings for the book,[5] which was a rather fragile romance about an eastern girl traveling via the Santa Fe Railway to find true love in the West; that its heroine looked suspiciously like Lillian Koerner is not surprising. After *Pilgrim's* demise, Harriman had a distinguished career as editor of *Red Book* and its associated publications, then on *Ladies Home Journal* under Edward H. Bok, and back to *Red Book* in 1918, where he remained for many years, as it became a two-hundred-page magazine, fat with advertising, and its circulation climbed to more than 280,000 copies monthly. It was during his first stint on *Red Book* that he gave Koerner illustration assignments that were vital to his economic health and the enhancement of his professional stature.

Editorially, *Pilgrim* emphasized current events and provided helpful hints for clubwomen and homemakers, including pages of the latest fashions and how to make them. It offered a fourteen-carat gold pen for $1.50 and a new *Pilgrim* subscription, or a special, thin-model, nickel-plated watch for $1.25 and a new subscription, and it piggy-backed itself with either *Harper's Bazaar, Good Housekeeping,* or *Cosmopolitan* for $1.50 for the pair for one year. Readers could get *Pilgrim* and *American Boy* for one year for $1.25, and the *Pilgrim* course of physical training for just $1.00: "How to live long and have good health. Eating, drinking, walking, sleeping, how to do each one according to the laws of nature." It used the best writers Harriman could afford, with such as Jack London, Clarence Darrow, Samuel Merwin, Brand Whitlock, Caroline Lockhart, Reginald Wright Kauffman, and Andy Adams appearing in its pages. (It is assumed here that what these authors sold to *Pilgrim* was unsalable elsewhere for more money.) Harriman's own appearances, both fact and fiction, are assumed to have been those he could not place elsewhere and which served to bulk *Pilgrim's* pages with but little drain on the budget.

Art Editor Koerner's title was a monumental misnomer. He *was* the Art Department. For example, the August, 1903, issue carried two fiction stories for which he did five illustrations and a feature article on "Paris at Play" for which he supplied six more. In addition, he did decorative borders for the several "department" pages and the drawings for the multiple pages of female fashions, with buttons, ribbons, furbelows, and folds where each belonged. For one Christmas issue, he illustrated six stories, signing different names to several of them, and did two full-page drawings that "stood alone" (artwork that had no connection with any textual material). What he had to illustrate varied widely, from "Cave Dwellers of Today" (4/1904), a fiction short about the sod-house frontier, for which he supplied his first western illustrations in the form of a prairie schooner and horsemen in cowboy garb, to an article on the Russian battleship *Tsarevitch* (2/1904), for which he did five drawings of battleships—three Russian and two Japanese.

What Jules Guérin did for *Scribner's* and André Castaigne did for *Century* in visually reporting the Lewis and Clark Exposition in Saint Louis, Koerner did for *Pilgrim,* and his first known Indian heads were part of the dozens of cameo-like renditions he did of Indians seen on its grounds. (Solon H. Borglum's sculptures of cowboys and Indians were on display, as was the work of Charles M. Russell.) He did all these things for $50.00 a week at a time when Charles Dana Gibson was under contract with *Collier's* for one hundred of his in-

tricate double-page pen paintings over four years at $1,000 each; when *Ladies Home Journal* held a prize contest for original cover designs in any medium that must be capable of reproduction in two colors and reducible to $10 \times 14\frac{1}{2}$ inches in which the first prize was $1,000 and was won by Maxfield Parrish; and when *Scribner's* was offering a set of four pastel drawings by Howard Chandler Christy, each 12×16 on a 19×24 inch backing, for $3.50 express prepaid. What was happening to Koerner is well described by a phrase from today's education jargon, "an enriching learning experience."

For the first time, he had to read fiction to find out *what* he could illustrate that would arrest the readers' attention and lead them into the story, and then *how* to illustrate it without giving away the story's plot or climax and without duplicating what the author already had done in prose. He also began his life-long training in composing visual images that *fit* the characters involved, and to do this he had to *get inside* the characters themselves, always hewing to the maxim that action springs out of character and character is described by action. He had to learn page layout and photoengraving techniques and grasp the delicate interrelationships of tone and shading and strength between the black-and-white artwork and its reproductive plate. Most of all, he had to learn how color reproduced, because *Pilgrim's* covers were done in two colors, that often looked like three, and color reproduction had not been a major subject in his newspaper training.

I have had upon my wall an original painting by Koerner rendered for a Saturday Evening Post *story ... which was painted in full color, although for black-and-white reproduction. The highlights were painted in blue—not white—and the reds and browns were used lavishly for the darks, while detail in shadow contained sufficient blue so that reproduction showed these areas even lighter than in the original, giving a splendid luminosity to the published illustration.*[6]

Thirteen *Pilgrim* covers have been identified positively as Koerner's during the months he was employed directly by it, with six more identified as his work thereafter,[7] and many of them smacked strongly of Lillian's face and figure. She was the only model he could afford. Thirteen of these covers "stood alone" which was contrary to the

THE PILGRIM

JUNE 1904

EDITED BY WILLIS J. ABBOT
Published by THE PILGRIM MAGAZINE COMPANY,
BATTLE CREEK, MICH.
CHICAGO: 1045 Marquette Building
NEW YORK: 150 Nassau St.
LONDON: 34 Norfolk St., Strand

VOL. VIII   NO. VI
Copyright, 1904, by THE PILGRIM MAGAZINE COMPANY,
Entered at the Postoffice at Battle Creek, Mich.,
as Second Class Matter.

10 Cents a Copy $1.00 a Year

The Lighter Side of the Fair

By KARL EDWIN HARRIMAN

OF COURSE, a great deal — a very great deal, indeed — depends upon one's idea of what constitutes fun. The acid-tainted dyspeptic who sat in a rocking-chair on the broad-shaded porch of the Inside Inn nursing a cold cigar and a gnawing ache in the pit of his stomach, certainly was not having fun from your point of view — or mine — we are not dyspeptics, but for his own part I am sure he was enjoying every weary moment of his visit to St. Louis. It was fun for him to have none; that's all. You've seen the type.

"Been here long?" I blandly inquired. One must exchange a word now and then even if it be with a stranger, when one is alone at a World's Fair. The Man from Waco up-rolled a yellow eye at me and snapped, as he bit viciously at his cold cigar: "Two days."

"Stopping on for a week or two?" It was not that I cared; I simply *had* to speak to some one in the crowd. He felt in his waistcoat pocket, wearily, for a match. "Goin' t' night," he answered tersely.

"Seen all you care to, eh?" If there was the least note of sneer in my voice the Man from Waco did not appear to notice it.

"Heven't seen anything; ain't moved off this piazzy. This is the fifth World's Fair I've been at and I ain't seen nothin' yet. Day and a half in Chicago, back in '93; three hours in Buffalo; two days in Paris (rained the hull time) day and a half in Nashville and b'golly I'm a goin' home t' night at 'leven forty — if I live."

Of course, it was the dyspepsia. There he sat unmoved by the kaleidoscopic crowd; the virgin beauty of the green grass fringing the roadway, the red roadway itself meandering among the State buildings that nestle so comfortably under the oaks of Forest Park. My heart went out to the yellow-eyed Man from Waco as it had not gone out even to the little Esquimau who sought to sell me a miniature icehouse on The Pike.

So, I said earnestly: "I'm downright sorry you've had such a bad time — missed all the fun — all the enjoyment the Fair has to offer."

He started as though something had stung him. "Who said anything 'bout missin' it all!" he exclaimed. "What do you s'pose I fetch my wife for? Wait till she comes in t' night an' you'll understand. She's doin' the Agricultural Building and the Filipinos today. She's got a wad o' money as big as a head o' lettuce an' she knows there's plenty more where that come from. You see," he went on, quite confidentially, and leaning toward me, his elbows on his knees, "You see, I send her out every morning to see the show, *and she sees it!* Don't you think she don't! When she gets in at night an' we've et, I make her sit down and tell me every blamed thing she's seen. It's just the same as though I seen it myself for her descriptive powers are sure amazin'. Besides, it means I ain't all done up come bed-time, with my feet like blocks o' wood under me, an' a pain in my stumick something powerful."

So you see the Man from Waco had his fun after all, only it wasn't our brand. Besides we haven't all wives like his. I saw them together, that same evening. Above them sputtered an electric, about them surged the crowd — pretty girls from Tennessee, pretty girls from Texas, pretty girls from South Carolina, pretty girls from everywhere — and a few men. He had lighted his cigar and was leaning forward, listening raptly. She was a stout, red-cheeked, wholesome, healthy woman — and she talked. Now and then his hand went mechanically to the lower button of his waistcoat, but his eyes were open wide, and his lips were parted as he listened. For half an hour she talked at him and then bustled away to view the illumination.

❧   ❧

I SHOULD like to know what were the words employed by the wife of the Man from Waco in her description of the illumination that night. I encountered her in the portico of Festival Hall, the proper view point if one wishes to gain a perfect appreciation of the magnitude and the transcendent beauty of the Exposition architecture. She stood there in all the glory of her two hundred pounds, her clear blue

Koerner's drawings for Pilgrim's *coverage of the St. Louis Exposition, 1904*

usual magazine practice of those days. Until about 1907, unrelated cover designs were reserved for holiday issues and the usual cover was a "come-on" for the leading piece inside; often it was merely an illustration from the inside story placed on the cover. Reproduced on poster board, these covers were used for newsstand displays to attract potential buyers. One of the leading cover artists of the first half of this century, Joseph C. Leyendecker, had this to say about the cover's function in the days when newsstands were plentiful and well stocked and vital to magazine distribution:

A cover is more related to murals, even sculpture, than to illustration. . . . The cover sells more copies of its magazine because it carries further and hits harder because it is a symbol; says what it has to say in a straight line. It carries further because a good cover has a distinct silhouette. The design pulls the reader in from a distance.[8]

The *Pilgrim* months were not all work and no play. The Koerners were too young and too alive for that, and Karl Harriman's home on Garrison Avenue made the center of a vivacious social group to which they belonged. There was time, too, for Koerner to discover the Michigan backcountry and its lakes, a land and a life completely new to him. Moose still roamed the woods, the loon's eerie cries made lakeside nights memorable, and there were still living remnants of the glory days of white-pine logging. Koerner sketched and sketched and absorbed, gaining the background, later expanded by whole summers spent in the Androscoggin region of Maine, that would enable him to illustrate successfully in the "moose-and-snowshoe," or north woods, genre of the outdoor-action school of American popular fiction.

A favorite Koerner haunt was Waupaskisco Beach on Goguac Lake, where a Battle Creek colony had week-end and summer cabins.[9]

The two whose pet and very private names for one another were "Dick" and "Boy" had begun their marriage with the idea that their separate careers in art would be pursued together. They gave a joint exhibition of oils and watercolors in the editorial rooms of *Pilgrim* which the Battle Creek *Journal* heralded as the beginning of the city's development as a center of the fine arts and not just "commercialism."[10] Whether any sales were made and for how much remains undetermined. It would not be surprising, however, to

Pilgrim *art: "Oh, how comfortable you look"*

see some of these early paintings appear on the market.[11]

Whether it was the stark comparison this joint exhibition made inevitable or simply a cumulative realization, "Dick" determined during their Battle Creek stay that "Boy" was the artist of the family and abandoned her artistic ambitions. Instead, she took over completely the management of the household and its purse, including its investment in later years when there was a surplus to invest. In the lean years, she followed the honorable maxim: "Use it up, wear it out, make it do or do without." Koerner used only the best paints and the finest of linen canvasses, and these materials and how he used them may explain why none of his surviving work, some of it more than a half-

The Koerners

cordially invite you and your friends
to attend an

Exhibition and Sale of their Original
Illustrations

including work in water colors, oils, pastels,
pen and ink and crayon
which will be held in the art and editorial rooms of
The Pilgrim Magazine

December first, second and third
nineteen hundred four

from nine o'clock in the morning
till five o'clock in the afternoon
and
from seven o'clock till nine o'clock in the evening

Announcement of Koerners' exhibition and sale

century old, has needed restoration but only cleaning. When he needed supplies, he ordered them and Lillian found a way to meet the bills. When the children came, and their arrival was long postponed, when her mother came to live with them in her crochety years, when Koerner's later fame drew coveys of clubwomen to visit his studio unannounced, Lillian handled them each and every one without interruption of her man at his creative work. It was a working partnership in the deepest sense and only one who has experienced a similar relationship can appreciate it fully.

On December 18, 1904, Koerner resigned from *Pilgrim,* although his work continued to appear in it for the next twelve months. They took an apartment overlooking the park in Detroit, where Koerner was to become art editor of a new paper, *The United States Daily,* so named more than twenty-five years before David Lawrence started his paper of the same name in Washington, D.C. It was not a Hearst paper, as has been stated erroneously, perhaps because Willis J. Abbott was involved in its birth, and it lived a little more than three months. The idea behind the paper stemmed from the success of the "trading stamp" promotions of the period. The paper itself, a respectably produced journal, served as the trading stamp involved. It was sold in bulk to merchants, without regard to their size or the nature of their wares, in amounts ranging from 50 copies to 5,000. A perforated corner of one page served as the coupon, on which the merchant wrote the customer's name and filed it away, every time the customer made a purchase of ten cents or more. When a sufficient number of these coupons had accumulated to the customer's account, they could be exchanged for premiums ranging from a silver teaspoon to a chromolithograph of Chief Lone Wolf to a fire-new automobile which Detroit was beginning to produce in numbers above the level of *curiosa Americana.*[12]

Financially unimpaired and considerably wiser in the ways of the newspaper world, the Koerners returned to Goguac Lake and rented a cottage on Waupaskisco Beach, where Bill proposed to spend the late spring and summer months in sketching and painting before embarking on the next step in his career; a step towards which they had saved religiously ever since their marriage. They had been there only briefly when Bill's old boss on the *Tribune,* William Wells, telegraphed him to come at once to help out on special-assignment work. Lillian was left to hold down the beach cabin and she stood the snow and wind blowing through its cracks and the screech owls crying in the dark until a flying squirrel spent all one pitch-black night banging against the door, which to Lillian's vivid imagination could only be sounds made by a wandering drunk bent upon ravishing any female he could find. She packed her things as soon as daylight came, managed to find a team and driver to take her to Battle Creek, and caught the train for Chicago, where she descended unannounced upon Bill's sister, now Mrs. Edward R. McCoy, and gave "Boy" a not unwelcome surprise.

Koerner's second stint on the *Tribune* lasted several months and appears to have been spent mainly on features for its Sunday magazine section. The fare this offered its readers may be judged from some of the titles he illustrated: "An American's Adventures Among the Most Exclusive Savages in the World," "Epidemic of Happy Marriages Between Rich and Poor," "To Go To the Heart of Africa in Search of a Flea," "What Strange Influence Has Interfered Five Times in Fifteen Months to Prevent the Wedding of Ab Fender and Millie Goings?" When Wells found a suitable replacement, the Koerners returned to Goguac Lake where Bill could improve his skills in what he had determined would be his forte, out-of-door illustration. Trumbull White, the first editor of *Red Book*, sent him a run-of-the-magazine story to do; the Battle Creek printing firm of Gage & Company commissioned fashion drawings for a dress catalog; and *Pilgrim*, of course, wanted whatever he could do for them.

On October 20, 1905, they boarded the steamer *Western States* at Detroit for the overnight run to Buffalo, whence they would entrain for New York, where Bill had been accepted for study at the Art Students League, a furthering of his professional education that he hoped to pursue for at least two years. They had one another, health, youthful confidence, and their carefully preserved savings. They also had a small sheet anchor to windward that was an integral part of the magazine era in which their whole lives were lived, and which requires some explication here.

The birth and maturation of the magazine era was inseparable from the promotion of mass consumer goods, and advertising became acquainted with the uses of psychology about 1903 through the work of Professor Walter Dill Scott at Northwestern University and Professor Harlow Gale of the University of Minnesota.[13] In this same year, *Collier's* issued the first of its annual "Automobile Numbers,"[14] which often were larger in pagination and illustrative content than the regu-

Koerner, Goguac Lake, about 1905

lar weekly issues they accompanied, and these made that magazine the first great advertising medium for the infant industry.

The first, full-page color advertisement in *Saturday Evening Post* appeared on September 30, 1899, for Quaker Oats, and by 1905, its rotund, apple-cheeked, smiling Friend, together with Cream of Wheat's white-capped chef, and Aunt Jemima, were indelibly identified with the products they symbolized. The lesson was not lost on C. W. Post, who was combatting Kellogg's monthly magazine *Good Health* with a booklet entitled *Road to Wellsville* extolling the virtues of his health-giving substitute for coffee, Postum, and his equally efficacious Grape-Nuts cereal.

(Grape-Nuts No. 1561—July, 1907, Magazines).

(Postum No. 1541—Aug. 1907 Magazines).

THE GOAL

is easily attained if you have **endurance, steady nerves, precision of movement** and a clear brain. These depend on the kind of food you eat;

Grape-Nuts

covers the entire field. Made of wheat and barley, including the Phosphate of Potash Nature places under the outer coat of these grains (wasted by the White Flour Miller) for the purpose of rebuilding worn-out and devitalized nerve and brain cells.

They go pretty rapidly in a long, hard game, but are quickly replaced by new cells when Grape-Nuts food is used—chewed dry, or with cream.

"There's a Reason"

Made by the Postum Cereal Co., Ltd., Battle Creek, Mich., U. S. A.

HAPPY DAYS

and cool, comfortable nights are the rule when the favorite beverage is

ICED POSTUM

Make Postum in the usual way, strong and rich, and have some always on hand.

When it is desired to serve it, add lemon juice, sugar, cracked ice, a little cream (if you like,) and squeeze a bit of lemon peel over the glass to get the oil for additional flavour.

Then you have a delightful, cooling, healthful beverage to serve friends on short notice.

"There's a Reason."

Postum Cereal Co., Ltd., Battle Creek, Mich., U. S. A.

Koerner art for Grape-Nuts and Postum ads: these are typical of the many illustrations Koerner did for the products of C. W. Post

Although Post never found a single identifying symbol for his products, such as those mentioned above, he did become one of the leading advertisers in the mass-circulation magazines,[15] and this affected the Koerners' early years in the East.

Lillian's father, Dr. W. I. Lusk, had been a prominent Battle Creek physician and she later recalled that:

C. W. Post, Mrs. Post and Marjorie [two years younger than Lillian] *had lived at our house where Mr. Post was a patient of my father, and he had been cured of stomach trouble in my father's sanitarium. Mr. Post experimented in our barn with bread* [sic] *formulas which he baked and crushed into what he called Grape Nuts for dyspepsia and ulcers.*

What effect this relationship had upon her husband's later employment by the Post Company remains unknown. From December, 1905, until well into 1910, Koerner supplied both black-and-white and color advertising illustrations for Grape-Nuts, Postum, and Post Toasties, which appeared in the leading magazines. Whether he did *all* the artwork for the Post products, as a newspaper article about him once alleged, remains unverified and, indeed, unverifiable, as these advertisements appeared unsigned. It brought him a small but steady monthly income during a period in his career when he needed it. After ending this Battle Creek connection, Koerner did only a minuscule amount of advertising art thereafter, which made him an anomaly among illustrators of his time and stature.

Norman Rockwell, who began his rise to membership in the nation's households with a cover for *Saturday Evening Post* in 1916, for which he received $75, made it his later practice to charge twice as much for an advertising picture as he did for a magazine cover: "It is common knowledge that there is more money to be made in advertising drawing than in any other type of illustration."[16] N. C. Wyeth once received more than $3,000 for one utility-company advertisement. A substantial number of Frank Tenney Johnson's western canvasses were done for the Minneapolis calendar firm of Brown and Bigelow;[17] F. B. Hoffman, another expert illustrator of western scenes, did work for Swift & Company; while Remington's western scenes sold

Kodaks and the film they used. Joseph C. Leyendecker painted the Arrow Shirt advertisements that created the masculine equivalent of the Gibson Girl, while Denman Fink, Gustavus C. Widney, and N. C. Wyeth did color work for Cream of Wheat that appeared for years. The dignified advertising for the Steinway piano used the work of Harvey T. Dunn, F. Luis Mora, Arthur I. Keller, and Ernest L. Blumenschein among many others, while Ivory Soap, Palmolive Soap, Woodbury's Facial Cream, and Colgate's Ribbon Dental Cream used a galaxy of the country's foremost illustrators to stimulate their sales.[18] So did any and every manufacturer who wished to reach the audience that the mass-circulation magazines provided, and collecting magazine advertisements became almost a national pastime.[19] The magazines themselves used illustrators to boost and hold their circulation. *Ladies Home Journal* offered "bedquilt designs" by Maxfield Parrish, Ernest Thompson Seton, Peter Newell, Jessie Willcox Smith, and Gazo Foudji, while *Collier's*, in its never-ceasing quest to reach the *Saturday Evening Post's* circulation, offered "Idle Hour Picture Puzzles," containing "famous pictures by Maxfield Parrish, Frederic Remington, Jessie Willcox Smith and other well-known artists."

Koerner's relative absence from this lucrative field was due to several factors. He disliked the time-consuming, speculative nature of much of this work, whereby a company such as Forbes Lithograph asked for sketches to present to calendar customers, then asked the artist to prepare a finished painting after the customer had indicated a preference, and did all this with no assurance that a sale would result. Koerner basically was too busy with magazine illustration to spend his time in such pursuits, and his few advertising illustrations after 1910 seem to have been done only when he was "between stories," which was seldom the case. More important, he seems to have *preferred* the challenge of giving visual life to a story's characters, of accepting the responsibility of enhancing and illuminating the author's story line, to advertising art.

The city for which Bill and Lillian were bound was the publishing capital of the nation, despite pretentious challenges from Boston, Philadelphia, Indianapolis, and Chicago. The "fiction factory" of Street and Smith celebrated its fiftieth birthday in the year of their arrival by moving into a new plant at Seventh Avenue and Seventeenth Street, whence it spewed forth two million copies of books and magazines a month. Prestigious publishing houses, such as Century, Harper and Brothers, Scribner's, Doubleday, Page and Co., operated on a somewhat different plane and the result was to make New York the major market for artists doing magazine, book, and advertising illustration.

Almost coincident with their arrival, *McClure's*, which was alive with "inside" color, listed its selections of America's leading magazine illustrators by their specialties:[20] *Great Character Drawings*—André Castaigne, Thomas Fogarty, Jay Hambidge, F. D. Steele, Sigmund Ivanowski; *Fascinating Children Pictures*—Reginald Birch, Fanny Y. Cory, Alice Barber Stephens; *Humorous Pictures*—A. B. Frost, W. J. Glackens, May Wilson-Preston, Orson Lowell, Charlotte Harding, Martin Justice; *Beautiful Girls*—Howard Chandler Christy, Henry Hutt, Frank Craig, J. H. Gardner-Soper; *Vigorous Realistic Pictures*—Ernest L. Blumenschein, Henry Reuterdahl, F. W. Taylor, Stanley M. Arthurs, W. J. Aylward, Frank E. Schoonover, Fernand Lungren. An examination of *McClure's* for 1900–1905 has shown that these selections were not confined to those artists whose work appeared on its covers and inside pages. Shortly afterwards, Arthur Rackham's illustrations for *Rip Van Winkle* caused Doubleday, Page and Co., to hail him as "the leading illustrator of the year"; the Scribner house was not averse to advertising in advance the artists whose work would grace their publications, including N. C. Wyeth, James Montgomery Flagg, and Harrison Fisher, and *Collier's* (9/1/1906) took a full page to say "A Few Words About Art" and to note that Walter Appleton Clark and Albert Sterner had joined the "well-known artists who already work 'exclusively' for *Colliers*." His ambition to join their company had turned Koerner's thoughts and finally his steps towards New York and the Art Students League.[21] He and Lillian were fortunate to reach there.

One of the largest and best built passenger ships on Lake Erie, *Western States* boasted two, powerful fifty-ton engines and seven boilers. Carrying fifty-five passengers, she cleared Detroit at six in the evening into the teeth of a gathering storm. Running ahead of it through the night, she was in sight of Buffalo harbor next morning when a full gale struck with winds estimated at seventy-two miles an hour, "faster than the running of an express train." The ship's master felt it impossible to enter Buffalo's harbor under such conditions and turned for the Canadian side of the lake. In so doing, "the boat was thrown upon its side, and passengers and everything movable thrown against the railings and everything fell that could fall. One car load of flour was precipitated into the boiler room."[22] *Western States* and eight other vessels made it to a safe harbor sixty-three miles from Buffalo and rode out the storm's trailing edge, before finally making port a full day behind schedule.

Mrs. Lusk received a more graphic account of the adventure in a letter from Lillian after imminent disaster had been averted.

Imagine a boat 300 feet long, 80 feet wide, 60 feet high, and five stories [sic] and having waves so powerful and high as to completely wash in the front of the fourth story, next to the pilot house, . . . Can you imagine the terrible plunging, wrenching, creaking, thumping, rolling and tossing, and the water from the waves rushing into the cabins and over the carpets. Everybody was deathly sick. All the passengers put on life preservers and prepared to jump into the waves. . . . The boat creaked and groaned as if it would break in two at any moment and we all expected to go to the bottom. William and I got our identification papers secured upon our persons, and clung together, intending to go down together. Through it all I was as calm and peaceful as if I were expecting chocolate cake instead of death.

We were on one of the two best boats on the lake, so we had a fair chance with the storm. Other boats would have gone down. . . . During the height of the storm the colored waiters in the dining room were frightened nearly into insanity. They were white with fear, and moaned, groaned and prayed. We could not get them to do anything for us. Captain Stewart is a brave man and showed great courage, and the passengers have all signed a vote of thanks to him. He, in company with the mate and pilot, never left their posts for 48 hours, not even to eat.[23]

The vessel had been reported lost and when she was sighted off Buffalo a crowd began to gather

Modeling class at Art Students League: Koerner is standing figure, second from left

to welcome her. Safely ashore, Lillian wrote to her mother: "We will go right on to New York. We will not stop at Niagara Falls. We don't want to see any more water!"[24]

Through a friend, they had arranged in advance for board and "accommodations" in the premises operated by Miss Jean Fields, a sculptor, and had specified "a view on the street and sunny windows." When they awoke their first morning, on individual cots placed at right angles to one another, they looked out on a back alley festooned with clothes lines and their assorted contents. This was partly overcome by the fact that Miss Field's guests were singers, actors, painters, and sculptors, and that she was "a delightful hostess at the table and at our 'At Homes' on Sunday evenings, when we had tea for the guests, all very gay and reportorially correct."[25]

Thus settled as comfortably as their budget would permit, Lillian began attending classes at Columbia Teachers College, "to learn something," where she studied under Nicholas Murray Butler, among others. She also found time to cover several pages of a small copying book with her own "Theories of a Wife" about child rearing. These activities partly filled the lonely times while Bill was studying at the Art Students League, and during his first year there, he attended classes in the mornings, afternoons, and evenings almost every day. Located on 57th Street, between Broadway and Seventh Avenue, the League was within easy walking distance for Koerner from their lodgings on 114th Street, just west of Central Park. Founded in 1875 as a split-off from the National Academy of Design, it was the first independent art school in the nation and the only one to hold "life" classes

Reproduction of nudes such as these by Koerner from Bridgman's "life" class precipitated the im-broglio with Anthony Comstock

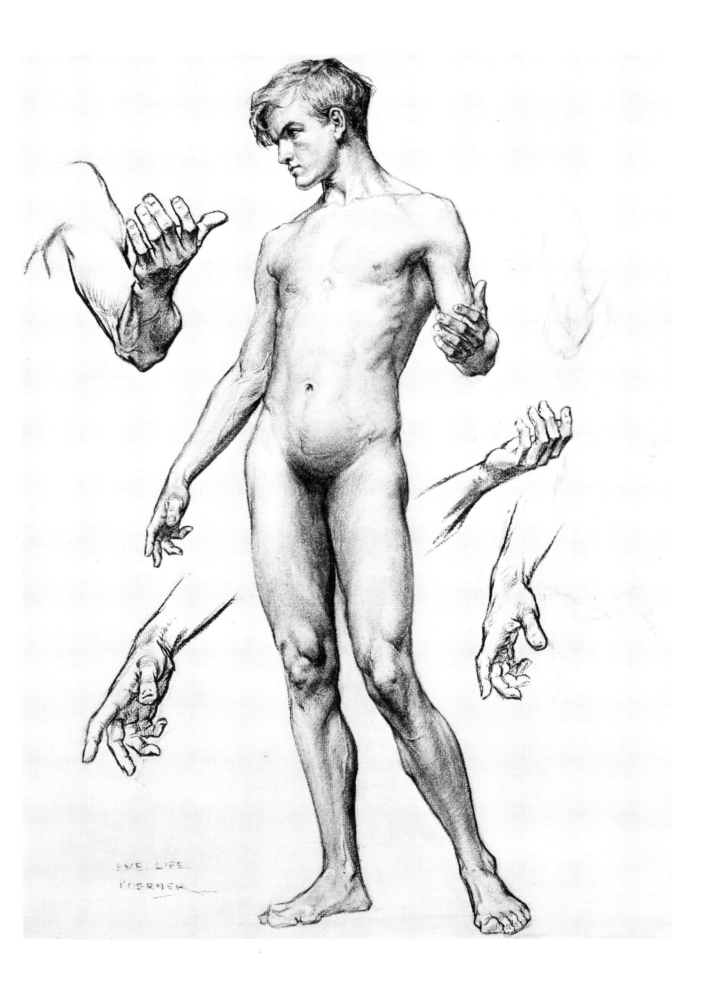

EVE LIFE
KOERNER

Pencil sketch while at the Art Students League

every week day. Its basic purpose was to give its students facility of expression, and it admitted women as students and mandated their membership on its Board of Control without apology or preachment.[26]

The Board consisted of twelve members, six of whom were elected each December at a general meeting of the League's membership; of these six, three had to be members of the outgoing Board, thus ensuring continuity in policy and practice. The six elected members then chose the other six to bring the Board to its required strength for the ensuing calendar year. Of its twelve members, four had to be current

students at the League and the League required work as a student before admission to membership. One of the Board's two vice-presidents had to be a woman and she could be nominated only by the female membership. This detailed account of the Board's composition lends emphasis to the fact that Koerner was chosen to join the Board in December, 1905, after being a student for a scant two months, and was again selected in December, 1906. The most important responsibilities of the Board were discharged each spring, when it established the program for the ensuing academic year and hired the faculty accordingly.[27]

Its distinguished faculty during Koerner's study there included Boardman Robinson, Joseph Pennell, Kenyon Cox, H. Siddons Mowbray, and Walter Appleton Clark. Gutzun Borglum joined its faculty in 1906, and Howard Pyle, called with reason "The Father of American Illustration," had taught there in 1904–1905 and was listed among its faculty for 1905–1906.[28] Of all the faculty, none made a greater impression on Koerner than did George B. Bridgman, one of the great teachers of his or any other time.[29] He was not an exponent of broad, luscious brush strokes but insisted upon the ability to draw, and told his classes that he had been drawing and painting *one* tree for thirty years but never had succeeded in getting *that* tree the way he wanted it.

You have to see the life *of the tree and only a great man can see life, ever-present life. Another thing you must grasp is that a tree has roots. An artist must realize that it must go into the ground with a root system as strong and as wide-spreading as its branches. Think of roots when you paint a tree and then your painting of a tree will not be on top of the earth; it will go into* the earth.[30]

Hans Peter Hansen had been Bridgman's top pupil until Koerner entered the class and the two waged a seesaw battle for first place in Bridgman's frequent "Concours," which entitled the winner to the choicest easel position to keep until the next competition brought about its retention or loss. At the end of the semester, Koerner received the Bridgman Scholarship in Drawing.[31] His work under Bridgman involved him in the League's imbroglio with Anthony Comstock,

Koerner did the cover (above) and inside art (following pages) for the Kalamazoo Suit Co.'s catalog while studying at the Art Students League

a United States postal inspector and secretary of the New York Society for the Suppression of Vice.[32]

The League's summer session in 1906 was held in Woodstock, New York, but Koerner did not attend. He and Lillian returned to Battle Creek and then to Goguac Lake. For the rest of his life, as the exigencies of his profession and the needs of his family permitted, Koerner's summers were times of meditation, self-appraisal, and renewal. He was not an artist who continually painted away his crop before it was half-grown. He sketched and painted away the summer days, finding tremendous release and relief after the punishing demands he had made upon himself in New York. The only remunerative work he did in this summer, other than for Grape-Nuts, were five wash drawings for a *Red Book* story, and the fall-winter catalog for the Kalamazoo Suit Company, for which he did thirty-three fashion illustrations and the cover.[33] He did one more of these style book–catalog combinations in 1907, probably of ladies' suits, for the S.F.&A.F. Miller Company in Baltimore. His remembrance of this work still was vivid in 1915.

It was an order for twenty or thirty drawings of suits, for which I was to receive something like four or five dollars for each drawing. I put infinite pains and care into the first drawing and was pleased with it. BUT—it took me three days to make it. I worked faster on the second but it took me two days. I sat down to think. At the rate I was going and considering the extreme transience of feminine styles, I figured that by the time I completed the set I would be too aged and infirm to draw, even if it should be the fashion to wear clothing. So I thought out a plan. I made two fine drawings: one with the left hand raised in a graceful gesture; the other with the right hand raised in an equally graceful gesture. Then I made tracings from these and added the details. I knocked off about three or four a day. There was a certain lack of variety, but the fashion man was more concerned about buttons and braid than originality so they were highly satisfactory.[34]

They returned to New York on October 1, 1906, where Koerner resumed his education at the League, taking more work with Bridgman

Two pages from the Kalamazoo Suit Co.'s catalog showing Koerner art

and modeling with Gutzun Borglum among his other studies. Lillian took an English course at Columbia, and taught a night class for a while at the Lincoln Club in the Bowery, where her pupils were boys of nine and ten who had proved too much for two male predecessors. They rented a veritable barn of a room, 40 × 40 feet, on the fifth floor of the six-story Lincoln Arcade Building, which Lillian transformed with burlap draperies hung on wires into a bedroom, kitchen-dining room, and Koerner's first professional studio of his own.[35] There was a sink with cold water already in place, and they bought a two-burner gas plate for $1.00; a bed-couch with wire springs, a low table for dining, some dishes

No. 1153. Novelty is the main qualification of this skilfully tailored skirt, and it is a gratifying example of the most recent vogues intended for general wear. Being unique in style, it offers a splendid opportunity for economical indoor dress, as a compromise on more pretentious designs. The construction is according to the latest circular models, with deep inverted pleats and large folds. When worn with a fancy waist, the charming grace of this garment is apparent to the most casual observer.

Made in quality A goods	....	$ 5.50
Made in quality B goods	....	6.50
Made in quality C goods	....	7.75
Made in quality D goods	....	9.25
Made in quality E goods	....	11.00

No. 1154.

No. 1154. This garment is an effective illustration of the tailor's art and will add an individual charm to the wearer's personality. An attractively unique feature is the panel front, the effect of which lends an air of distinct exclusiveness. Thirteen gores are included in the skirt, and they are arranged with deep kilts specially created with the idea of both service and beauty. Indeed this design has few equals. It will win immediate and unqualified admiration wherever worn.

Made in quality A goods	....	$ 4.50
Made in quality B goods	....	5.50
Made in quality C goods	....	6.75
Made in quality D goods	....	8.25
Made in quality E goods	....	10.00

No. 1153.

EXTRA SIZES COST 10% MORE. ALL SKIRTS OVER 30 WAIST OR 43 LENGTH ARE EXTRA SIZES

13

for $3.50, and, most costly of their investments, an easel and a model stand, to say nothing of paints, brushes, and canvas. Their shelves were made out of orange crates and wooden boxes made their chairs, while the bath and lavatory were down a drafty hall, beyond the rickety elevator that rattled and creaked up and down all day and far into the night.

The previous tenants of this man-made cavern had been a theatrical troupe which had used it as a practice room for their dance routines. Lillian felt sure that they had left because the floor was monstrously uneven and continually dusty.[36]

Their basic food budget was one dollar per day—meat, vegetable, bread, butter, milk—and

Lillian shopped the stores and markets on Amsterdam Avenue to get the best bargains she could find. A case of beer lasted them a long time, unless too many thirsty League friends came calling, the bottles being cooled by wrapping them in wet dish towels and standing them on the sill of the open window. Oranges for Bill's breakfast were an infrequent luxury: "He never knew that I liked oranges until, shall I say, we were affluent." Frugality was their watchword because it had to be. Koerner won the William T. Evens Prize of $50.00 for the "most practical drawing," and won another small monetary stipend for the "best design for a magazine cover," which helped their budgetary problems. His work for Grape-Nuts and Postum paid the rent, as nearly as can be ascertained, and internal evidence in the corpus of his and his wife's papers for these years suggests that he did work for Hearst's New York *American,* as Willis J. Abbott was chief editorial writer during this period. A tattered fragment in this same corpus is part of a color advertisement for "Columbia Brand" macaroni, but where this work appeared remains unknown.

Too much erosion of their savings was prevented by Koerner's first consistent appearance in a magazine other than the ill-fated *Pilgrim.* Karl Harriman sent him six stories to illustrate for *Red Book* for which he produced at least twenty-two black-and-white wash drawings. The stories were magazine-run, boy-girl fiction, and the illustrations were distinguished largely by their strength of line and clarity of composition. One half-page, that showed two couples in the tonneau of a left-hand drive automobile, did convey a sense of movement. Koerner, Gustavus C. Widney, and Walter J. Enright were the only illustrators in these six issues of *Red Book* who went on to do much work for the other leading magazines in the first decade of the present century. He also turned out five illustrations for two stories in *The Home Magazine,* and demonstrated his versatility thereby. One was a college football yarn, "The Left Guard's Pass," and the other was a boy-girl romance in a western setting, "The Wire Cutters," by Grace McGowan Cooke, who contributed to leading magazines in the early stage of the western story's development.

His cameo of the hero's head gave him cleanly chiselled features, a neckerchief, and a modified

Head sketch while at the Art Students League

forest ranger's hat, the heroine took up almost one long column and resembled Lillian, while the major illustration filled a quarter-page and showed the villains swooping down on horseback upon the story's romantic leads.[37] In this illustration, even more than in the automobile drawing mentioned above, Koerner's early sense of movement in space was apparent. He perfected it throughout his career, using it with particular effectiveness in his later vignette work. "In my personal opinion," said William Moyers, "Koerner and later Benton Clark were the premier ones in the use of vignette. They could really make a spot exciting."[38]

There was not the budgetary leeway to permit much theater-going, which both of them relished, and they only read about most of the attractions that graced the "Great White Way" in 1907,

including the first of Flo Ziegfield's many "Follies." A "Card of Admittance" to the annual exhibition of the New York Water Color Club cost them nothing. Inexpensive entertainment as well as education was ever present at the great Bronx Zoological Gardens and the American Museum of Natural History, where a former Clinton boy and student of Herr Stich, Bruce Horsfall, was making fossil drawings. Koerner's sketch book was always with him on these junkets and his account books in later years listed the expenses of many visits he paid these institutions to bring verisimilitude to his illustrations.

As the slow spring nudged itself towards summer, Koerner was invited by two fellow-students, Wilson C. Dexter and Robert W. Amick,[39] to spend the summer months with them at a cottage in Maine. They assured him that they would help Lillian with the cooking and household chores. The foursome traveled by steamer to Portland, thence by train to Wilton where they transferred to a horse-drawn "Mountain Coach" for the twelve miles to Webb Pond, near Weld. This was Koerner's first taste of rural New England and Maine was one of the last strongholds of early rural America, its people, animals, artifacts, and values. Koerner loved it and returned to it again and again in succeeding summers. His affection for the land and the self-reliant, fiercely independent human beings who wrested a living from its thin and stony soil was reflected in the paintings and drawings he did for *Harper's*, which continued to use the "rural New England" story that had been a mainstay of American fiction in the latter nineteenth century long after it had passed from the pages of *Century*, *Scribner's*, and *Atlantic*.

While these summer weeks were filled with sketches and impressions that would be of value in Koerner's future, they also were weeks filled with pondering that future: what to do and where to do it? They had survived the Panic of 1907 which had not rippled out from New York with sufficient force to affect their savings account in Battle Creek's Central National Bank but others had not been so fortunate, including Maynard Dixon who had moved to New York just in time to lose his modest grubstake.[40] The aftereffects of the Panic continued to limit the market for illustrations, as N. C. Wyeth noted with some self-esteem in a letter from Wilmington, Delaware, on November 29, 1907: "In spite of *hard times* and the fact that most of the fellows [artists] here are idle as far as ordered work goes, I have *Scribner's, Century* and *Saturday Evening Post* hot on my heels."[41] It was a poor time to embark upon a full-time career as a freelance artist, and the temptation was strong to return to Chicago and the *Tribune,* where he was always welcome, and where *Red Book* was published.

Their dwindling savings account, plus the continuing work for Grape-Nuts, provided a thin cushion of solvency and it was on this basis that Koerner wrote a letter regarding possible acceptance for instruction by Howard Pyle. At this stage in his distinguished teaching and illustrating career, Pyle conducted a composition class in his Wilmington studio each Saturday evening and set aside a brief period each working morning to critique the work of those who wanted it. There was no charge for attendance, but Pyle insisted on the right to determine those whom he would accept.[42]

This was not a "school" in the sense that Pyle's teaching at Philadelphia's Drexel Institute and at Chadd's Ford, Pennsylvania, had been. There students had come to him with only preliminary training, or none at all, and he had coaxed those who could meet his exacting standards into artistic maturity. That he had done his job well is attested by the fact that of the thirty-five artists mentioned by Frank Luther Mott in his five-volume *History of American Magazines* as having had significant effect upon magazine growth and stature, eight were Pyle students and Pyle, himself, was among those listed. In 1907, he was giving of his time and formidable talents only to men and women who had had professional experience and were actually working artists. Some resided elsewhere and came to him only occasionally, but most resided in Wilmington, where they executed their professional assignments and brought their work to Pyle for instruction, guidance, and stimulation. He treated them as professional equals and would not accept dilettantes, or those who talked about art for art's sake, or who indulged themselves in esthetic fancies without professional production. It was what Pyle had seen in Koerner's already published work that brought a letter of acceptance from Miss Gertrude Brinckle, Pyle's long-time secretary and confidante. About mid-September, 1907, the Koerners arrived in Wilmington and took a major step up the ladder of his long career as one of the nation's foremost illustrators.

1. This was part of Chicago's continuing efforts to supplant the effete East as disseminator of culture for its own hinterland. *Blue Book* and *Green Book,* both semi-pulp magazines, later were added to the *Red Book* stable and folklore holds that each title was derived from the cover of a brothel directory in different cities.

2. Ross H. Coller to W.H.H., 6/14/1970 *et seq.* Coller, a veteran Michigan newspaperman and student of Battle Creek history, at this time was press relations representative for the lower house of the Michigan legislature.

3. The last name is sometimes spelled Abbot; his autobiography, *Watching the World Go By,* has been useful.

4. Coller, 8/2/1970.

5. One of these was stamped into the front cover of the book, as was the custom in the days before dust wrappers or jackets.

6. Ben Duggar, *Professional Art Magazine,* 2/1940, 6.

7. H. W. Ryan to W.H.H., 5/1/1970, transmitting research in the Library of Congress.

8. *Saturday Evening Post,* 6/25/1932, 40.

9. "I do not know exactly how to describe the colony which existed at this beach," said Coller, "except that the place was dominated by what you might call 'deep thinkers.' They were nature lovers, art and music enthusiasts, students of astronomy and the like." All one summer at the lake, Koerner was followed constantly by "a wide-eyed, open-eared youngster who literally pumped him dry of his knowledge of drawing, painting and illustrating," and was quite content to be paid for what posing he did by a plate of chocolate fudge from Mrs. Koerner. Before he learned the proper handling of canoes, Koerner essayed to take his bride across the lake to a dance one evening and tumbled them both into its waters "in our best bib and tucker," a fact which did not deter them from attending the dance, bedraggled but with undampened spirits. Coller to W.H.H., 6/28/1970 and 8/12/1970.

10. The titles of their studies included "The Sweetheart," "Lillian," "The Reconciliation," "Chicago by Night," "Mother and Child," and "Sunset." Undated clipping, Koerner Papers.

11. Some of Koerner's later work has appeared in an auction at New York's Parke-Bernet Galleries in the past few years. This renewed interest in Koerner has been stimulated in part by a comprehensive hanging of his paintings at the Amon Carter Museum of Western Art, Fort Worth, Texas, 1969.

12. The theory was that the trade attracted to the store would enable the merchant to find a profit in buying and distributing the paper, while its owners would find their profit in the advertising receipts. It was a good theory,

perhaps, but it was unconscionably complicated and that spelled its doom, although Abbott later insisted that its failure was due to the opposition of the city's established *Free Press* and *Evening News,* which threatened merchants who deigned to participate in such a scheme. Abbott also maintained that his effort to sell the paper to Hearst as its future darkened was blocked by the fact that the existing Detroit papers pledged $50,000 to *The United States Daily's* owner to prevent Hearst's entry into their domain. Abbott, 247–49; Coller, various letters; G. W. Stark, Detroit *News,* 3/31/1941; Koerner, *Narrative.*

13. Frank Luther Mott, *American Journalism, A History: 1690–1960* (3rd. ed.), 593.

14. This annual automobile number appeared with the second January issue each year for many years.

15. Post's claim for the efficacy of his products involved him in a protracted legal battle with *Collier's,* which regarded him as a "faker" and his claims as hogwash. See *Collier's,* 9/28/1907 and 12/17/1910, for an outline of this skirmish.

16. Anon., *Norman Rockwell, Illustrator* (3rd. ed.), 129.

17. Harold McCracken, *The Frank Tenney Johnson Book,* virtually ignores this aspect of Johnson's artistic career.

18. *Time,* 2/5/1973, carried a full-page color spread for Datsun automobiles by Peter Hurd.

19. These color advertisements were confined at first to the inside front cover and both sides of the back cover, which were of heavier, coated stock than the inside pages.

20. The issue for 11/1905 had 202 pages of advertising and 112 pages of text, including Rudyard Kipling's "With the Night Mail," a science-fiction forerunner.

21. Koerner, *Narrative* indicates that Mrs. Lusk felt that her daughter was being taken to the sink of iniquity of the universe.

22. Koerner Papers, undated clipping, Battle Creek *Moon.*

23. Koerner, *Narrative.*

24. *Ibid.*

25. *Ibid.*

26. Anon., *Years of Art: The Story of the Art Students League of New York,* 21.

27. Letters from Lawrence Campbell of the Art Students League were of great value in unraveling the League's method of selecting its governing body.

28. Lawrence Campbell to W.H.H., 6/29/1970. There is some question still of Pyle's actual presence in this season.

29. Koerner's son studied under Bridgman at the League thirty years later and holds him in high regard to this day.

30. Koerner, *Narrative.*

31. He received two other awards during his studies at the League.

32. In January, 1906, the League issued the first number of *The American Student of Art,* to be published monthly from October to July, with the purpose of providing material for serious students of art. The June issue carried three male nudes by Koerner, E. E. Clark, and C. J. Martin. Such an incitement to impurity and obscenity did not escape Comstock's attention and, in due course, he arrested the League's bookkeeper, a young lady of nineteen years, on charges of selling and distributing material inimical to public morals. The students promptly responded with cari-

catures of Comstock with wings and a halo; they suspended an effigy of him, as fat as they could stuff it, from a third-story window of the League's building; one of them composed a sonnet in Comstock's honor which condemned him as "a sexless clown who shunned love's hallowed fire," and a statuette of Comstock was presented to the bookkeeper, which showed him as a meager ascetic with one foot—a cloven one—resting on the shattered form of the Venus de Milo, while his right hand clutched a mallet. The New York press had a field day with the case and members of the League visited Washington to complain to the Postmaster-General that Comstock was abusing his official position. On December 29, 1906, Comstock wrote a letter to the bookkeeper, agreeing to dismissal of the charges against her as a "Christmas present," and the case was withdrawn from the Court of Special Sessions two days later. This victory did not remove Comstock from the attention of the Society of American Fakirs.

This was a group within the League which selected its members annually from students and League members. Each spring, the Society held an exhibition of "Fakes" in a room above that in which either the Society of American Artists or the National Academy of Design was holding its annual exhibition. The Fakirs were boisterous and ruthless in their burlesques of such trends as *art nouveau,* then on the wane, or the latest imported rage of Impressionism, or the subject painting of everyday American subjects that was the current "crest of the wave" in indigenous Art. They spared no sacred cow or canon, much less an artist, no matter how famous. They advertised their annual exhibition by staging a parade in costumes of their own contriving while playing papier mache instruments, and they usually "lost" their parade permit, which got some of them sent to jail and brought them additional free publicity.

Koerner and Jo Davidson, a bear of a man, were the two biggest members of the Fakirs and the leaders in rowdy antics. A fellow-student of Koerner's remembered him as being tremendously strong in his arms, and remembered, too, that in one of their impromptu "pushing" contests Koerner inadvertently broke an opponent's arm. They also assembled upon occasion at a beer garden on Columbus Circle to drink Pabst beer, which Koerner told his wife was "cooling," when she joined them there one day. Their annual exhibit of "Fakes" in 1907, when the phrase "It's a lemon" was popular, featured a "Fake" Anthony Comstock who stamped and stormed among the exhibits, among which were nudes of all sizes and kinds in every medium imaginable, affecting to regard them with shame and horror. The League's catalog for 1907–1908 was sprinkled liberally with nudes without reaction from Comstock. This account is based on *Years of Art,* 86–88, 169–71; Koerner, *Narrative;* clippings in the Koerner Papers; telephone interview, 5/7/1970, Andrew Dasburgh.

33. Koerner cannot be charged with responsibility for the company's slogan: "We *suit* you by mail with garments new/Made to your measure in Kalamazoo." A copy of the catalog is in the Koerner Papers.

34. Quoted in Lewiston (Maine) *Journal,* 9/14/1915.

35. Koerner, *Narrative* is the basis for this account of their second year in New York.

36. Besides being uneven, the floor at night became alive with mice and cockroaches and Bill was awakened one

night by a screeching yell from Lillian, who had been awakened by a mouse crawling up the sleeve of her night-gown. He leaped for the bare light bulb that gave the only light, spied the mouse which she had shaken loose from its precarious hold, and dispatched it with suitable im-precations to the accompaniment of encouraging cries from his thoroughly shattered wife. Next morning, when she took the elevator down to the street, Bill having already departed for the League, the grizzled elevator operator looked at her pityingly and asked, "Heard you scream last night. Did he hit you?"

Another diversion that intermittently plagued their nights was a banging and thumping on the floor above, with occasionally the sound of a solid object hitting it with the impact of a dropped piano. Their one light bulb on its long cord jerked and jiggled and swayed in arcs, while dust filtered down on them and their household goods. One especially noisy night, after they had been awakened by the commotion from above, Koerner slipped on his bath-robe and went out the door, muttering "I'll give 'em Hell" as he went. The noise subsided and then resumed as he returned. "Did you give them Hell?" asked his wife. "No," came the growled reply. "They told me!" The cavernous studio above was occupied by George Bellows, and the noises came from his study of pugilists in action, whenever he could afford their services, in preparation for the paint-ings that made him the Goya of the American prize ring. Thereafter, he was as considerate of his downstairs neigh-bors as his studies permitted, and Koerner learned much about anatomy in action at Bellow's invitation.

37. *Home's* page size was 10½ × 13¼ inches trimmed; its circulation is unknown.

38. William Moyers, Albuquerque, New Mexico, to W. H.H., 3/26/1973. "Bill" Moyers is among the outstanding artists of the West today.

39. Both became well-known magazine illustrators in the period 1910–20.

40. Harold G. Davidson, *Edward Borein: Cowboy Artist*, 61, says that Borein reached New York in December, 1907, which was after the Koerners had left.

41. Wyeth was in his "western" phase at this time and *Saturday Evening Post* was using his western illustrations as an offset to Remington, who was under exclusive con-tract with *Collier's* for magazine work.

42. Henry C. Pitz, *The Brandywine Tradition*, 148–49.

Chapter V
THE RUNGS OF THE LADDER

ONCE the center of Sweden's effort to gain a slice of North America and steeped in colonial history and traditions, Wilmington contained a juxtaposition that would seem incompatible, or at least incongruous, to many today. Ever since Thomas Jefferson had encouraged a Huguenot immigrant to produce gunpowder there, a commodity Jefferson felt was vital to the well-being of the infant republic, it had been a major center of its manufacture and of explosive ingredients in general. Now into its second century, its major firm was turning its energies to the new field of industrial chemicals with such success as to make du Pont a household name today.

Thanks to Howard Pyle's residence, it long had enjoyed stature as a center of American art and this was enhanced when Pyle resigned from Philadelphia's Drexel Institute in 1900 and thereafter conducted his school in Wilmington. His students had found quarters there while under his tutelage and many of them then had made it their home while pursuing the profession that Pyle had taught them. They were a clannish group, within which were subtle gradations based more on the time and place they had begun their work with Pyle than on artistic ability.

Heading the "squirearchy," as it were, were the Drexel students, such as Elizabeth Shippen Greene, Jessie Willcox Smith, Alice Barber Stephens, Stanley M. Arthurs, and Frank E. Schoonover. The next echelon comprised those who had been students in Pyle's Wilmington "school," and included N. C. Wyeth, Harvey T. Dunn, Allen Tupper True, and others. Then came those like Koerner, numbering Douglas Duer, Anton Otto Fischer, William H. Foster, Thomas D. Skid-

more, Henry J. Soulen, and Gayle Porter Hoskins, the last of whom had attended the Art Students League in New York while Koerner was there and had preceded him to Wilmington. These gradations also were followed roughly in the various groups of studios in Wilmington. The first two groups tended to concentrate in the studios adjoining Pyle's own, or the newly completed Rodney Street Studios, while the others found working quarters in the Orange Street Studios and those maintained by Henry Downard. Elizabeth Greene, Jessie Smith, and Alice Stephens made a self-contained colony within a colony and produced gorgeous color illustrations for editions of *Mother Goose* and *A Child's Garden of Verses,* as well as covers for *Good Housekeeping* and *Ladies Home Journal* among others.

That there was some friction between members of the Pyle-ians is understandable, given the premise that a colony of artists could introduce Hell to Paradise. That there was not more of it seems due to the remarkable camaraderie that Pyle engendered in his students. There was personal friction between Schoonover, at this point regarded as Pyle's strongest student, and Wyeth, young, cocksure, and aggressive, who was challenging all of Pyle's pupils, past and present, with his productivity and its magazine acceptance. This seems due in part to Schoonover's subtle air of superiority and his social milieu—he already was a member of "The Players" in New York and was traveling in Europe in 1907—and in part to Wyeth's inward feelings, which he did not always suppress, that "Illustration is built on superficial techniques and everything that's artificial."[1] This seems rather surprising in a young man who had offered *McClure's* exclusive use of his skill in illustration for thirty weeks for the sum of $4,000.[2] Neither the distinctions nor the personality conflict mentioned affected Koerner. He made friends easily with men, he was restrained with his personal opinions to the point of taciturnity, and, above all, he had come to Wilmington to study and to work.

Oliver Kemp, already known for his hunting scenes,[3] was one of those Koerner met at his first Pyle session. He helped the newcomer to find a house at 1008 Kirk Avenue, "a little short street with nice neighbors on either side and always a cat or two on the back fence. We acquired a cat that howled with the rest."[4] Koerner first tried sharing a studio with Alfredo Demarest, but soon found a third-floor room in a vacant house to use as a studio until taking one of the Downard Studios at $16.00 per month when Watson Barratt moved out. His later neighbors in these studios were Anton Otto Fischer, Mary Ellen Sigsbee,[5] who became Mrs. Fischer in 1912, and William H. Foster, who then specialized in illustrating "speed" stories of automobiles, trains, and boats. Mrs. Lusk came to live with them, after retiring from teaching, and "she could not understand why we did not have a tea kettle instead of a saucepan to boil water in for tea, why we only had three plates, three cups and the plated silver Mother Koerner had given us for a wedding present."[6] She also could not understand, and never did, why her daughter's life was centered on what her husband did and needed.

What he needed most during those first months in Wilmington was encouragement. Pyle was a jolly and a cordial man in his fifty-fifth year, who combined Quaker simplicity with a touch of Swedenborgian mysticism in his sincerity, enthusiasm, dramatic force, fertility of imagination, driving energy, and earnestness of purpose. He felt that too great a dependence upon models was stifling, because it emphasized imitation not imagination, and he demanded of his pupils that they possess imagination first of all, and then artistic ability, color sense, and draftsmanship, firm and solid draftsmanship.[7] He taught art and illustration as one and he taught it as a religion, always insistent that "illustrations be made to fill out the text rather than

to make a picture of some scene described in it."[8]

Pyle had an amazing ability to get inside his students' minds and hearts and bowels. "How [he] did reach *in* and *down* and fairly *tore* at one's weak spots! It was like salt on an open sore, but it cleansed and healed."[9] When he told Koerner that his work lacked "spiritual quality," it was taken to heart to such an extent that, barring the old reliable breakfast food-and-drink advertising, Koerner did no commercial work at all during his first six months under Pyle's tutelage. He drove himself to grasp and to feel everything that Pyle could teach him and he drove himself, too, in improving his ability to portray women and dogs, two subjects that had plagued him. Lillian posed for him far into many nights, as he made studies of her hands, forearms, fingernails, elbows, ears, and nose—memorizing every bone and muscle in light and shadow that he might be free from models to endow these intimate details with both dimension and depth.

What his work with Pyle meant to him is shown clearly in excerpts from his only major writing for publication: a tribute to Pyle upon the latter's death. That he was the one of all the Pyle students who was asked to do the piece was a compliment he appreciated.

Howard Pyle has passed. The place that he filled in art, literature, and in national affairs is vacant, and there is no one to take his chair. The man has left us—the master lives. He lives now just as he has lived, by his work and by his influencing others to work toward individual expression of all of that which is true, beautiful and noble. He believed in America. He believed in the latent power of American art—of American culture and genius. He supported his beliefs, and proved their substance, by establishing the first distinct school of American illustrators the country had ever known, and this school made an American art free, straight-forward and sincere.

A great man never loses his greatness, the quality of fruitage assures the greatness; and the reaping of the harvest of good works was rich and full for this man who held all the strength of genius and but a few of the weaknesses. He gathered into his highly sensitive, tense, and truth-loving nature all that was of use, and, in turn, he gave freely, broadly, universally. The world has lost a useful man. Utility and Purpose were the keynotes of his long and steady activity. He looked forward, never backward; in his progress in art and in literature he kept a true course, and, during this process of his development, Howard Pyle pursued his own path, uninfluenced by the artistic currents of this or any other country.

"Tell about life in your own way," he has said to his students. "Paint ideas, paint thoughts, then you will be of use; your work will be needed." And as he taught others how to do, just so did he practise himself. . . .

Believing, as he did, that good was an essential quality in all mankind, he was able to make us love his fiercest pirates, his boldest sea-robbers, his most bloodthirsty scenes of plunder and conquest. We love his buccaneers as wildly as we do gently love his Joan of Arc, or that wonderful and mystical series on "Travels of the Soul." He was capable of raising us from the depths of human emotion to the heights of spiritual experience. He almost touched the one elusive and purely creative art, for at times his pictures had the power of music.

Howard Pyle taught, fought, sang, laughed and sobbed through his work. His pictures, in point of composition were simplicity itself, and in their straight-forward way of appeal, one felt the frank, open-hearted sincerity of their creator. In color, he caught the rare and subtle tints of nature; he understood her moods, her shades, her tones, her atmosphere as one with less trained senses and grosser soul could never know or feel; and, although his imagination seemed boundless, yet it was always held true and wholesome by his sense of justice to his fellowmen, his reverence for high morals and religion and his love for truth.

Howard Pyle was not a narrow specialist, and although he became the authority in his favorite field, he seemed to know the essential points of a subject upon whatever line he touched, or was called upon to discuss with his students. He understood the heart of things and he learned this great throbbing pulse, through his own personal efforts in untiring study and observation.

Not a stylist, not an imitator, but a man with a purpose, was Howard Pyle. This raised him higher than his pictures, higher than his power as an author, and he lives, not alone in his own

productions of brush and pen, but through the lives of many, many notable men and women who owe their inspiration, their training, and the stability of their work to Howard Pyle—the master—the master who found himself in finding others, who believed that he received as he gave, and who worked like father with children, with those who came to learn from him. . . .

Howard Pyle lived not for himself. For thirty years or more he has been giving, giving, giving himself to us. Where brush limited his giving, his pen took up expression and we have his "Robin Hood," his "Twilight Land," his "King Alfred" stories, and his "Man of Sorrows," besides other books and the many short stories which have appeared in the magazines, especially in Harper's Monthly. *In point of production Howard Pyle has lived his four score years and ten; he has fulfilled his youthful promise as a genius of rare order; he has established the American School of Illustration, and foremost in the field, has taken his illustrious place as our representative American illustrator. All this accomplished in the artistic world alone, not including his acknowledged mastership of the short story and his literary career. He was able, in the last few years, to reach the very heights of his desires—the painting of mural decoration. . . .*

His future work is past, Howard Pyle lives. His name and memory can never die. He, the man, and his, a man's works, will be the inspiration that will bring out all that is best and pure and lofty in the younger generations of artists—to all of those who listen and learn of him.[10]

Koerner's work was among that displayed at the First Annual Exhibition of Paintings by the Pupils of Howard Pyle in Wilmington, November 12–16, 1912. Lillian was one of the forty-two "Patronesses" for the exhibition, which included other wives of resident artists and four du Pont matrons. To collect and preserve the work of Pyle, and "to further the interest of Art in Delaware," the Wilmington Society of the Fine Arts incorporated after this exhibition.

Pyle was not the only one from whom "Bill" Koerner, so he was called by his Wilmington friends, learned in Wilmington. Harvey Dunn, who had married Tula Krebs, the daughter of a local explosives manufacturer, frequently drifted into Bill's studio to criticize and talk shop, and did an oil portrait of him at work in his studio. Stanley M. Arthurs, outwardly reserved and very dignified but with a latent twinkle always in his eyes, gave advice on how to see "top light" and "edges" and how to balance light and shade.[11] Schoonover was another who gave Koerner of his expertise,[12] and Schoonover at this time was the nation's foremost portrayer of the Canadian Arctic and sub-Arctic, having spent many months in the "bush" around Hudson's Bay, at a time when the north-woods story was a staple of American popular fiction.[13]

The most lasting friendship and the one with the greatest impact upon Koerner's later life was formed with Frank Stick, who had recently married Maud Hayes, Wilmington's outstanding female model, whom Lillian saw as "a beautiful, graceful Maryland girl with a hint of a drawl . . . beautifully tantalizing." Stick belongs properly with such great animal and wildlife illustrators as Carl Livingston Bull, Lynn Bogue Hunt, Carl Rungius, and Paul Bransom, and he did fish, both fresh and salt-water, better than any of them. South Dakota-born, six years younger than Koerner, Stick had studied at the Chicago Art Institute before joining Pyle's special classes about 1904, being then in his twentieth year. The two couples made a compatible foursome, canoeing on the Brandywine, fishing the unpolluted Delaware River and its ocean approaches, and striding along on the ten-mile hikes that were Koerner's favorite diversion on non-working Sundays, and which caused Lillian to wonder upon occasion if they could not afford a trolley ride back to town.

The problem faced by most aspiring illustrators once was expressed succinctly by Wesley Stout, who succeeded George Horace Lorimer as editor of *Saturday Evening Post*.

The young illustrator must take what the gods give and be thankful. Until he wins his spurs, he gets, if anything, the odds and ends of magazine work. This month it may be a circus yarn, next month a railroad story, weeks of idleness and then a Western or a lumberjack story. Or worse, if he does the circus story passably, he may, like a type actor, get himself labelled in editors' minds as a circus specialist, though he knows little and cares less about the Ringling boys.[14]

There was plenty of diversity in the work Koerner did in 1908 and he did not have to seek it. Karl Harriman sent him all that he wanted to handle from *Red Book*—fifteen cents per copy and 350,000 monthly circulation—which was on the verge of billing itself as "The Largest Illustrated Fiction Magazine in the World." It also was one of the very few mass-circulation magazines in this period to give the illustrator a credit line in its table of contents. Most printed the illustrator's name in agate type beneath one of the story illustrations and *Saturday Evening Post* did not do even this until December 14, 1907.[15] In common with many of the monthly "quality slicks," *Red Book's* illustrators worked from six to eight weeks ahead of the issue for which their story was scheduled,[16] sometimes only a month if the schedule got jammed up, which afforded time for the artist to receive proofs of his work before it appeared. Printed on quality coated stock these proof sheets had a clarity that all too often was muddied by the presswork of the production schedule.

Koerner did six stories for *Red Book* in 1908, receiving a minimum of $100 per story,[17] depending on the number of illustrations each required. Their titles reflect their story lines, from "A Postponed Proposal" to "The Freshman Full Back," for which he did a full-page frontispiece, as it was the lead story, by Ralph D. Paine, and three black-and-white drawings. For "What the Buyer Bought," a story of young love in an Alpine setting, he did four black-and-white wash drawings and provided ten separate decorations for its pages, these being small line drawings of such things as churches, goats, an Alpine village, and a mountain climber. He also executed a book assignment in this year, contributing the frontispiece and two illustrations to *The Lackawannas at Moosehead*, one in a series of juveniles by George Selwyn Kimball that fell between the *Three Little Peppers* and the adventures of *The Rover Boys*.

This income, plus the metronomic regularity of his cereal-and-beverage advertising work, was more than enough to meet their fixed charges, about $40.00 per month for both house and studio rental, and their living expenses. Koerner's studio supplies were extra, of course, but Lillian made her own dresses and the costumes that he often required in order to get the hang and the sheen and the feel of them into his illustrations. When Wilmington's summer became oppressive, and Koerner once maintained that it could make a man perspire while taking a cold shower, they hied themselves off to Michigan's lake country, after paying a visit to his mother in Clinton and his sister in Chicago, and renewing their friendships in Battle Creek. It was a relaxing summer, as Bill had gotten ahead of his advertising commitments before leaving Wilmington, and they returned to the rented house in Kirk Street and the Downard Studio refreshed in body and spirit. They both now knew that he could succeed as an illustrator, which is what he had dreamed of being since his boyhood days, and this was a comfort and a sustaining article of faith between them.

The ensuing year justified their confidence. Enough work came his way to merit Harvey Dunn's laughing description of Bill's studio as "The Grist Mill." At least two of his Grape-Nuts advertisements appeared in color on the back covers of the leading magazines and he kept up a steady production of their black-and-white "inside" inducements to purchase. He did eight fiction stories for *Red Book,* which required twenty-nine illustrations and several page decorations. One of these was by James Branch Cabell, "A Fordyce of West Brook," and the most unusual was "A Daughter of Two Lands" by Onoto Wautauna, which required him to transform an American-born, modishly dressed Japanese girl into a true daughter of Old Nippon in three illustrations. Taking some samples with him, he also sallied forth to "show his wares" to various editors in New York and Philadelphia.

His New York sortie brought an assignment from *Success,* then a weekly with a sworn circulation of 301,000 copies and an advertising rate of $800 per page. It was financed by J. N. McGraw, of technological journal fame, and used covers by J. C. Leyendecker as often as it could get them. Its editor was Samuel Merwin, an accomplished fiction writer in his own right, whose seven-part serial "Tho 'twere Ten Thousand Mile" in *Pilgrim* had been illustrated by Art Editor Koerner before he left it. The page size of *Success,* almost 10 × 14 inches, permitted the signature *William H. D. Koerner* to appear on the larger of the two illustrations he did for "The Autobiography of a Stolen Kiss" by Vale Downie, whom he would illustrate again in *Harper's Monthly. Success* had embarked upon muckraking after that journalistic art form's circulation-building crest had passed, and despite its fulminations against the rule of "Uncle Joe" Cannon, the autocratic Speaker of the House, it was sliding down the muckraking wave into desuetude,[18] and Koerner did no more work for it.

His foray into Philadelphia brought more lasting results, as it provided his first direct contacts with the Curtis Publishing Company's two great magazines, *Ladies Home Journal* and *Saturday Evening Post.* In this year the *Journal's* sixty to eighty "inside" pages were laden with advertising, and it had a monthly circulation approaching 1,250,000 copies, at fifteen cents each or $1.50 per year. Its Holland-born, bachelor editor, Edward H. Bok, did not edit it for the intellectual type but had built it into the most important journal for women in the nation by making it a magazine for what women wished to be and by idealizing the average woman for what she was. He was not averse to writing signed editorials along the lines of "My Quarrel With Women's Clubs," which stimulated reader response, and he probably published Rudyard Kipling's famous poem "The Female of the Species" (11/1911) for the same reason.

Bok used the best fiction writers he could find—Mrs. Humphry Ward, Grace S. Richmond, Kate D. Wiggins, and Maurice Maeterlinck, for examples—and published articles by Helen Keller, Jane Addams, and Jacob Riis, while Theodore Roosevelt contributed a page, "The President," in 1906–1907. His magazine had been one of the first to use color illustrations on its inside pages, possibly the first of the general magazines to change its cover design each month, a pioneer in running its fiction over into the back advertising pages, and its artwork always had been distinguished. In this year, Harrison Fisher was doing many cover paintings, of "The Girl I Like Best" type; artists such as C. Coles Phillips, F. Graham Cootes, George and Worth Brehm, Will Crawford, E. L. Blumenschein, Peter Newell, F. Luis Mora, and Emlen McConnell appeared inside; and Maxfield Parrish had been commissioned to do seventeen panels, each 10½ × 5½ feet, for the dining room on the ninth floor of the new Curtis Building in Philadelphia, where meals at cost were served to 2,400 employees daily. Its artist-of-all-work was C. M. Relyea, virtually a staffer so often

(text continues on page 86)

A Gallery of
Frontiersmen, Cowboys, Indians, and Others

Before the Long Rifle Triumphed, oil/vignette, 32 × 50, for "The Long Rifle" by Steward Edward White, Saturday Evening Post, *7/12/1930 (Collection of Hal du Pont)*

Bound West, watercolor/charcoal, 19 × 28, for "As It Was in the Beginning," by Conrad Richter,
Saturday Evening Post, 9/14/1935

Trek of the Mountain Men, oil on canvas, 28 × 40, for "Mountain Man," by Stewart Edward White,
Saturday Evening Post, 7/11/1931 (Collection of Dr. Dean Mawdsley)

Tomahawk and Long Rifle, oil on canvas, 28 × 40, for "Fur Brigade," by Hal G. Evarts, Saturday Evening Post, *5/12/1928 (Collection of Robert Rockwell)*

Rocky Mountain House, oil on canvas, 28 × 40, for "The Long Rifle," by Stewart Edward White, Saturday Evening Post, *2/14/1931 (Collection of William E. Weiss, Sr.)*

Shotgun and the Law, oil/vignette, 20 × 30, for "Stepsons of Light," by Eugene Manlove Rhodes,
Saturday Evening Post, 9/25/1920 (Diamond M Foundation, Snyder, Texas)

Trail Herd to Wyoming, oil on canvas, 22 × 72, for "North of 36," by Emerson Hough,
Saturday Evening Post, *4/14/1923 (Whitney Gallery of Western Art — W.H.D. Koerner Studio,*
Cody, Wyoming)

Caballada, mixed media, 27 × 34, for "Ranchero: Hacienda," by Stewart Edward White, Saturday Evening Post, *3/26/1932*

The Lynchers, oil on canvas, 22 × 30, for "Stepsons of Light," by Eugene Manlove Rhodes, Saturday Evening Post, *10/2/1920 (Collection of Calvin Moerbe)*

Steep Trail, oil/vignette, 38 × 28, for "The Hermit of Three Buttes," by Ben Ames Williams, Saturday Evening Post, *5/10/1930 (Collection of Gene Patch)*

Moving the Herd, oil on canvas, 26 × 56, for "Short Grass," by Hal G. Evarts, Saturday Evening Post, 5/21/1932 *(Whitney Gallery of Western Art—W.H.D. Koerner Studio, Cody, Wyoming)*

Welcome for the First Trail Herd, oil on canvas, 26 × 36, for "North of 36," by Emerson Hough,
Saturday Evening Post, *5/19/1923 (Citizens Bank of Abilene, Kansas)*

Slicker Weather, oil/vignette, 29 × 34, for "Maid Most Dear," by Eugene Manlove Rhodes,
Saturday Evening Post, *8/16/1930 (Collection of Dr. Harold L. Manhart)*

Double Rush, oil/vignette, 12 × 24, for "Tumbleweeds," by Hal G. Evarts, Saturday Evening Post, 9/9/1922 *(Collection of Tom Pickett)*

Chuck Wagon, oil/vignette, 14 × 28, for "Tumbleweeds," by Hal G. Evarts, Saturday Evening Post, 9/2/1922

*Faithful Pedro, oil/vignette,
36 × 20, for "City of Refuge,"
by Lloyd Osbourne, Saturday
Evening Post, 9/29/1923
(Collection of Alice Taggares)*

Woman at Yellow Wells, oil/vignette, 30 × 49, for "Women at Yellow Wells," by Oliver LaFarge, Saturday Evening Post, 11/24/1934 (Tracy Collins Bank and Trust, Salt Lake City)

Heading for Winter Quarters, oil/vignette, 26 × 25, for "Lost Ecstasy," by Mary Roberts Rinehart,
Saturday Evening Post, 5/7/1927 *(Diamond M Foundation, Snyder, Texas)*

The Trader Who Cheated, oil on canvas, 36 × 30, for "North of 36," by Emerson Hough, Saturday Evening Post, *5/26/1923 (Collection of Pete Taggares)*

Red Man's Meat, oil/vignette, 17 × 41, for "Travelling the Old Trails," by Emerson Hough, Saturday Evening Post, 8/2/1919 (Collection of Fallis L. Oliver, Jr.)

Little Bull Buffalo, oil/vignette, 18 × 18, for "Fur Brigade," by Hal G. Evarts, Saturday Evening Post, 4/21/1928

Untitled, watercolor, 10 × 8, for "Folded Hills," by Stewart Edward White, Saturday Evening Post, *9/3/1932*

Fighting Fury, oil/vignette, 33 × 60, for "Fur Brigade," by Hal G. Evarts, Saturday Evening Post, *4/28/1928*

Stolen Ponies, oil on canvas, 33 × 60, for "Fur Brigade," by Hal G. Evarts, Saturday Evening Post, *5/5/1928*

Buffalo Hunter, oil/vignette, 14 × 30, for "North of 36," by Emerson Hough, Saturday Evening Post, *5/12/1923 (Collection of John Beaupre)*

Crow Raiders, charcoal/watercolor, 15 × 28, for "Mountain Man," by Stewart Edward White, Saturday Evening Post, *8/22/1931 (Charles B. Goddard Center, Ardmore, Oklahoma)*

Squaw's Revenge, oil/vignette, 21 × 15, for "Fur Brigade," by Hal G. Evarts, Saturday Evening Post, *5/26/1928*

Their Peltries Traded, watercolor/charcoal, 12 × 24, for "Mountain Man," by Steward Edward White,
Saturday Evening Post, 9/19/1931

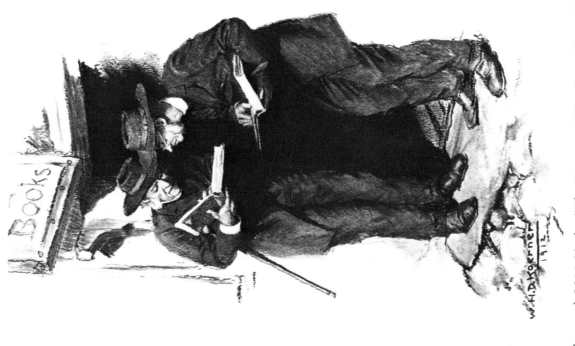

Untitled, charcoal, 16 × 12, for "The Business Side of the Church," by James H. Collins, Saturday Evening Post, 3/1/1913

Where Rocks Made Fences, oil on canvas, 26 × 36, for "The Gift on the Altar," by Mary E. Mitchell, Harper's Monthly, 9/1918

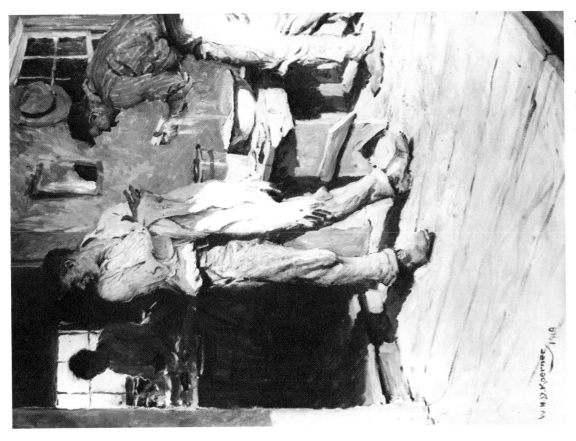

Prelude to Chuck, oil on canvas, 30 × 20, for "The Man Who Slept to Noon," by Will E. Ingersoll, Harper's Monthly, 6/1918

The Squall, oil/vignette, 20 × 16, for "Black Pawl," by Ben Ames Williams, Red Book, 12/1919 (Collection of Hal du Pont)

When Steam Plowed Through, oil on canvas, 28 × 40, for "Power," by Arthur Stringer, Saturday Evening Post, *3/28/1925 (Collection of Hal du Pont)*

The Oil Game, oil on canvas, 28 × 36, for "The Maxim—Caveat Emptor," by Wilbur Hall, Saturday Evening Post, *9/22/1917 (Collection of G. N. Parrott)*

Boilin' Over, oil on canvas, 28 × 40, for "No Thoroughfare," by Ben Ames Williams, Saturday Evening Post, *1/30/1926*

The Strike Breakers, oil on canvas, 28 × 40, for "Power," by Arthur Stringer, Saturday Evening Post, *3/7/1925 (Collection of Hal du Pont)*

Watassi Tribesmen, oil on canvas, 27 × 52, for "Back of Beyond," by Stewart Edward White, Saturday Evening Post, *1/15/1927*

The Biplane, oil on canvas, 28 × 36, for "White Man," by George Agnew Chamberlain, Woman's Home Companion, *12/1918 (Collection of Hal du Pont)*

Simba, Simba, oil/vignette, 24 × 17, for "Back of Beyond," by Stewart Edward White, Saturday Evening Post, 1/15/1927

Elephant Trackers, oil/vignette, 23 × 19, for "White Man," by George Agnew Chamberlain, Woman's Home Companion, 12/1918

The Knothole, oil/vignette, 22 × 17, for "The Bachelor," by Lowell Otis Reese, Saturday Evening Post, *2/7/1920 (Collection of Casey Meyers)*

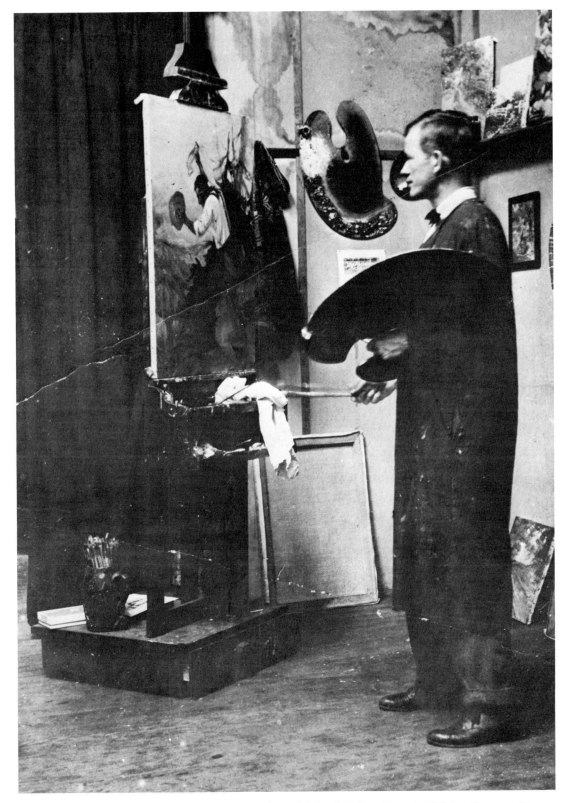

Koerner at work in his Wilmington studio, dubbed "The Grist Mill" by Harvey Dunn, about 1909

did his work appear, and Koerner's first assignment was to do two illustrations for the last (6/1909) in a set of "series" stories,[19] "Husband and Wife Sketches" by Grace S. Richmond, because the *Journal* was dissatisfied with the work Relyea had been doing for these pieces. Another assignment followed immediately, and he continued to do work for the *Journal* over the next ten years as his schedule permitted.

More important to Koerner's career and to his impact upon the western field he finally made his own was the *Saturday Evening Post*, between which and *Ladies Home Journal* no love was lost. One reason for this was the hard fact that the *Post* had fifty-two opportunities a year for advertising revenue to the *Journal's* twelve, and it was crowding Bok's magazine for top-rank in both revenue and influence in the Curtis organization. Another and perhaps more important reason was that George Horace Lorimer was as formidable a personality as was ever Bok. Kentucky-born, Chicago-reared, a graduate of Yale in the same class (1888) with Amos Alonzo Stagg, Lorimer had served a stint as a newspaper reporter in Boston before going to work for P. D. Armour's meat-packing company. His rise in the Armour organization had been rapid and he was earning the very respectable annual salary of $5,000 when Curtis hired him to make something out of a moribund little Philadelphia weekly, with less than 10,000 circulation, which Curtis had acquired for $1,000. Ten years later, when Koerner made his first contact with Herbert Johnson, then its art editor and for many years its political cartoonist and Koerner's abiding friend, its issues averaged fifty-two pages and circulation was approaching 1,250,000 copies weekly. It was what Will Rogers later called it, "America's greatest nickelodeon."[20]

Lorimer accomplished this amazing feat because he sensed the mood of the nation's rapidly expanding middle segments more accurately than any other editor of his time, and continued to gauge the nation's mood most accurately for many years. In this, he was aided immensely by the fact that he had traveled in England and on the Continent in his youth with his father, a leading evangelist of Baptist persuasion, and that his travels for Armour's company had given him first-hand knowledge of the *whole* nation he loved passionately but without jingoism or false sentimentality. He knew it as a congeries

of sections, each with its own likes and dislikes, special interests, and resources. He measured human values by achievement, not inheritance, and while he was an evangelist for business, he was not an apologist for its sins, which he also knew from first-hand experience. He feared the status quo and unwonted power, no matter in what hands it rested, and he made political progressivism, as well as the Progressives, an integral part of his editorial policy. He espoused conservation long before the nation abounded in ecological activists, too often echo-activists, because he knew that the nation's natural resources were dwindling too fast before the swelling onslaught of industrialization. While his magazine would be castigated by "Mencken and the little Menckenoids,"[21] as the mainstay of "booboisie" values, it should be remembered that Lorimer let Clarence Darrow argue the workingmen's side of the open-shop question in his pages; that he printed five articles by William Jennings Bryan when that eater of wild honey beside Platte River still was seeking to save the nation; and that he published six articles by Leon Trotsky on the Russian Revolution, which gave that firebrand an audience larger than he could reach by any other medium in the stronghold of imperialistic capitalism.[22]

His editorial pattern for the *Post* combined ". . . large portions of plain common sense, homely democracy, shrewd pragmatism and faith in the recognized virtues."[23] To get what he wanted, Lorimer personally read some 500,000 words of manuscripts per week for many years, then selected what he wanted, and chivvied the Art Department to get the *right* illustrator for each story. Lorimer then personally approved each illustration before it went to the engraving department. He also selected the covers in what became a weekly routine. Fifteen or more paintings would be lined up against the wall outside Lorimer's office and he would walk by as if he were reviewing troops, wearing his coat and vest even on the muggiest summer day in a Philadelphia without air conditioning, and make his choices. Then he would scrawl his initials on the ones he had chosen and go about his other tasks. Norman Rockwell worked out his own system for dealing with Lorimer's predilections: ". . . it was my practice to submit five sketches at a time because it seemed to be a policy with him *never* to accept more than three out of five. I generally made up three that I really liked, and put in two fillers."[24]

One problem that never bothered Rockwell was Lorimer's policy concerning any illustration —be it for the cover or for a story or for advertising—that showed too much leg or other feminine charm; those that did were either rejected or retouched by the artist into acceptance. Koerner's major brush with this taboo came with some of the last illustrations he did for the magazine, those for Nordhoff and Hall's "Pitcairn's Island," wherein he first portrayed the Polynesian women's breasts *au naturel,* a manner not unnatural to them, and then had to disguise the bare facts without completely denying their existence.[25] Lorimer was no teetotaler—no friend of Irvin S. Cobb could be—but he resolutely refused to accept either liquor or cigarette advertising, as well as that for real estate and financial opportunities, even when the magazine needed additional revenue. In 1910, it became taboo to show wine glasses or steins in story illustrations. No other magazines were so free from the influence of their business offices as were the Curtis publications, and Lorimer would switch a story even in its final page proofs if he suspected that the advertising department had made a tie-in for the issue in which the story had been scheduled to appear.

In 1909 its weekly contents averaged one serial installment, three short stories, and four articles, which required twenty-three pieces of art and up to ten photographs, the latter being used for article illustration only.[26] William Allen White, the Sage of Emporia, Kansas, was a nonfiction regular in this period, receiving $1,000 each for his contributions, while other good nonfiction writers were paid $500 per article. Short stories were purchased in the $500–$1,000 range depending on the author and how badly Lorimer wanted the story, with serials bringing their authors about the same amount per installment. J. C. Leyendecker's covers for the Thanksgiving, Christmas, and New Year numbers already were on their way to becoming annual fixtures, and the other covers for this year reflected Lorimer's emphasis on the masculine appeal of his magazine: about equally divided between "pretty girls," most of them by Harrison Fisher, and wildlife by C. L. Bull and Paul Bransom, plus Oliver Kemp's hunting and camping scenes.[27]

Henry Raleigh was the standard illustrator of Montague Glass's "Potash and Perlmutter" stories, which gently spoofed the New York garment trade and broke the barrier against Jewish ethnic characters. Harvey Dunn was illustrating Brand Whitlock's Civil War stories, and both he and Frank Schoonover tried their hands at H. J. Stabler's Deep South "darky" yarns. May Wilson Preston illustrated a two-part suffragette story by Mary Roberts Rinehart, already one of the nation's highest paid writers;[28] W. J. Aylward supplied the sea scenes for a short story by Jack London; and other artists appearing regularly included Will Grefé, Orson Lowell, Stanley M. Chase, F. R. Gruger, Sarah Stilwell-Weber, and George Gibbs, better remembered today as a novelist and portrait painter. The authors they illustrated included Richard Harding Davis, William J. Locke, Richard Washburn Child, Emerson Hough, Rupert Hughes, Peter B. Kyne, and Eugene Manlove Rhodes.

Koerner's first assignment was a western short story by George Patullo, "The Gunfighter: Padden Meets His Match," which had a variant of what became a basic plot in this genre: a cold-eyed Texan was hired to eliminate a homesteader in the middle of a large ranch's unowned range, but succumbed to the blandishments of the delectable daughter.[29] It was distinguished, as was most of Patullo's western work, by his personal knowledge of locale and the character types he used. Koerner's three illustrations, one of which ran across the top of the story's first page, were marked by the fact that the heroine's face no longer resembled Lillian Koerner's and that his horses were tremendously alive. It is believed that he received less for this story than he was receiving from *Red Book* in this year, which may explain why he was absent from Lorimer's pages until 1912, plus the fact that he opened up new outlets for his work that kept him busy.

The Koerners spent the summer of 1909 at Webb Pond in Maine, where Lillian began to develop a latent interest in antique furniture and furnishings, such as rope-strung spool beds, handmade quilts, and rag rugs. This interest persisted and expanded, as their income grew and they finally got a home of their own. Koerner did no more work this summer than was absolutely necessary, and spent his days in sketching and long-distance swimming, an exercise which

Koerner, Christmas, 1910, while at Naaman's-on-Delaware

he enjoyed and at which he excelled. They returned to Wilmington at summer's end to take part in a venture that appears unique in the annals of American art, a self-contained, masculine artists' colony.

The project had originated in June with three of Pyle's last regular students—Percy V. E. Ivory, Herbert Moore, E. Roscoe Shrader—each of whom was established as an illustrator, Ivory perhaps more prominent than his friends,[30] and each of whom ostensibly was unmarried. They asked Koerner, older than any of them at almost thirty-one, to join them and his wife to become chatelaine of their manor, so to speak. Professionally, the idea had much to recommend it. The four men each had expertise that could be tapped by the others, and if any of them was asked to do work and was too busy, he had an inside track in recommending one of the others for the assignment.[31] Each had his own "morgue"

of clippings and photographs that could be shared, and each had his own collection of costumes and artifacts; Ivory possessing a group of gorgeous costumes that he had acquired on a visit to Mexico. Added reasons for establishing their colony were its physical and financial attractions.

Located near Claymont, Delaware, in an orchard adjacent to the Delaware River, it was just eight miles from Wilmington and twenty-one from Philadelphia by trolley, a matter of some importance to men who owned not one automobile between them. A commodious, two-story dwelling was on the property, the rifle slits in its thick stone walls attesting to the conditions that had surrounded its construction,[32] and it was steeped in the Colonial traditions that Pyle had imparted to his pupils—General Washington, "Mad Anthony" Wayne, the Marquis de Lafayette and "Light Horse Harry" Lee had skirmished around it and been sheltered by it. A functioning well and a stone outbuilding stood on the property and its owner had agreed to rent them the dwelling; install a furnace, running water, and one bathroom in it; provide them one acre of garden ground; extend harvesting privileges from the orchard; and construct four separate studios adjacent to the dwelling.[33] All this for a total rental of $60.00 per month! He did want them to sign a four-year lease and Koerner had balked at this stipulation.

His reasons were made clear in a letter to Herbert Moore before he left to spend the summer in Maine.

Four years is quite a long time for four fellows to bind themselves to keep a house because of the chance of change, marriage, or family affairs, and to us it seems rather a long period to bind ourselves for we do not know how things would work out if we should have a family or if either of our mothers should need our help and home. . . . So much depends on the manner and ability Mrs. Koerner has in running such a house. The aim of all is to have it a success—professionally and domestically—and if a success, then a continuance, providing we can make some plans in case of children or mothers, and in considering these plans for future years, we would like you to realize that these two—children and mothers—are always provided for—'tis the safest and best way.[34]

The main house and servant quarters at Naaman's-on-Delaware, 1909–11

The result of Koerner's hesitation was that the final agreement contained the proviso that if he wished to withdraw at any time after October 1, 1911, and the others could not find a replacement, the landlord would reduce the total rental by one-fourth.

Upon returning from Maine, Lillian plunged into the task of furnishing the living quarters, and clerks at Wanamaker's and other Philadelphia stores were somewhat bemused to wait upon four men and one young woman deciding on patterns and prices for draperies, glassware, and the like. The Koerners were allotted a bedroom–sitting room suite with fireplace downstairs, which also contained the dining room, parlor, and kitchen, while the three men drew lots for their respective upstairs bedrooms that opened off a large room that became the artists' "commons." A live-in cook was obtained, as well

as a maid-laundress who had been "Little Eva" in the first company of "Uncle Tom's Cabin" and declaimed her lines as she ironed and cleaned the house.[35] Both these were Lillian's responsibility. A handyman to tend the furnace, help with the gardening, and serve as male model when needed was given living quarters in the barn, and the colony at what they named "Naaman's-on-Delaware" became operative on October 1, 1909.

Certain houses rules were established. Each man sat at the head of the Queen Anne dining table for one week, Koerner leading off so the others could learn to carve by watching him. When Koerner came around again, it was time for Lillian to pro-rate the expenses and for each colonist to "pay up." She sat always at the foot of the table with the tea and coffee service. No individual pets were permitted, but one colony pet was forthcoming in the form of "Jeff," a bejowled and bench-legged bulldog, that quickly learned to enjoy being tossed back and forth by the feet of four grown men lying on their backs on the lawn. Unexpected visitors were politely discouraged at the door by Lillian, while invited guests for afternoon tea and meals were permitted only on week-ends. Harvey Dunn once brought Watson Barratt, Henry J. Soulen, Douglas Duer, and Henry J. Peck from Wilmington for supper in his brand new Pierce-Arrow touring car which he drove as though he were Jehu himself.[36]

The rule against week-day visitors and guests was broken for one man, who was welcome any time he appeared and for good reason. William "Pop" Hines was art director for Street and Smith, which then was publishing at least five magazines in addition to a veritable torrent of books. Hines paid $20 per black-and-white illustration, up to $100 for a magazine cover, and the work had to fit his specifications exactly: "He would crop the head off Whistler's Mother if he thought it would fit the page better."[37] *Popular* was their big magazine at this time,[38] being published semi-monthly with a circulation exceeding 300,000 copies, about nine-tenths of which stemmed from newsstand sales, and an advertising rate of $300 per page. It was an all-fiction magazine, patterned after Frank Munsey's once successful *Argosy,* and generally used one serial installment, one novelette, and four short stories per issue. It did run Jack London's "The Abysmal Brute" complete in one issue (9/1/1911), paying him $1,200 for it after it had been rejected by what London called the "first rate" magazines. It used no inside illustration but its covers were designed to attract the masculine eye. Koerner did three north-woods covers for it during his two years at Naaman's, thus joining such as Charles M. Russell, N. C. Wyeth, W. Herbert "Buck" Dunton, Harvey Dunn, Frank E. Schoonover, J. C. Leyendecker, and Oliver Kemp.

His Naaman's years brought Koerner's work for Grape-Nuts and Postum to an end. No reasons appear in his surviving papers, but it is logical to assume that he now could spend the time they had consumed in doing more challenging work—work more to his liking—for more income. He continued his *Red Book* work in these years, supplying thirty illustrations for

eight stories, and this reached its peak in 1915, when he furnished it seventy-two illustrations for twenty stories, and continued on a diminishing scale until 1925. In addition to the Street and Smith covers, he did a hunting-camp scene for what is believed to have been *Field and Stream;* a cover for *Fleming's Farm and Livestock Almanac,* which extolled the merits of "knee sprung" and "lump jaw" cures, among other nostrums and appliances purveyed by a firm of chemists at Chicago's Union Stock Yards; and he did a 24 × 36 inch oil painting for the Philadelphia calendar firm of A. M. Collins which depicted four hunters and their guide "Around the Camp Fire."

It was during these years that he began his continuing custom of asking for the return of his work, once it had appeared, and most of his publishers were happy to comply. The Scribner firm retained all work done for them, often copyrighting it in their name, which well may explain why Koerner illustrated but one story for their magazine and none of their books.[39] During these years, he offered some of the work returned to him for sale through the firm of Gabriel and Levy, 78 Fifth Avenue, New York and Three Rue de Choiseul, Paris. How many paintings were sold or for how much or how long this association endured remains unknown.

More important than these facets of his Naaman's years was the inception of Koerner's long association with the venerable New York publishing house of Harper and Brothers. His first assignment was a color cover for *Harper's Weekly* and he did at least ten more covers for it over the next sixteen months. All but one of these involved the automobile in various settings and actions, from Florida's palms to the Grand Canyon, which reflected the *Weekly's* awareness of the nation's growing love affair with the automobile. Its editor was George Harvey, concurrently editing *North American Review,* who was given to marching in the annual parade of suffrage-minded women down New York's Fifth Avenue in the company of John Dewey and Oswald Garrison Villard, owner-editor of the New York *Evening Post.*[40]

The *Weekly* was on the wane in 1910, with a circulation around 70,000 copies for its thirty-six pages, including covers of almost bedsheet size, 11 × 16 inches, at ten cents per copy, $4.00 per year.[41] It had not been profitable for many

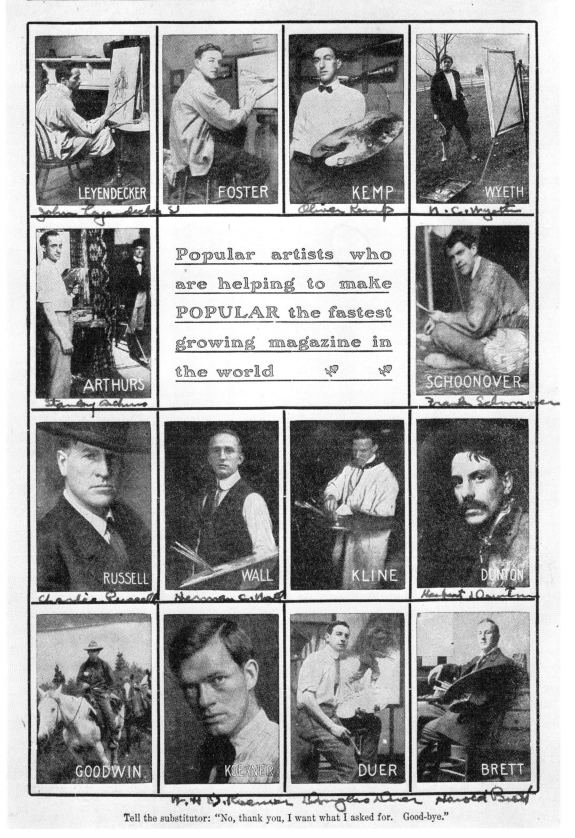

Popular *took a full page to advertise the artists who did its covers. Those shown are F. X. Leyendecker,* William H. Foster, Oliver Kemp, N. C. Wyeth, Stanley A. Arthurs, Frank E. Schoonover, *Charles M. Russell,* Herman C. Wall, *Hibberd V. B. Kline,* W. Herbert Dunton, Phillip R. Goodwin, Koerner, Douglas Duer, *and* Harold M. Brett. *Those whose names are not italicized had been pupils of Howard Pyle. Harvey T. Dunn, another Pyle pupil, also did covers for* Popular *in this period, 1910–15. The magazine carried no inside illustrations*

years but had been kept alive because its publishers believed firmly that there was more to their business than black ink. It paid its illustrators well, $100 per cover and $45 per black-and-white drawing, and this fact, plus the prestige that still lingered from its glory days, brought its pages such prominent illustrators of the period as Elizabeth Shippen Greene, John Wolcott Adams, Arthur William Brown, Angus MacDonall, Rollin Kirby, J. J. Gould, and Peter Newell. It still billed itself as a "Journal of Civilization," and published such articles as that by Kenyon Cox (3/15/1913), one of America's foremost easel painters, on the Cubist fad that followed Marcel Duchamp's "Nude Descending a Staircase," in which Cox described Cubism's true meaning as "nothing less than the total destruction of the art of painting" and urged art students to distrust all short-cuts to art or to glory. It was one of the few periodicals of its day to accept liquor advertising, which included that presenting the ready-made advantages of "Hueblein's Club Cocktails," later examples of which appear in today's major magazines in full-page four-color inducements to consumption.

It also hewed to the line that had made it famous: that of a fighting, political journal for which the visual vehicle was its opening, full-page illustration. Its Thomas Nast in these last years was E. W. Kemble, and his major targets were the Republican Party in general and its maverick offshoot, Theodore Roosevelt, in particular. One of Kemble's slashing drawings showed Henry Cabot Lodge as a battered gladiator defending the party of "Privilege and Broken Promises" (12/3/1910), while yet another showed two prizefighters in the ring, Robert La Follette being the "Progressive Champion of the Senate" and Nelson Aldrich the "Machine Champion" (2/26/1910). One of his treatments of Roosevelt (10/10/1910) showed him sitting on the knee of "Marse" Henry Watterson, the famous Kentucky editor, in what can be regarded as a very early version of the standard pose later assumed by Edgar Bergen and Charlie McCarthy, while another showed T.R. as mostly teeth throwing a spear into President Taft's back through an open window of the White House (10/14/1911). Yet another showed Roosevelt astride a hybrid mount composed of donkey and elephant components, while the cover for this issue was done in color by C. J. Budd and showed

Woodrow Wilson in academic robes riding an enthusiastic donkey above the caption "The New Rider" (7/13/1912). It is this work by Kemble that lends credence to the belief that the *Weekly*, despite its declining circulation, did influence Wilson's elevation to the presidency.

Another feature of the *Weekly* was its double-page, pen-and-ink or wash drawing center spread, whereon Thomas Nast had lambasted whatever seemed iniquitous in the body civic or politic and which Charles Dana Gibson had filled with his Junoesque "Girl" besieged by suitors young and old and infinitely superior to them all. In these latter years, James Montgomery Flagg often did his renditions of the same theme which showed their debt to Gibson's earlier work. Another double-page in this period showed a cowboy down in a stampede by Stanley L. Wood (12/3/1910), which was derived from Remington's earlier work, and many of them dealt with automobile happenstances.

The double-page "spread," or "split" or "double truck," presents the artist with a technical problem, because his work only can be "continuous" when it will be reproduced on the two center pages of a folded form known as a signature. Even here, the "gutter" where the signature is stapled or stitched to the cover is an annoyance. On any other pages in the signature, the reproductive plate must be broken into two parts and only great care, virtually impossible to achieve in high-speed printing, folding, and binding, will bring its two halves into perfect alignment. For this reason, many artists when confronted with a "split" tried to gloss over in the illustration itself where the gutter would fall in printing. Koerner faced this problem first in the *Weekly* with a drawing that showed a hunter making coffee over his fire and looking up to see a bear beside his rifle, which he had placed at a safe distance (6/4/1910). In this one, he did a continuous picture, because of the *Weekly's* suitable pagination. In the later ones he did for other magazines, he usually did them as separate parts and so acute was his sense of the relationship between creative work and its reproduction that there was little gutter "loss."

The *Weekly* ran one fiction piece per issue generally of the outdoor-action type, and Koerner illustrated at least five such for it, one of which marked the first time that his "inside" illustrations had been given color reproduction (12/16/1911). It was only two colors to be sure, but nonetheless color. This was a logging-and-lumberjack piece by Herbert L. Walker, entitled "The Lawyer's Christmas Socks," for which he did four illustrations.

For far longer than any of its taste-making contemporaries—*Atlantic, Century, Scribner's*—the Harper firm conducted its operations by their original idea of a publishing house as being an almost familial group of author, artist, and publisher happily associated to advance the great cause of literature and to be of mutual service. In no case was this evident longer than in their monthly magazine, cited in this work simply as *Harper's*. It stubbornly resisted the trend towards becoming a journal of contemporary affairs longer than the others mentioned above, and it clung with equal persistence to the belief that certain illustrations were served better by hand engraving for reproduction purposes. Nelson Demarest and F. A. Pettit, as well as the artist, were getting credit on the "plates" they engraved, including work by Koerner, as late as 1920.

Well into the first decade of this century, *Harper's* pace was so leisurely that artists were allowed as much as six months' lead time in making their illustrations. Artists whom it had come to know were sent galley proofs from which to illustrate, with the request that they prepare such illustrations as they deemed suitable to the equivalent of so many "magazine pages," and without detailed instructions as to numbers or scenes or sizes or story locations. Its cover consisted of chaste decorations around the logotype, but its inside pages were rich, even opulent, in color, which in quantity and quality were the equal of *Scribner's* and superior to *Century*, with Howard Pyle's influence more noticeable than in the others. They made a distinction in the illustrator's credit line between "pictures" and "drawings," with the former including oil, gouache, and watercolor paintings and the latter pen-and-ink and wash work.

In 1910 it boasted a circulation of 125,000 at thirty-five cents per copy, $4.00 per year. It was a fat magazine of 160 inside pages, 6-3/4 × 9-3/4 inches, sandwiched between two advertising sections aggregating 128 pages, almost half of which dealt with books by all the leading publishers. Additionally, *Ladies Home Journal*, *American, Collier's*, and *Cosmopolitan* used full pages to proclaim their own coming attractions. Its editor since 1869 had been Henry Mills Alden, who would complete a half-century in that capacity. Three or more poems graced each issue by Witter Bynner, George Sterling, Richard Le Gallienne, Sara Teasdale, and others, including Owen Wister; William Dean Howells was the proprietor of "The Editor's Easy Chair," later conducted with éclat by Bernard DeVoto; and a section devoted to humorous verse and cartoons, by such as A. B. Frost and E. W. Kemble,[42] was a monthly feature. Alden generally used one continued story (serial) installment per issue with six or more short stories and up to five articles rounding out its contents. His authors included Sir Gilbert Parker, A. Conan Doyle, Rudyard Kipling, Joseph Conrad, Arthur Bennett, Booth Tarkington, Clarence Day, Jr., Basil King, Simeon Strunsky, Margaret Deland, Mary E. Wilkins Freeman, Inez Haynes Gillmore, Ellen Glasgow, Fannie Heaslip Lea, Katherine F. Gerould, Henry S. Canby, John Burroughs, and Clarence Budington Kelland.[43]

The "recorders of New England's decline" had made the life of that region popular magazine fare in the last quarter of the preceding century and *Harper's* continued to use stories of rural America long after they had vanished from the pages of its literary competitors. Their leading male contributor in this genre was Irving Bacheller, a former newspaperman, whose *Eben Holden* had sold almost 300,000 copies in its first year of publication (1900–1901) and has been termed the *Lorna Doone* of American fiction. Its hero was an elderly farm hand, tough as a pine knot, filled with sententious wisdom and dry humor, a great story teller—the archetypal bumpkin who was more than he appeared.[44] It was a deep, rich vein of Americana that can be mined no more because the nation that was its mother lode has vanished.

Bacheller was working this vein for *Harper's* in 1910 and Koerner's first assignment was "Keeping Up With Lizzie," for which he made eight wash drawings. He did another, "Socrates to the Rescue," thereafter and illustrated Bacheller's two books that were made from his *Harper's* stories. In the illustrator's world before World War I, regular appearance in *Harper's* was a *coup* not counted by the majority of the more than five hundred artists tabulated for this study. To appear in color in its pages was a mark of distinction and to have work selected for color reproduction as the frontispiece of an issue was an accolade to be cherished.[45] Koerner earned them all and more than once. As did every right-minded magazine above the pulp level, *Harper's* had a taboo against using the same author more than once in a single issue. This did not, however, apply to illustrators and Koerner's work appeared twice or more in single issues of many magazines, *Harper's* included, throughout his later career.

His association with *Harper's* continued for fifteen years and its highlights are reflected in selected letters.

July 3, 1912

Dear Mr. Koerner:

Your note of June 29th has just reached me.

You are a little behind time on the illustrations for "The Voice" book, but the delay really is not serious, and we hope you will be able to deliver the drawings within ten days.

Irving Bacheller has revised and enlarged his stories published in the MAGAZINE under the title of "The Talk Trust" and "The Jewel Trust," and we are going to publish them in book form under the title of "Charge It." You will remember that you made four pictures for these stories. We intend to use these in the book, and we would like to have two more, provided you can deliver them without fail about August 1st, or certainly not later than the 8th or 10th. Can you undertake this work? If so, we would like to have the pictures and we would pay you $100.00 for the two.

If you can find four more good subjects—instead of only two—*well separated,* we will take four for $150.00.

Proofs by accompanying mail. The book cut should be about 3-5/8″ × 5-5/8″.

Very truly yours,

Joseph W. Harper

December 10, 1912

Dear Mr. Koerner:

"The Forbidden Road" will come first, please, followed by the other two stories. We will reproduce one of the Memory drawings, "the group" in color. It is drawing so near the holiday season, and as I may not have the opportunity again, I wish to send to you and Mrs. Koerner, my most

sincere wishes for a Merry Christmas and a Happy New Year.

While you are in no sense a protege of mine, yet I have been largely responsible for your introduction to Harper's, and when our confidence in people is justified by their good works, our faith in general, is strengthened, and the effect is good and wholesome. I have watched your steady improvement with great pleasure, and I am sure your advancement will continue.

Sincerely yours,

W. E. Mears[46]
Art Editor

February 4th, 1913

Dear Mr. Koerner:

I wish to congratulate you on the success of this large picture for "The Blue Jay's Nest," and we appreciate too, the fact that you do not slight the Weekly work, because we do not pay as much for Weekly illustrations as we do for the Magazine. This too, though so many men fail to see it, strengthens you, because all work that is slighted, for any reason, has a deteriorating effect, and I am glad you are so mindful of your own work, not only for the present, but for that steady developement which day by day secures a sure future.

You are progressing finely, and it is a great pleasure to watch your progress, and to tell you of it.

Sincerely yours,

W. E. Mears

April 17th, 1916

The Treasurer
Harper & Brother, Pub.
New York.

Dear Sir:

I have been anxiously looking for a check from you, will you please send me one right away, as I need it very much.

Very truly yours

W.H.D. Koerner

[*4/18/16—Check for $200 mailed today.*]

April 7, 1917

Dear Mr. Koerner:

Your letter advising us that you will not be

able to handle any work until June 15th has been received.

We have another Barcy story, probably the most interesting one of the lot, and under no circumstances do we care to give this to any other artist to illustrate, for your pictures have been very successful and we want you to continue to make illustrations for these stories. Is it at all possible for you to work this story in, so that we might have it by the 5th or 7th of May? It seems as though we are always asking you for favors, but at the same time I am sure you realize that if we did not think well of you and your work, we would not make these numerous requests.

We are anticipating that you may be able to do this for us, so we are sending to you, registered, the manuscript entitled "Then Came David," from which please make two (2) page pictures.

Sincerely yours,

W. E. Mears

[*They got them on the 8th of May.*]

May ?, 1917

Dear Mr. Koerner:

Mr. Harold MacGrath, author of the "Luck of the Irish" for which you made the very good, Irish-Chinese scrap picture, has just written us how much pleased he is with it, and so I am passing his kind word along to the poor artist person.

All of us here also like the picture very much, and we feel that it's helping a lot to sell the book. Mr. MacGrath has asked us to give him the original drawing, and this we wish to do. I find, however, that it has been somewhat marred by the lettering we had to paint on it for the jacket, so I must beg you to kindly re-touch the canvas. I am forwarding it to you by express prepaid, and you may return it by express marked in my care.

I am sorry to bother you with this re-touching, but I know that in the circumstances you will feel like doing it.

Thanking you for your courtesy, I remain

Very truly yours,

Joseph W. Harper

P.S. Or better,—please forward the picture by express to Mr. Harold MacGrath, 1618 James Street, Syracuse, N.Y., and please prepay the expressage, and let me know what the amount is, and I will see that it is remitted to you.

January 14, 1925

Dear Koerner:

As far as delivery date is concerned we can give you until the 5th of March as the schedule of the story has been changed.

I have been thinking over our conversation and while my feeling for you and your work is very strong I would not ask you nor would I want you to work for Harper's at a figure so much less than you receive from other publishers. You would be unjust to yourself in doing it and I would be wrong to ask you, so to be absolutely fair I think probably the best way to do is to send the manuscript back and I will try to place it elsewhere. We have lost some of our best illustrators because with our limited circulation we find it impossible to compete with some of the larger magazines, and yet I believe we still maintain a certain standard which is recognized in spite of the difference in cost.

Sincerely,

Mears

It was not all work and no play in the Naaman's colony, and Lillian Koerner prefaced her recall of those years by saying, "When the fellows were not *in* a story, the one thought we all had was to have a good time and as cheaply as possible."[47]

I keep saying "we"! We, "we," the five of us, had good times together. We went tobogganing over the farm hills in winter with a long coaster with me in the center. Again, the fellows carried Schrader's non-tippable canoe down over the rocks of Naaman's Creek to the Delaware River, and I sat on the bottom, as ballast they said, when the river waves hit us and we returned drenched but exuberant.

Week-ends we were "at home" to visitors. The men opened their studios and turned their easels to the wall, took off their painting coats and made ready for guests. We never knew just who might come or how many.[48] *Once the handyman killed an opposum and Mary [the cook] baked it and served it for dinner. We gagged but said nothing.*

Usually in good weather, or before the men went out to their studios, we would walk to Claymont for the mail. Sometimes we sang and could really tune up with such songs as "After the Ball is Over," "On the Banks of the Wabash,"

"Bird in a Gilded Cage," "The Bowery." Before dinner, when the men came in with a hand-full of paint brushes to wash, they would go to the bathroom, get their pails and Ivory Soap with warm water, and really make a "Bathroom Quartette." William was deep bass. It was a real concert from where I heard it downstairs.

Our Christmas party [1910] was for a few friends and one or two house guests. The fellows put on a tableau, exquisite and solemn, of the nativity. Herbert Moore's biblical costumes contributed to heighten its beauty. In the center they posed me as "Mary," with a bundle in my arms as the "Christ Child." I have often wished that our tableau could have been seen for more than just Christmas Eve. It was almost better than a sermon. Christmas Day was great fun, too. We invested in a bottle of Port Wine and gave a toast to each present and to the dignity of the old house. At our [table] places, we had appropriately folded white paper as place cards and on each I had painted with watercolor a rope of holly. On mine, the fellows had written on the outside "Mrs. Koerner" and on the inside:

> *There was a young girl nick-named Dick*
> *Who managed four men mighty slick;*
> *They all toe the mark*
> *When her eyes 'gin to spark*
> *For she carries a great big stick!*

My place gift was a policeman's club. William's card read:

> *There was an old groucho named Bill*
> *Who married a young maiden called Lil*
> *But—this here decree*
> *Sets the Young Lady free*
> *And Bill has to swallow his pill.*

His place gift was a bogus bill of divorce, so I kissed him and he grinned, dear Boy.

If their Naaman's years were ringed by innocence, gentility, and clean mirth, it can be noted that such were hallmarks of both Bill and Lillian

Koerner. They were also years that brought an income which did not drain but added to their savings. A reasoned estimate of Koerner's earnings during the second full year at Naaman's (1910–11) approximates $2,500.[49] Their share of the colony's operating and household expenses does not appear to have exceeded $1,200, which left a comfortable surplus. Why they left Naaman's at the end of their second year, as Koerner thoughtfully had stipulated could be their option, remains unclear.

The colonists drew lots for the lares and penates they had purchased jointly, and Koerner then purchased from the others whatever furniture they were willing to sell that his wife desired—two Queen Anne drop-leaf tables, two old chests, and four lyre-backed chairs. Henry J. Peck, another Pyle student, and his wife replaced them at Naaman's, and the Koerners returned to Wilmington. There they rented a narrow house at 1502 Van Buren Street, on its descent to Brandywine Park, which had enough room for Lillian's mother to have her own quarters instead of the room-and-board arrangements that had been her lot during the Naaman's stay. Koerner rented a studio for $15.00 per month at 1008 Franklin Street, next to that of Anton Otto Fischer, where he remained for several years before paying $18.00 per month for a studio at 1616 Rodney Street that adjoined Frank Schoonover's.[50]

"There is a priceless memory I have of William that I would like to add to the many expressions that you have by now. You know Bill worked next to me in the Wilmington studios and during many trying periods in my own work, his cheery "Good Morning" and "Get to Work" that floated through the walls of the studio was a great incentive for a hard day's work. That and his unusual capacity for long hours of successful picture production have served as a guiding light for my own programme. We will all miss him but he left a monument of creative imagination."[51]

---

1. From his letter in *The Wyeths*, it is clear that Wyeth wrestled with the question of art versus illustration for many years. The letter containing this quotation was dated 1/25/1907.

2. *Time*, 2/3/1975, 52, states that Arthur G. Dove was earning $12,000 a year in 1907 as an illustrator, when he eschewed illustration to become an abstract artist. Based on the record compiled of Dove's magazine appearances,

1900–1910, the figure quoted seems high, although Dove may have been doing advertising work as well as magazine. He returned to magazine work in the 1920s.

3. Kemp was doing camping-hunting covers for *Saturday Evening Post* in this year.

4. Koerner, *Narrative.*

5. Daughter of Admiral Charles D. Sigsbee, of *Maine* fame.

6. Koerner, *Narrative.*

7. Charles D. Abbott, *Howard Pyle, A Chronicle,* 217.

8. *Ibid.,* 163. See also Jessie Trimble, "Founder of an American School of Art," *The Outlook,* 2/23/1907, 453–56.

9. *The Wyeths,* 606.

10. *New Amstel Magazine* (Wilmington, Del.) 11/1911, 477–82. It is believed that Lillian had a major hand in preparing her husband's words for publication.

11. Anon., *Stanley Arthurs.* This publication of the Wilmington Society of Fine Arts gives Arthurs high rank among Pyle's pupils and successors. He was one of the very few who called Koerner "Billy."

12. John F. Apgar, Jr., *Frank E. Schoonover, Painter-Illustrator* is a selective bibliography.

13. N. C. Wyeth removed to Chadds Ford, Pennsylvania, March, 1908, and it does not appear that he and Koerner had much contact in Wilmington.

14. *Saturday Evening Post,* 6/25/1932, 36.

15. It did not list illustrators in the table of contents until some years later.

16. *Collier's* allowed ten days and *Saturday Evening Post* two weeks.

17. Harrison Fisher reputedly was earning $60,000 per anum in this period from his illustrations of "pretty girls" for various magazines.

18. Mott, *Magazines,* V, 286 *et seq.*

19. A "series" is distinct from a "serial," because it uses the same cast of characters or one major character in a series of independent stories, not in connected installments of a longer work. Famous "series" during Koerner's career were such as C. B. Kelland's "Scattergood Baines," Norman Reilly Raine's "Tugboat Annie," and Guy Gilpatric's "Mister Glencannon" stories.

20. John William Tebbel, *George Horace Lorimer and the Saturday Evening Post,* has been invaluable in relating Koerner's career to that magazine.

21. The phrase belongs to Eugene Manlove Rhodes.

22. Lorimer's image as an ogre of reaction stems from his stout opposition to certain precepts and actions of Franklin D. Roosevelt and his New Deal.

23. Mott, *Magazines,* IV, 685.

24. *Norman Rockwell,* 197.

25. One of Koerner's cover compositions (see Chapter IX) showed a Crow "Buffalo caller" holding up a bison's skull to the rising sun. Lorimer rejected it because of the skull.

26. Martin Justice and Lejaren A. Hiller, two prominent magazine illustrators of this period, already were experimenting with photographing posed models for their story illustrations. The results were not very successful.

27. Ed Clinkhammer wandered into Idaho's Salmon River country about 1900 and found a bench above the river to his liking. There, three days by pack string from the nearest road, he built his cabin, set out his orchard, and stayed until he died a half-century later. The walls of his cabin, even the attic, were covered with covers cut from his favorite magazine. Interview, Hal G. Evarts, Jr., La Jolla, California, 3/14/1970.

28. Her *The Man in Lower Ten,* illustrated in color by Howard Chandler Christy, was fourth on the best-seller list in 1909, which was topped by Basil King's *The Inner Shrine.*

29. Pattullo's place in the development of the western story is discussed in Chapter VIII.

30. Ivory had illustrated Joseph Conrad's serial about South America's revolution against Spain, "Gaspar Ruiz," in *Saturday Evening Post,* 7/28–8/25/1906, and appeared frequently in its pages thereafter.

31. When the Providence Lithograph Co. asked Koerner to do a series of Biblical scenes, he recommended Moore, who got the assignment. Moore later became a well-known designer of stage settings and other theatrical appurtenances in New York.

32. Portions of it dated from 1640.

33. The premises were demolished in the mid-1970s to accommodate an interstate highway.

34. Koerner Papers.

35. Koerner, *Narrative.* The cook raised chickens and warmed the new-hatched chicks against her capacious bosom.

36. Frank Schoonover once suffered a broken arm in an accident while riding with Dunn.

37. Quentin Reynolds, *The Fiction Factory,* 209.

38. The others were *Ainslee's, New Story, Smith's,* and *Top Notch. Popular* discovered Zane Grey; was the first to publish Edgar Wallace's stories in the United States, paying him $100 per story, and was regarded by Lorimer as an incubator of authors for his *Saturday Evening Post,* including such as Mary Roberts Rinehart, Octavus Roy Cohen, and Courtney Riley Cooper.

39. Gordon H. Gerould, "Pseudonymous," 10/1914, for which he did six soft-pencil-with-watercolor wash drawings and received $250 therefor. With this sum, the Koerners purchased a Victrola and records. Scribner's habit of retaining all artwork and copyrighting it in their name ruptured their relationship with N. C. Wyeth.

40. This prelude to the Nineteenth Amendment began in 1910 with a march of three thousand suffragettes, including the Collegiate Equal Suffrage League in caps-and-gowns, each wearing a sash and waving a flag of yellow, the movement's chosen color. Sixty-three automobiles in the procession showed that the suffragettes truly were *a la mode du temps.* Furnas, 889.

41. It was sold to the McClure organization in 1913 and died with the issue of 5/13/1916. It was re-born in the 1970s.

42. Frost had created "Brer Rabbit" and "Brer Fox" for the "Uncle Remus" stories and Kemble often did humorous drawings of rural "darkies."

43. Kelland's "Simeon Small" stories in *Harper's,* 1915–18, were the forerunner of "Scattergood Baines," who made his very first appearance in the *Saturday Evening Post,* 6/30/1917, and appeared regularly thereafter until Lorimer had had enough of him. Kelland then took "Scattergood" to *American,* where he endured for years and

years and years.

44. Frank Luther Mott, *Golden Multitudes*, 203.

45. Posters made from these frontispieces and from book illustrations were used by the Harper firm for newsstand and bookstore display in promoting their wares. One such was a Koerner illustration from the March, 1916, issue of the magazine. The poster was 13-3/4 × 20-3/4 inches overall, with the artwork measuring 7-1/2 × 11 inches, and the legend in bold orange-and-black type.

46. Mears was an artist and illustrator in his own right and he and his family became close and fast friends with the Koerners. When his wife died suddenly and unexpectedly, Lillian Koerner became virtually his children's surrogate mother.

47. Koerner, *Narrative*, as are the excerpts which follow.

48. One of these visitors was John Wallace "Captain Jack" Crawford, the "Cowboy Poet," who was a friend of Schrader's.

49. Approximately $12,500 in terms of 1974 dollars. (Ward C. Krebs, vice-president, Wells Fargo Bank, San Francisco, to W.H.H., 8/22/1974.) This income was net before taxes and there were no taxes in that simpler time save on real property, and that was their landlord's concern. For contrast, Charles Dana Gibson received $10,000 in this period for illustrating R. W. Chambers' risqué serial "The Common Law" which is said to have brought *Cosmopolitan* a 70 per cent increase in circulation.

50. The rent increased to $24.00 per month, including telephone, in 1924. The four studios in a row on Rodney Street seem to have been the prized ones in Wilmington. They sat on a lot above street level and were commodious with excellent skylights.

51. Frank E. Schoonover to Lillian Lusk Koerner, 9/9/1938, Koerner Papers.

Chapter VI
MAINE SUMMERS AND "SATURDAY EVENING POST"

THE NEXT SIX YEARS were part of the "ragtime era," symbolized in *Life* by John Held's drawing of a pretty young miss conversing with a handsome youth while holding a cigarette in one hand and a cocktail in the other. Kenyon Cox inveighed against what he termed the "shock your grandmother" trend in American art, and the hands on *Cosmopolitan's* editorial clock were settling towards the "sex o'clock" position that became fixed after World War I. Gene Stratton Porter, author of *Freckles* (1904), *A Girl of the Limberlost* (1909), and other best-sellers, reacted to criticism of her work as purveying falsely sentimental pictures of life by saying:

They are living pictures from the lives of men and women of morals, honor, and loving-kindness. . . . Am I the only woman in this broad land so born and reared? Was my home the only one with a moral code and religious practise? Are there not homes by the thousand in which men and women are true to their highest ideals?[1]

And Zane Grey made ninth in the list of ten best-sellers for 1915, with *The Lone Star Ranger,* that had a Frank Tenney Johnson frontispiece.

These were years when *Ladies Home Journal* was challenged for supremacy in circulation and advertising in its field, as *McCall's* climbed from 1,000,000 to 1,250,000 despite raising its price to $1.00 per year, *Pictorial Review* soared from 350,000 to 1,250,000 at $1.00, *Woman's Home Companion* gained 280,000 to reach 1,000,000 at $1.50, while the *Journal* added 250,000 to reach 1,500,000 at $1.50. *Collier's* ran the first ten of Sax Rohmer's "Fu Manchu" stories in 1913, with Joseph Coll's spidery lines providing

visual menace to augment the text. In this same year, *Collier's* first listed illustrators on its front cover (12/13/1913)—Alonzo Kimball, William Glackens, Franklin Booth, Henry McCarter, Penryhn Stanlaws, and Henry Raleigh—and *Cosmopolitan* (7/1914) listed Charles Dana Gibson, Howard Chandler Christy, and Harrison Fisher on its cover, together with the issue's leading authors—Rudyard Kipling, Rex Beach, Gouverneur Morris, R. W. Chambers, G. R. Chester, and Arthur B. Reeve.[2] And on December 16, 1916, P. F. Collier and Company advertised that the lack of space in its files would enable the sale of "charming Christmas gifts—25¢ to $15.00" consisting of original artwork for covers, illustrations, and decorations from both the magazine and the books the Collier firm published.

Harry Conway "Bud" Fisher, who had begun his career on the newspapers of San Francisco, his birthplace, was said to be earning $150,000 per year from his "Mutt and Jeff" cartoon strip. The place of the motion picture as staple fare in entertainment diets was attested by Street and Smith launching *Picture-Play Weekly* at five cents, as competition for *Motion Picture Magazine,* and its climb within one month to 100,000 circulation and a price of ten cents. When *Photoplay* asked Koerner if he could do work for it, his reply that he would not accept "any pink tea stories" ended the correspondence. The dust wrapper or jacket for books replaced the former decorated or illustrated cover of the book itself in these years, and that the wrapper was intended to do what the advertising poster had done previously is borne out by a letter to Koerner from Joseph W. Harper:

If you can make a good picture for printing in two colors, that is in black and yellow or black and orange or something like that, please do so. We would like to avoid three printings if possible. Did I give you the size of the book? It is 5" × 7-5/8" and your picture should be made in proportion.

The action scene that he did from one of the book's incidents brought him $75.00 and the comment from Mr. Harper, "We all here feel that it is helping a lot to sell the book."[3]

It was during this period that Koerner began to do virtually all of his work in oils, even though it was for black-and-white reproduction, because he felt more at ease thereby and could get into a painting's mood and feeling with greater authority. He did black-and-white work—wash, charcoal, pen-and-ink—when the assignment lent itself best to these mediums, or when they were requested specifically, and he did some of his vignette work in watercolors because it was not so "heavy" for certain reproduction processes.[4]

Koerner's first and only experiences as a thespian came during these years when Wilmington's artists produced two humorous plays written by Miss Gertrude Brinckle, for which Frank Schoonover was the director and general factotum.[5] In the first of these, "The Magician of Badgab," Koerner played "Alkandra, the Faithfull," while in the second opus, "The Heart of the Painter's Desert," he was "Chief Arrow-root." Neither was a major part but Lillian was dumfounded that her "Boy" could act at all, or would even consent to try. He exhibited in at least three of the annual exhibitions sponsored by the Wilmington Society of the Fine Arts during these years, and one of his entries was judged "Best Landscape" in the 1914 exhibition. Entitled "The Birches," this was a painting done for his own private concerns and then discarded. Lillian found it and had it framed for entry without his knowledge. In these years, too, Lillian began her acquaintance with Christian Science, which came to occupy a prominent part in her life thereafter.

The most important aspect of these Wilmington years was the completion of the Koerner family. Ruth Ann was born on October 18, 1913, after more than ten years of marriage, and Koerner, who often had said that he really did not care whether their union was blessed with children, who had sworn during Lillian's pregnancy never to touch small children, was the first to lift his daughter from her mother's side after her delivery. During Ruth Ann's first six months, he kept a photographic record of her progress week-by-week; then on a biweekly basis for another six months, and then on a monthly basis through 1915. The pictures he took of Lillian holding, feeding, and bathing the baby, plus those he took of the infant's own poses and moods, eventually became grist to his mill, but they had not been taken with this in mind.

When Ruth Ann was three months old, Koerner did a painting of mother and child that won the prize for the "Most Popular Painting" at the Wilmington Exhibition held in 1914. He was offered $1,000 for it but he refused to sell, nor would he submit it as a cover possibility to *Ladies Home Journal*, of which Karl Harriman now was managing editor. In his own mind, he felt that he never could paint another like it and it was to be Ruth Ann's when she grew up and had a home of her own. So it became and remained. Her brother, named for his father, was born on April 27, 1915, and the "1-2-3-4 Koerners," as their Christmas cards later showed them, were complete.

The Koerners had shared their last unencumbered summer together for many years in 1912 and it was a memorable one for them both. Leaving Mrs. Lusk in Wilmington, they visited "Mother" Koerner in Clinton and assorted relatives and friends in Chicago and Battle Creek. Then they entrained for Minocqua, Wisconsin, about seventy-five miles north of Wausau in the Lac du Flambeau country of the Chippewas. A team-and-wagon jolted them along for some three hours to the shore of Squirrel Lake, whence an asthmatic motorboat conveyed them to an island where Frank Stick (who had moved from Wilmington to Chicago in 1911) had invited them to spend a month with him and his family. The cabin was so constricted that Lillian observed in later years that they must have built the beds inside *after* the cabin had been completed.

Frank Stick, as noted earlier, was one of the great wildlife painters of his day, and he knew how to do what he painted other men as doing. Koerner learned how to fish, and boat, muskellunge, which is perhaps a freshwater angler's supreme test, while wall-eyed pike and black bass added to their larder. Chippewas still harvested wild rice by bending the full, yellow heads over the gunwales of their birch-bark canoes and flailing them onto its bottom. Mallard ducks fed on these wild rice beds, for it was September, and so did coots and helldivers, the provender making even their meat approach palatability. Stick brought in only basic supplies to his cabin and fish and wildfowl and rice were a welcome addition to the larder. The loon's cry at night and the bark of the fox made poignant reminders of their first summers together, while the deep silence all around them was a benison after the Naaman's years and work and Mrs. Lusk. Carefree as two children for a blissful month, they came all alive with the ecstasy of living, which was not lessened when Koerner, standing on the one-plank dock, as a full moon rose behind the fire-scarred trunks along the lake's eastern shore, was so startled by the splash of a deer entering the lake behind him that he toppled backwards into the chilly water—hat, Mackinaw, boots, and all.

Ensuing summers were spent in a rented cottage with room for Mrs. Lusk—three bedrooms, a large living room furnished with antiques, combined dining room and kitchen, and a large,

Koerner at Stick's cabin on Squirrel Lake, Wisconsin

Frank Stick, left, and Koerner in the Wisconsin back country

Bill and Lillian inspect the framework of a Chippewa structure near Squirrel Lake, Wisconsin

screened-in porch—on Lake Cochnewagan, near Monmouth, Maine, and Koerner established his summer studio in the empty hayloft of a nearby barn. A summer studio was mandated by the fact that the demand for his work outstripped even the demands of an enlarged family. Significant, too, is the fact that Koerner enjoyed his work and that he was growing in his sensitivity to stories and their characters and in his ability to express that sensitivity powerfully and swiftly. This brought the *Saturday Evening Post* a letter from George Patullo.

Please convey to Mr. Koerner my hearty thanks for his illustrations to "In Pursuit of Hicks." They are bully—especially the one where "Mom Bastido" is sitting in the hammock. I hope he will get a crack at some more of mine. His people are human.

Patullo was not the only author to ask for Koerner's illustrations; others included Martha Ostenso for her prize-winning "Wild Geese," Stew-

art Edward White, and Emerson Hough for "The Covered Wagon," which made a significant contribution to the development of the western story in the post–World War I years. In the last named story his horses' heads became what they were becoming in this earlier period—the most natural, especially in repose, of any done by an illustrator whose work has been examined in the course of this study, Frederic Remington and Charles M. Russell not excluded.

Koerner's work and the magazines in which it appeared had not gone unnoticed by the former business manager of *Pilgrim*. Hiram M. Greene now was editing the *Illustrated Sunday Magazine*, a weekly supplement carried by seventeen newspapers—the Detroit *Free Press*, Memphis *Commercial-Appeal*, Minneapolis *Tribune*, and Des Moines *Register-Leader* among them—which is not to be confused with the Sunday magazine supplement appearing in the Hearst papers. Greene commissioned at least three full-page, black-and-white illustrations from Koerner, with his only stipulation being that they "pull down" for reproduction to 8-7/8 × 7 inches, for which he paid $100 each.[6] This apparently evolved into the *Sunday Monthly Magazine*, again not a Hearst publication, for which Koerner did three wash drawings for a western short story by Patullo.

Only about 5 per cent of Koerner's total production was done for the magazines controlled by William Randolph Hearst and almost half of this was done for *Good Housekeeping*. Founded in 1885 as a family journal with literary pretensions, it had been a heavy user of reader-written articles until Hearst acquired it in 1911 and began to increase its fiction content, as well as carrying only "Money Back" advertising, forerunner of the magazine's later "Seal of Approval."[7] It was the "runt of the litter" in this period, among the women's magazines, with a monthly circulation around 300,000 copies, at fifteen cents per copy, $1.50 per year, but it weathered the traumas of the Great Depression better than most in this field to reach more than 2,000,000 copies per month and become probably the most profitable monthly then being published.[8]

During the four years, 1913–16, that Koerner's work enhanced its pages, William F. Bigelow edited a magazine, 7 × 10 inches, with 144 pages of text, sandwiched between front and back advertising sections averaging in aggregate 128 pages. It had three art editors during these

Koerner and catch, Maine, 1915–18

Summer scene in Maine, 1915–18

Maine sketches

years, who used C. Coles Phillips, Penryhn Stanlaws, and James M. Flagg for cover work, mostly pretty girls and children in beguiling poses, and such as Henry J. Soulen, Gayle Porter Hoskins, Lejaren A. Hiller, A. B. Wenzell, Herman Pfeifer, Clara Peck, G. Patrick Nelson, Lucius W. Hitchcock, and George Wright for inside work, very little of which was in color. An average issue contained a poem, by such as Ella Wheeler Wilcox; one serial installment— Coningsby Dawson, John Galsworthy, and William J. Locke; six or more feature articles, among which Rose O'Neill's "Kewpies" in color were regular fare;[9] the usual "departments" for a magazine of its type; and six short stories. These latter ran heavily to "series" stories, with Wallace Irwin's "Togo," illustrated by Frederick

Strothmann, regularly presenting the humor of a young Japanese confronted by the American version of western civilization, and Dorothy Dix regularly contributing her "Mirandy" stories, illustrated by E. W. Kemble, of rural "darky" characters.

Koerner illustrated nine such "series" stories by William Johnston over three years. These were built around "Eddie Randall," aged ten, the youngest of three brothers, who was called "Limpy" because of a birth defect that was slowly, very slowly, responding to treatment. The stories had a warm and wholesome family setting and revolved around "Limpy's" triumphs over his handicap in the process of growing up. Koerner responded to their milieu but he had to wrestle with his depiction of "Limpy," simply

Field work in Maine

because he was extremely sensitive to the tribulations of any and all of God's creatures that
were marked by a mistake at the Hands of the
Potter.

His work for *Collier's, The National Weekly,*[10]
began in 1914, as the clouds of World War I
darkened Europe's lives and began their slow
spread westwards against the prevailing winds
of public opinion in the United States. It continued intermittently for the next decade but
was never an appreciable part of his illustrative
career, quite probably because his time became
more and more committed to *Collier's* arch-rival
in the weekly field. In the opening decade of
the century, *Collier's* inside pages had been
bright with color, including the truly opulent
Arabian Nights plates by Maxfield Parrish and
the dramatic compositions of Frederic Remington. In 1914, its pages were color-less, save for

the covers and the advertisements for long-van-
ished makes of automobiles—Overland, Franklin, Hudson, and Peerless among them—and for
Mecca, Murad, and Fatima cigarettes.

Collier's had pioneered photojournalism as
early as the Spanish-American War, with the
work of James H. Hare, and even though Frederic Remington had covered the later Russo-
Japanese War for it, Hare's photography of the
conflict made an outstanding feature of its pages.
Jack London's article on the San Francisco disaster of 1906 had been given sixteen pages of
photographic illustration.[11] By 1914, its photojournalism section had been standardized at four
pages, and the magazine gave the Mexican Revolution and Pancho Villa extensive photographic
coverage, as well as reportage by James Hopper
and George Patullo.

Mark Sullivan was its editor in 1914, turning

out a magazine of thirty-six pages, each 10-7/8 × 15 inches, with a weekly circulation of 500,000 copies at five cents per copy, $2.50 per year. It would double its circulation by 1917, when Peter Finley Dunne became its editor, largely because it realized that "Fiction was the backbone of circulation." Towards this end, *Collier's* conducted a contest for short stories in 1914 that was judged by Theodore Roosevelt, Ida M. Tarbell, and its editor. The first prize of $2,500 was taken by J. B. Connolly with "The Trawler," a story of the sea; the second prize of $1,000 went to Ceylon Hollingsworth for "Saleratus Smith," a humorous "darky" yarn; with twelve other awards of $500 each. Its first ever serial began on November 29, 1913, by Amèliè Rives, also the Princess Troubetzkoy, and ran for at least sixteen installments. It carried these, as well as its short fiction, into the back of the magazine among the advertisements.

Its standard format in 1914 was one serial installment, using Hamlin Garland, H. G. Wells, Maude R. Warren, for examples; two or three short stories, with Sax Rohmer and Beatrice Grimshaw frequent contributors,[12] and three feature articles on such topics as the presidential chances of Senator William J. Borah of Idaho, and the alleged murder of Mary Phagan in Atlanta by Leo M. Frank, a Jew, which was one of the nation's most celebrated cases. Grantland Rice's baseball articles were almost weekly fare during the season, and Walter Camp's annual All-American college football team selections were accompanied by *Collier's* annual All-Western college eleven, no members of which came from west of the University of Minnesota for the five years they were examined. This emphasis on sports reflected the magazine's aim at a masculine audience, and explains in part its failure to catch *Saturday Evening Post*, which aimed at the same masculine audience but hit its distaff members as well.

F. De Sales Casey was its art editor and he divided the covers about equally between pretty girls by Penryhn Stanlaws, Haskell Coffin, J. K. Hare, and Sarah Stilwell-Weber and more dramatic compositions by F. X. Leyendecker, a football specialist, Worth Brehm, Frederick Dorr Steele, Z. P. Nikolai, and Louis Fancher. He gave his inside illustrators a credit line under the author's name, which of course appeared below the story title, and they included Henry Raleigh, D. C. Hutchison, C. W. Ashley, Arthur E. Becher, Ernest Fuhr, Denman Fink, Remington Schuyler, R. M. Brinkerhoff, F. R. Gruger, Frank Schoonover, J. N. Marchand, George Harding, Henry J. Peck, and M. L. Blumenthal. Henry Reuterdahl, then the nation's foremost painter of the U. S. Navy, sailed for Europe shortly after hostilities were declared to paint the war for *Collier's* which reflects the fact that *Collier's* carried more war coverage and fiction before 1917 than any other magazine in its class. A letter from Casey to Koerner (10/7/1914) indicates some of the factors that an illustrator had to take into account in his work.

When you are making the drawings, please bear in mind that the requirements of our presses must be taken into consideration. The figures must be silhouetted or made to stand out clearly. You must either keep them light in tone, with the backgrounds dark, or dark in tone, with the backgrounds light. Our presses will not print dark drawings.

Koerner's first work for *Collier's* was "The Lynching of the Night Marshal" by C. Hilton-Turvey, which qualifies as a semi-western because of its setting on the "sun-baked plains" of Kansas and the fact that boots and big hats were evident in the illustrations. The hero was not lynched, despite the story's title, because the man against whom he vented his spleen while wearing his badge of office, thus incurring the town's animosity, turned out to be a swindling land promoter. The townies then ran *him* out of the marshal's bailiwick when the latter told them, while looking at the rope they had made ready, that he, himself, had been a victim of this same man elsewhere.

His major illustration for "The Hospital Ticket" by James W. Fitzpatrick featured a lumberjack brawl in a bunkhouse, and most of the other stories he did for *Collier's* were of the outdoor-action variety—horse races, Afghanistan, Papua, the West—with one notable exception. This was "Candles for St. Nicholas" by I.A.R. Wylie, a French Army story that climaxed with an officer's son's prayer to St. Nicholas "to help me grow up quick" so he could assist his father in the defense of *la belle Patrie.* Koerner's painting of the son holding a candle while his mother held him close later appeared on the cover of the annual report of the private Harlem Eye and

Ear Hospital in New York by means that remain unclear to this day.[13]

Koerner received his first assignment from *Country Gentleman,* which Curtis Publishing Company had purchased two years before, in June, 1913, although he did no more work for it until four years later. This assignment soon brought him a letter (6/9/1913) from Herbert Johnson, art editor of *Saturday Evening Post,* which spoke for itself.

You mentioned some illustrations that you have in hand for the Country Gentleman *as interfering with the prompt delivery of our Woolley series. In that connection I wish to make entirely clear to you that there is no connection between the art departments of the* Country Gentleman *and the* Post *and that you are not working for the same people when you make illustrations for these two publications. With most of the men who work for the* Post *regularly, we have an understanding that* Post *work is to take precedence, as a rule, over other work in their hands.*

I hope you will understand that work for Country Gentleman *should not be allowed to interfere with the delivery of* Post *drawings any more than any other outside publication. Let me know if you can deliver the first installment of the Woolley series about the first of July and how soon the following installments will come to us. The galleys will be sent to you as rapidly as they reach my desk.*

Johnson's concern over "prompt delivery" is understandable. His view of the *Post's* "precedence" over other magazines, even other Curtis publications, was offset by the fact that the *Post* paid *promptly* and on acceptance for the work of both illustrators and authors,[14] while many other magazines paid only upon publication, and this was a matter of some importance.

The "Woolley series" had brought Koerner back to the *Post* in 1912, and deserves some mention for what it represented. Lorimer had written "Letters From a Self-Made Merchant to His Son" because he could not find qualified American writers interested in business matters.[15] These letters have been credited with giving impetus to the *Post's* climb in circulation and Lorimer continued to use business articles by other writers for as long as he lived, ate,

slept, and breathed the *Post's* successful life. These created "a new fictional genre, the hustling American business story,"[16] and they kept Koerner busy.

Between May 4, 1912, and January 22, 1916, he illustrated forty-seven such articles, primarily by Edward Mott Woolley, James H. Collins, and Forrest Crissey.[17] Given Lorimer's emphasis on the business article, illustrations for these pieces were not for any hack brush, and in fact they received better illustrative treatment than much of the *Post's* fiction in these years. It appears that these stories were accepted, galley proofs sent to the illustrator, and then article and illustrations were stockpiled to be used whenever a slot in the magazine needed filling. Edward Hungerford's "The Yardmaster's Job," for example, was completed by Koerner on June 2, 1914, and did not appear until March 13, 1915. This explains in part why Koerner appeared three times in the *Post* of September 20, 1913: a short story by Kennett Harris, and two business articles by Collins and Will Payne.

A study of these articles has shown that four of them by Collins reflected a continuance of the turmoil in religious circles between individual salvation and social involvement that had racked the churches in the first decade of the century. Upton Sinclair's *The Profits of Religion* earlier had charged the churches with being tools of the moneyed interests and, in 1908–1909, *American* had published a hard-hitting series by Ray S. Baker entitled "The Spiritual Unrest." In 1913, the year after Koerner illustrated Collins's articles, Winston Churchill's *The Inside of the Cup* led the best-seller lists with a theme that embodied the argument for recognizing the social values in the teachings of Jesus of Nazareth.

The study of Koerner's *Post* work in this period has shown that the *Post* was not always punctilious in what it did with an illustrator's work, before returning it to him as it did with Koerner. One illustration Koerner did for "The Slipper Tongue," a western short story by William J. Neidig, showed a man riding as though the milltails of Hell were on his heels while leading two saddled horses. This appeared again, without credit line or payment, to provide visual relief for the text of George Patullo's "Ways That Are Dark" (4/4/1917), which presented reasons why Mexico was such a fertile ground for anti-

United States propaganda. One of Harvey Dunn's illustrations for Eugene Manlove Rhodes' previously published "The Come On" also was used for this article, again without credit to the artist. One of Koerner's drawings of locomotives with steam up in a railroad yard, a piece of line work that would not embarrass the memory of Edward Penfield, was used without credit or payment, eight months after it first appeared, to give visual impact to an article by Forrest Crissey about scrap iron.

Even though they had had their Wilmington house wired for electricity after the children came, the fans it made possible availed little when summer came to the Delaware coast and it came early in 1916. After advising various art editors that he planned to be in Maine for six months, Koerner shepherded his flock out of Wilmington during the first week in May. He undoubtedly hoped that nothing would occur like the previous summer's *contretemps*, when Mrs. Lusk's brother from California with his large family had descended upon them and stayed to the tune of "ten quarts of Jersey milk" per day. He was almost inured to his wife's passion for antiques and had been cured of remonstrating with her for "spending all our money" after one of her excursions, when she had him lift down her purchases from the hayrack wagon that had brought them and her back to the rented cottage and showed him her acquisition costs:

> .20 for one curly-maple, spool-bed with acorn finials and extra bed spring;
> .15 for one commode, with bowl, pitcher, and slop jar;
> .28 for four reed-seat Hitchcock chairs;
> .10 for one pine, hooded cradle;
> .18 for one Boston rocker;
> .10 for one nursing rocking chair;
> .10 for one hooked rug with original dog pattern,
> _____
> $1.11 Total Expenditure

They barely had gotten re-settled in their cottage, with Koerner getting underway in his hayloft studio on work that he had brought from Wilmington, when he received a letter (5/19/1916) from K. M. Goode, assistant art editor of the *Post*, who fancied his sense of humor.

Roll up your sleeves and clean up your palette

—I've got a real job coming for you, grabbed right out of Harvey Dunn's hands. Stewart Edward White is now writing a novel about Africa called "The Leopard Woman," or Why She Doesn't Change Those Spots. It is a whale of a story with magnificent illustration possibilities. Moreover, Mr. White has sent in numerous photographs of considerable pictorial value and recommended several books with more pictures. That's how I came to think of you. All you will have to do is to copy the photographs in colors on a big canvas and put your signature in some fairly conspicuous place. This you should be able to do as well as any man I know of and, with the opportunity, you ought to be able to put yourself on the map like the German Kaiser. Along about June first the stuff will be ready. If the baby is sick or there is any other reason why you can't make a killing, please tell me now and forever after hold your peace.

Koerner's prompt reply brought this response from Goode (5/23/1916):

When your letter first arrived I thought it was a manuscript and turned it over to the regular readers, but when they got to the part about seeing a beautiful rainbow at 4:30 a.m. they returned it to me on the grounds that it wouldn't be a fit story for us to print anyhow, as we aim to discourage such effects.

Any man that is sleeping under five blankets ought to be able to paint Africa to perfection, or even warmer spots.

I am having shipped to you the photographs. Please be careful of them as they belong to the author and, after you have painted pictures of Africa, he may want them to recall what Africa really looks like. Enclosed is a letter giving the titles of the books. By the time you have read them, you won't waste paper writing about a frog.

Mr. Dower [Art Editor] says to tell you that he has become so attached to the picture that he hasn't had the heart to part with it, but he expects to take an anesthetic soon and let us ship it while he isn't looking.[18]

The letter to which Goode referred had been written by White to his New York agent, Galbraith Welch, Inc., of which Carl Brandt was manager.

. . . the illustrator should get copies of my three books African Camp Fires, The Land of Foot Prints *and* The Rediscovered Country *to supplement these* [54] Kodaks. *By use of a reading glass a great many small details of costume, etc., can be observed. A little pains in the illustrating of this story will obviate the usual criticisms of such things from the expert who knows what he is talking about.*[19]

Koerner telegraphed Brentano's Book Store in New York to send the three books posthaste and went to work.

Africa was popular fare and had been ever since Theodore Roosevelt's adventures had given it to the public consciousness with more force than anything since H. M. Stanley had been encountered by Dr. Livingstone. Lorimer had scheduled the story for publication the moment he had read it, and the illustrator damned well had to meet the deadlines for each of the eight installments with four illustrations for each. One month to the day after Goode's first letter had advised him that "The Leopard Woman" was on his horizon, Koerner's first set of illustrations reached the *Post* and evoked this response (6/19/1916) from Walter Dower, its art editor.

Good work! "The Leopard Woman" just made her entry into the office and though she has with becoming modesty kept well in the background, the surrounding people and country are splendidly done and the whole effect and atmosphere of the pictures are mighty satisfying. Mr. Lorimer gave them the once-over and thinks they are bully. Personally, I think they are easily the best you have ever done for the Post, *which should mean your very best, for I would hate to think you are doing better things for someone else than you do for us.*

Here's the best of luck to you on the following installments and please bear in mind that the pictures must come in weekly and if it is a possible thing, let them appear Friday instead of Monday; in other words, try and get installment No. 2 in here this week Friday and the balance weekly thereafter.

A certain quite tangible form of nervous prostration invades the offices when Mr. Lorimer discovers on Monday morning that a serial installment did not get in, so if you want to do a little life-saving on the side you will get your

pictures here the latter part of the week instead of the first.

For eight consecutive weeks, stripped to the waist as he worked in the hayloft, Koerner produced four paintings per week for "The Leopard Woman." He wrapped them in birch bark for expressage after he exhausted the local supply of packing materials, and ordered pints of "Pale Artists Quick Drying Varnish" to speed the process. Family legend holds that the birch bark adhered to one set of paintings and that they had to be re-done. If so, this simply accentuates the fact that between May first and September first of this summer, Koerner produced fourteen additional illustrations for stories in *Good Housekeeping* and *Harper's.* This total compares quite favorably with N. C. Wyeth's production during the same time span of this same summer—at least twenty-eight book illustrations, "besides two magazine stories for Scribner's, several Collier's stories, a subject picture and a Pierce-Arrow advertisement."[20] It is doubtful if any others of Pyle's students ever matched these two for quality work under pressure.

In a more practical vein, his work brought him a letter (7/28/1916) from Doubleday, Page and Co. of New York:

We are planning to use several of your illustrations in Stewart Edward White's book "The Leopard Woman" which is now running serially in "The Saturday Evening Post." In this connection we would like to have made especially, for [dust] *wrapper purposes, a picture of the heroine, to be reproduced in four colors. The drawing should be made approximately 18″ × 24″ as it must be reduced in the reproduction to 5″ × 8″.*[21]

Will you please let us know at once if you could undertake this drawing for us, and at what price?

His work for "The Leopard Woman" also brought him African stories from other magazines and thereby hangs a tale. One of the country's leading fictioneers, who used exotic settings to give a fillip to his wares, decided to do a two-part story laid in Africa. Deeming that field research was a necessity, he bade farewell to his wife of many years and sailed for the Dark Continent, taking with him his "great and good friend" secretary, without advising his wife of the fact. When the story came to Koerner, he followed his usual practice of seeing the characters from what the author said they did. Again, this was in keeping with the valid fiction maxim that "Action springs out of character and character is described by action." The story was a forerunner of Ernest Hemingway's later pieces, in that it involved a White Hunter and a fair-skinned woman on safari. In writing the story, the novelist unconsciously described himself and his secretary in the leading roles, and he did this so well that when Koerner's illustrations appeared in print, the wife recognized the pair and promptly sued for and obtained a divorce. Despite this *contretemps,* or perhaps because of it, the author continued to work the African scene as late as 1934 with a serial in *Collier's.*

Koerner did not illustrate the seven short stories about Africa that Stewart Edward White contributed to the *Post* (7/21–1/27/1917) in the wake of "The Leopard Woman." These were done by Harvey Dunn and his work did not reproduce as cleanly, nor was it as expressive as Koerner's.[22] Correlating these dates of appearance with the *Post's* production schedule and with what Koerner was doing at the same time, it becomes clear that he simply was too involved with serials for other magazines at the time the first of these seven was scheduled by the *Post.* Once Dunn had been given the first to do, it was not *Post* policy to change illustrators. Another factor is simply that at this same time, Koerner and his family were engrossed by the details of preparing to move into the first and only home of their own.

1. Quoted in Mott, *Golden Multitudes,* 214–15.

2. *Ladies Home Journal* did not list illustrators even in the table of contents until the issue of 11/1929.

3. Harold MacGrath, *The Luck of the Irish,* 1917, which used the dust-wrapper painting for the frontispiece as well.

4. *Collier's* to Koerner, 10/7/1914, Koerner Papers.

5. Held in Wilmington's New Century Club, 4/24/1916 and 4/20–21/1917. Schoonover to Lillian Koerner, 3/23/1947, Koerner Papers.

6. They were completed 5/27 and 1/28/1912; 1/17/1913.

7. Mott, *Magazines,* V, 125–44, *passim.*

8. *Ibid.*

9. O'Neill and her "Kewpies" went to *Ladies Home Journal* in 1925.

10. Mott, *Magazines,* IV, 453 *et seq.* has much on *Collier's.* It joined *American* and *Woman's Home Companion* in 1919 to make the Crowell-Collier stable complete.

11. London's piece, "The Story of an Eyewitness," was one of seven articles on this disaster that appeared in the issues of 5/5–19/1906. William Kent contributed "Shake: A Personal Reminiscence" to the issue of 12/29/1906.

12. Grimshaw's exotic tales of romance and adventure in the South Pacific were a staple of this segment of the outdoor-action school of popular fiction. W. T. Benda illustrated many of these with the *masques* that became his trademark.

13. It was used as the front cover of the hospital's annual report for 1920, and Koerner's first knowledge of its acquisition by the hospital came when it appeared in the gravure section of the New York *Tribune* (5/8/1921), "an appealing painting by W.H.D. Koerner," to stimulate the first public appeal for funds made by that non-sectarian institution.

14. The *Post* made its decision on stories and articles within seventy-two hours of receipt and purchased first North American serial rights only, which was in marked contrast to other magazines that bought *all* rights. Its speed sired the fable that a *Post* editor picked up the mail at the North Broad Street station and dropped the rejections in the outgoing box before taking the others to the office.

15. Tebbel, 28. These began to appear in the *Post,* 8/3/1901, and were followed with a similar series, "Old Gorgon Graham" which began 10/3/1903. Both appeared later in book form.

16. Fred Lewis Pattee, *The New American Literature, 1890–1930,* 56; Lorimer also serialized Frank Norris's *The Pit,* 9/20/1902, *et seq.*

17. See the appendix for titles and dates.

18. This was a painting of a western sheriff that Koerner had done for a *Post* story and had promised to give to a friend.

19. Copy in Koerner Papers.

20. *The Wyeths,* 908–16, *passim.*

21. He did the dust wrapper, and seven illustrations from the serialization were used in the book. Koerner's compensation is unknown.

22. Dunn had opened his own art school at Tenafly, New Jersey, in 1915 and here and later at the Grand Central School of Art in New York, he became the foremost teacher of all of Howard Pyle's pupils. Dean Cornwell is regarded as the strongest of his students.

Chapter VII
STUDIO AT INTERLAKEN

A MOVE from Wilmington had been in the Koerners' minds for some time; that they decided upon Interlaken, New Jersey, produced a minor rift in the long friendship between Koerner and Frank Schoonover. Bushkill, Pennsylvania—on the uppermost reaches of the Delaware River—where A. B. Frost lived and painted for many years, had been Schoonover's residential target as early as 1906. He had acquired property and was either building a house or had just completed it when Bill and Lillian visited him there in 1916. It appears that Schoonover had an income apart from his painting and stained-glass work. Koerner most assuredly did not and Bushkill was too far removed from magazine publishers for an artist whose livelihood depended on steady assignments from these gentry. Schoonover also had a knack for being abrasive, unintentional in Koerner's case, and it is logical to assume that Koerner considered this facet of his friend's personality, multiplied it mentally by what family propinquity might do to increase its incidence, and said to himself "The Hell with it"!

Their selection of Interlaken stemmed directly from Frank Stick, who had moved from Chicago to New York, where he was illustrating steadily for *Field and Stream*. Its editor was Warren H. Miller, who lived in Interlaken and commuted daily to New York, a not interminable journey under normal conditions. He had persuaded Stick to settle there and Stick then convinced the Koerners to do the same. In addition to the warm friendship between the two families, Interlaken, then a political part of Asbury Park,[1] had advantages of its own. It was cooler in summer than Wilmington, for one thing, and it was a secluded, residential community, not a manufacturing city. It was closer to New York and the reference resources there that Koerner used so often at $4.50 round-trip train fare, albeit not nearly so handy to Philadelphia as was Wilmington, and it had attractive values in real estate to accompany its natural advantages.

Interlaken was all of a peninsula, heavily wooded with maple, pine, and birch, that jutted into Deal Lake, almost making it two separate bodies of water. Its entrance gateway was not far from Asbury Park and the breakers, sand dunes, and fishing of "the Shore" along a narrow gravelled road. No public transportation connected the two, but a veritable "Toonerville Trolley" ran from Asbury Park to Allenhurst, within easy walking distance. Begun in the 1890's as an ambitious real estate development that did not materialize, its east-and-west avenues had been given names with a uniform suffix—Windermere, Bendermere, Grasmere. Certain restrictions had been established by its original promoters, including the size of houses and their design, and among those still retained in 1917 was that prohibiting any type of commercial establishment, even medical practice, from being conducted within its confines. Artists and writers were permitted because theoretically their work was "taken out" and not sold on the premises, as in a shop.

After its initial promotion, Interlaken had slumbered along, attracting people with moderate to ample means who appreciated its natural and relatively unsullied natural beauty. It slowly attracted a nucleus of people connected with the arts, foremost among them being Yvette Guilbert, once a darling of the Foliés Bergere and Moulin Rouge and widely believed to have been the favorite model of Toulouse-Lautrec. Another was Charles Abels, son of the one-time resident agent for the real-estate developers, who had won fame on the Paris stage as a female impersonator and later renown at home as an interior decorator. Both still resided in Interlaken when the Koerners became residents.[2] An air meet at Interlaken in August, 1910, had brought it unexpected publicity, resulting in some real-estate transactions, when one of the planes crashed into the grandstand erected for the occasion and injured fourteen spectators, none fatally.[3] In 1917, farming still was being done on the spacious blocks platted by the original developers but never built upon.

The house they bought at 86 Grasmere Avenue, Grassmere to the Koerners, was surrounded by stately maples, with pine and birch along its eastern exposure.[4] Verandah-ed on two sides, it boasted three stories and fifteen rooms, ample enough for Mrs. Lusk's own private floor, which caused Lillian to estimate that its care would require at least three hired help. Lacking these, she substituted "a good broom, strong muscles and a happy outlook on life." She learned from Maud Stick to prepare for winter by buying barrels of potatoes, turnips, flour, sugar, and coffee, which were delivered free and which were stored in the capacious "cellar," as such were known then. Whenever weather and season permitted, the fish man, fresh-vegetable man, and ice man made their appointed rounds with horse-and-wagon; in summer, a flower man joined them in the daily procession. When the children reached school age, she occupied her spare time—between mothering, housekeeping and cooking, modeling for her husband, protecting him from intrusions upon his work, and being a gracious hostess at their formal entertaining— by buying old and run-down properties, making them presentable, and selling them to people she felt would be an asset to the Interlaken community. At least one of these transactions yielded such a substantial profit that she foresightedly purchased an annuity for herself and husband.

Their home had been built as a summer residence and until they installed a bigger and better, coal-fired furnace, winter mornings did not conduce to idle dawdling. It also boasted a de-

tached one-car garage, formerly the carriage house, with quarters on its second story for the nonexistent live-in help. They would not own an automobile for almost two more years, when they bought the first in a long line of Buick models, each of which came factory equipped, in Koerner's view, with a distinctive carbon-knock "ping."[5] Until the first of these entered their lives, the garage was transformed into Koerner's studio by the addition of a skylight and a potbelly heating stove. In later years, the second floor became Bill, Jr.'s preserve for the practice of photography, at which he became expert, and for diagnosing the idiosyncracies of the outboard motors that often powered his racing hull on Deal Lake.

Koerner personally designed his new, vaulted studio building, and supervised its construction, moving into it about mid-June, 1919. Located behind the house, which thus protected it from casual visits by idle passersby, its ground floor was taken up by an entrance-waiting room and a dressing room for the models he used infrequently; a "glass house" where the models posed; a huge fireplace with supplementary heating stove; and his commodious studio proper, flooded with northern light from an expansive skylight by day and by spotlights at night. The second-floor mezzanine opened onto storage rooms for costumes and draperies and the "morgue" of clippings that were indispensable to his work.[6]

For many years, the studio was the scene of informal Saturday night dances for the Koerners and their friends. The floor was waxed, candles lighted, and the Victrola and dance records were brought over from the house, as were home-baked cookies and a non-alcoholic fruit punch. On one occasion, a young artist who was studying both with Koerner and Frank Stick managed to spike the punch and Lillian, next morning, wondered whatever had possessed her to do a solo dance the previous night before an admiring throng. In later years, it became a similar center upon occasion for their teen-aged children and their friends. It was in this studio that the long trail "Big Bill" Koerner had begun to walk at the Chicago *Tribune* came to climax. Before this transpired, his country's entry into World War I presented him with an unexpected hazard.

Lillian is authority for the statement that her husband was one of the artists who was asked by the Committee on Public Information to go

The studio at Interlaken, New Jersey, with a corner of the residence visible at left

overseas and paint American troops in action. This committee had been established by presidential proclamation one week after the United States officially entered the war against Germany, and was headed by George Creel.[7] Primarily a propaganda bureau, not a censorship device, it had a Division of Pictorial Publicity headed by Charles Dana Gibson, with Louis Fancher as its production director and F. De Sales Casey, formerly art editor of *Collier's,* as secretary. Even without this request, Koerner was faced with the need to establish his father's naturalization. Without such proof, he technically was an "enemy alien," and anti-German sentiment was rampant. The German language was driven from the schools, German music was eliminated from concerts, the Germania Building in Saint Paul, Minnesota, became the Guardian Building, and sauerkraut became "liberty cabbage." It was not until June 18, 1917, and

then only through the efforts of an old friend in Clinton, W. D. Jacobsen, that Koerner established that his father had taken out his first papers for naturalization on May 2, 1882. Six months more elapsed before Koerner proved definitely that his father had been granted citizenship in the Clinton courts on September 15, 1884. This delay partly explains why Koerner did not join his fellow illustrators—Wallace Morgan, Walter J. Enright, Harvey Dunn, Walter Jack Duncan, W. J. Aylward, Harry E. Townsend, André Smith, Ernest C. Peixotto—with a captain's commission in the Army Engineer Reserve Corps at $2,400 per annum.

In common with many other illustrators, Koerner did war-related posters as requested by Gibson's subcommittee.[8] One of these was designed to recruit lumberjacks in the Pacific Northwest for the job of producing, under Army supervision, the Sitka spruce that was vital to airplane

At work in the Interlaken studio

manufacture. The request came to him with this notation: "The War Department has asked us to bear in mind that the average lumberjack is a man of meager education, and that a poster to attract his attention and lead him to the recruiting office must be compelling, gripping, something with a punch in it and easily understood [completed 8/4/1917]."

James Montgomery Flagg, "the playboy of the illustrators' world,"[9] did the most famous poster of them all, with Uncle Sam seeming to lunge forward out of the poster saying "I Want You!" Food-conservation posters were done by Henry Raleigh and Alice Barber Stephens; Arthur William Brown did a billboard in front of the New York Public Library;[10] Adolph Triedler did a poster for the First Liberty Loan, to which Koerner subscribed $1,500 through the Seacoast Trust Company of Asbury Park; the Fourth Liberty Loan drive was assisted by a stone lithograph from George Bellows, and N. C. Wyeth did posters for the Red Cross and for the Navy's recruiting efforts. This sampling supports the premise that the graphic arts provided the visual impact then that television does today.

A letter to Koerner from John E. Parker (6/29/1918), art editor of *Ladies Home Journal* and a close personal friend, reveals another facet of the illustrators' involvement in depicting their country's war effort.

Should we decide to publish in The Journal *battle scenes of the American troops abroad, would you be interested in trying to work out for us any subjects along this line? When I say battle scenes, I do not mean sugar and water subjects but the real fighting.*

Such pictures, of course, would have to be constructed from newspaper data, and from whatever photographs that might be available in this country. The proposition may sound almost impossible under these conditions, but if we are going to show any of our military actions in the magazine, there seems to be no other way to accomplish it. It is true that the Government has sent official painters abroad but there is no telling when any of these paintings will reach this country.

In the event of our taking up the American battle pictures, we would want to see small sketches in color before the actual drawings were started in order that we might know what to expect. As for the subjects selected to paint, that point would have to be decided as the American troops get into full action on the western front.

Just at the moment we are not ready to go ahead with the proposition, but I wish you would let me know how it strikes you in a general way, and if you would be interested.

As with much of his outgoing correspondence, no copy of Koerner's reply has survived, but it is known that he did not accept this assignment. This did not deter the *Journal*, which published a series of color plates (11/1918–4/1919) on the exploits of American troops in France by Frank Schoonover and Gayle Porter Hoskins, neither of whom had gone overseas.

Koerner's unavailability for the African short stories by Stewart Edward White in 1917 was due in part to the fact that he already had committed himself to a six-part serial for another magazine; when an illustrator took on a serial,

he obligated himself to do it on schedule, at least Koerner did, which meant not accepting work he could not fit around the serial's schedule until it was finished. The magazine in this case was *McClure's*, which had started the magazine revolution or era, as you prefer, in 1893.[11] Ida M. Tarbell's biography of Napoleon had been its first big circulation builder, and she followed it with a biography of Abraham Lincoln that boosted it from 175,000 to 250,000 copies per month. Anthony Hope's "Rupert of Hentzau," illustrated by Charles Dana Gibson, had not hurt its steady climb, and neither had Rudyard Kipling's "Captains Courageous," "Stalky and Company," and "Jungle Tales." Some of William Macleod Raine's earliest fiction appeared in its pages, stories of the Scottish "Hielands" that appealed to S. S. McClure's plaid pride. It had inaugurated the muckraking epoch with Ida Tarbell's "History of the Standard Oil Company," which required four years of her life and $50,000 of S. S. McClure's money to prepare and ran for two years in the magazine. Lincoln Steffens had been an associate editor for some time, and Willa Cather was its managing editor for almost five years.

In 1917, its managing editor was Charles Hanson Towne who was publishing a magazine of sixty-eight $10\frac{1}{2} \times 14$ inch pages, at fifteen cents per copy, with a sworn circulation of 563,000 copies monthly.[12] He listed his authors and illustrators on the covers, without distinguishing between them, and he sometimes listed people who did not appear inside the cover of that particular issue. His tastes in covers ran almost exclusively to pretty girls, most of which were painted by Neysa McMein until she went overseas; thereafter her sketches "from Life at the Front" began to appear regularly. Although *McClure's* was on the road that brought it to bankruptcy in 1921 and its eventual acquisition by Hearst in 1926, it still was on a parity with *American, Cosmopolitan,* and *Hearst's* in quality and quantity, if not in advertising, and was far superior to *Everybody's* and *Munsey's*, both of which were losing the circulation and advertising fight.

Towne generally used two serial installments, or a whole novel, in each issue by authors of the caliber of Edith Wharton, Sophie Kerr, and Gertrude Atherton; three or more short stories from Dana Gatlin, Mildred Cram, Susan Glaspell,

Volume XLIX
Number 1

McCLURE'S

MAY
1917

FREDERICK L. COLLINS, *Editor*   CHARLES HANSON TOWNE, *Managing Editor*

MLLE. ROLAND   JIMMY ALLEN   MOLLIE.   BILLY   MA CREEL   CREEL.

The OLD MAN

A King in Babylon

The Great New Mystery Novel

by **Burton E. Stevenson**

Illustrations by W. H. D. Koerner

*"When I was a King in Babylon
And you were a Virgin slave"* HENLEY

MUSTAFA

DIGBY

I AM writing this story because Creed thinks it ought to be written, in justice to ourselves and to Jimmy Allen. The truth is bad enough, but it is mild as milk beside the outrageous tales which have been flying about the studios since we came back from Egypt without our leading man.

I have tried to convince Creed that it is his job—that his long and varied experience in ripping scenarios open and turning them inside out and upside down should give him a terse and vivid style. His spoken style, as I happen to know, is extraordinarily terse and vivid! But he has snorted indignantly and accused me of trying to shirk a clear duty. He has pointed out to me, most feelingly, how a director has to sweat and slave all day trying to drive a glimmer of intelligence into a bunch of wooden actors, and then sit up all night laboring to inject some dramatic value into the rotten stuff passed out to him by the scenario editor; while a camera-man's life was one of elegant leisure, untroubled

if once I get it set down on paper, I'll be able to think about it less. Yes—and there's another reason. Jimmy Allen was a good sort; he did a lot for me, first and last, and I can't bear to think of the ugly gossip. . . .

I shall never forget the morning that Creed had his great idea. We had about finished the feature we were working on, and Creed was more than usually disgusted with it. Everybody could see that it was old stuff, and in spite of the artistic touches and unexpected twists which Creed had succeeded in giving it, I doubted if it would get across. And for more than a week he had been digging around among the scenarios in the office trying to find something which would do for his next production. But the more he dug, the more hopeless he grew.

"Not an idea in the lot,"

These nine portraits were considered by Koerner to be one illustration

Earl Derr Biggers, and Julian Street; at least two articles, many of them about business by James H. Collins and Edward Mott Woolley; while Melville Davisson Post contributed legal articles, including a three-part series on "Fraud as a Fine Art" (12/1917 *et seq*). A poem per issue, Ella Wheeler Wilcox appearing frequently, and the department on foods and drugs, that was standard for most magazines such as *McClure's,* rounded out the contents. Towne had no problem in commissioning top-flight illustrators for the simple reason, if Koerner's records are any guide, that he paid slightly less than *Harper's* but more than *Red Book, Saturday Evening Post, Collier's, Country Gentleman,* and *Ladies Home Journal* in this year. Also, Towne paid promptly. Oliver Herford's caustic half-page

drawings, debunking whatever he felt needed it, were a regular feature; Tony Sarg and W. T. Benda made some of their earliest "slick" appearances in its pages, while Anton Otto Fischer, James M. Flagg, Arthur William Brown, Frank Schoonover, F. R. Gruger, Frederick Dorr Steele, Thomas Fogarty, and May Wilson Preston were among its regular artists.

Koerner's major work for *McClure's* included a three-part serial, "Caught on a German Raider" by F. G. Trayes, which gave him a chance to do some seascapes, and a novel by Gertrude Atherton, "The White Morning," published complete in one issue. Heralded in advance by *McClure's* as "A Torrential Novel of Modern Germany," this prose portrayal of two rebellious daughters of a Junker family bordered on being anti-German propaganda as much as fiction. Koerner's illustrations were character studies of the principal characters, not military scenes. The six-part serial mentioned earlier as preventing Koerner from doing Stewart E. White's African short stories was written by Burton E. Stevenson, a prolific and popular writer of the period. It was entitled "A King in Babylon" and concerned the trials and tribulations, dangers and romances of a motion picture company on location in the Near East, where a professorial archaeologist was opening an ancient tomb. Needless to say, it abounded in camels, slave girls, desert warriors, ancient curses on tomb defilers, and similar appurtenances.

His lead illustration, which made a partial border for the first page of the issue in which it appeared, consisted of nine full-face drawings —one for each of the principal characters—and each was richly detailed and distinctly different from the others. Koerner considered these nine portraits to be but one illustration and charged *McClure's* accordingly.[13]

Russia's "October" Revolution brought Koerner the opportunity to do most of the work he did during this period for *Metropolitan*,[14] which was as urban-oriented as its name implied, and had begun its life in 1885 as a ten-cent "artists' models" and "nude in art" magazine. It became more respectable in 1898 with the use of material by Theodore Dreiser and Alfred Henry Lewis,[15] and came full cycle, perhaps, when it published Vachel Lindsay's poetry in 1914. In this same year, it serialized the life story of Dr. Anna Howard Shaw, leader of the "Women's Movement for Equality in America," and published the first story from the European front by John Reed, who had "covered" the opening stanzas of the Mexican Revolution for it earlier. This coverage may have been a factor in lifting it from its 125,000 copies per month to about 300,000 in 1918, but it did not prevent its slide from 124 pages of text and 48 of advertising to 70 inside pages, including advertising. Neither did the fact that in 1918 it could bill itself as "The Magazine Colonel Roosevelt Writes For," because of a page by T.R. in each issue. In one of these (2/1919), he devoted his space to "unraveling the twisted confusion into which the Wilson Administration has thrown almost every important feature of governmental policy."

It was an outsize magazine, 10-3/4 × 14 inch

pages, compared to its principal competitors— *McClure's, Red Book, Cosmopolitan*—and it cost more, at twenty-five cents per copy, than did they. Its four front-and-back cover pages held its only color work, and its advertisements were dominated by Lucky Strike and Fatima cigarettes, with virtually none of the lucrative automobile and cereal foods advertising that enhanced the profitability of its competitors. Nonetheless, its brilliant managing editor, Carl Hovey, put out a respectable magazine, with an editorial policy that was anti League of Nations and pro compulsory subscription to the nation's Liberty Loan drives, just as there was compulsory conscription for the young men who paid their shares of the costs of war with their bodies.

Hovey paid his illustrators well and "pretty girl" covers by Rolfe Armstrong and Edna Crompton were the rule. Clarence Day, Jr. illustrated the pieces he wrote himself on such topics as "The Abolition of Rich Uncles"; Clarence F. Underwood illustrated love stories of the "urban boudoir" type; W. T. Benda, Worth Brehm, and George Wright handled boy-girl and wartime-leave romances; May Wilson Preston presented her amusingly languorous yet alive women in light love stories; while Dalton Stevens, Henry J. Soulen, and Arthur I. Fuller did baseball, action, and exotic stories. Leslie L. Benson drew the assignment to illustrate F. Scott Fitzgerald's "The Beautiful and Damned" when Hovey began its serialization in September, 1921.

Including a full-page portrait of its author being received by President Woodrow Wilson, Koerner did thirty-five illustrations in various media for "My Life" by Maria Botchkareva, as told to Isaac Don Levine.[16] A peasant girl who either turned to or was trapped into a brothel, whence she was rescued by the love of a young soldier who then was killed in combat, Maria secured the tsar's permission to enlist in his armed forces as a rifle soldier despite her sex. In one illustration—Maria bathing nude in a wooden tub as her male fellow soldiers watched from the middle distance—Koerner gave her a towel for not quite enough covering and came as close to putting raw sexual vibrations into a scene as in any other illustration he ever did. His powerful rural sense was admirably suited to Russian peasant life and countryside, and an illustration of Maria bayoneting a German soldier was solid and massive without blood-lust sadism. The final installments of Maria's story concerned her participation in the "Russian Women's Battalion of Death" which was formed to combat the "Red" terrorists on behalf of the "Little Father." It was a powerful story that gained verisimilitude from the fact that Maria was not a sylph-like, glamorous figure but as solid and enduring as the soil from which she sprang and Koerner showed her for what she was. In the context of its times, this story and others in the leading mass-circulation magazines pertaining to Bolshevik usurpation of Russia's embryonic constitutional government certainly had some effect in preparing the climate of opinion that produced the country's first "Red Scare" in 1919, which gave Attorney General A. Mitchell Palmer his niche in American history and translated the meaning of "SOS" into "ship or shoot" for imported Marxists and their indigenous sympathizers.[17]

Radical sabotage on the home front was the theme of one of the three serials, all outdoor-action type, that comprised the bulk of Koerner's last work (1917–19) for *Country Gentleman.* It was set in the steeply yet smoothly rolling hills of eastern Washington known as "The Palouse" and famous for its wheat-raising capabilities. There Zane Grey played out the conflict in "The Desert of Wheat" between "Wobbly" (I.W.W.) agitators, who espoused pacifism as a cloak and sought to thwart the harvest of food-and-feed grains so necessary to the war effort,[18] and the "good guys" loyal to their country, despite their Germanic and Scandinavian ancestry. There was a love story, as well, for added reader interest. Koerner supplied eleven illustrations for the serial's twelve installments, most of which were reproduced on a type of newspaper stock the magazine was using in this wartime period and thus lacked the clarity of detail that was Koerner's hallmark.[19] In book form, *The Desert of Wheat* ranked third on the best-seller list for 1919, which made the fourth consecutive year that Grey had appeared thereon. Koerner sold two of his original paintings to a man who had liked them in the magazine, despite their muddy reproduction, and received the munificent sum of $40 for the pair. Their whereabouts today are unknown, as is so for many of Koerner's originals which he either sold after magazine use or gave away to personal friends and friends of his editors.

One of the other serials he illustrated for *Country Gentleman* was a five-part north-woods action story by Ben Ames Williams, a prolific writer, whom Koerner illustrated many times. The last was a ten-part saga about the efforts of a young man, well ahead of his time, to transform Minnesota's cut-over timberlands into productive agricultural use, despite opposition from urban forces which wished to build a power-generating dam that would flood out the results of his labors. The author of this serial, Henry Oyen, deserves to be better known as a writer in the vein that Rex Beach and James Oliver Curwood made famous. Koerner was asked to illustrate another Zane Grey serial, a twelve-part story tentatively titled "Columbine," which made its appearance (6/7/1919) as "The Mysterious Rider." The request came when he was already as fully committed as he cared to be and the illustrations for it were done by Frank B. Hoffman, whose cow-work scenes and horses were adequate but whose humans were too slickly depicted to convey a strong sense of their respective characters.

Country Gentleman: A Journal for the Farm, the Garden, and the Fireside was a different magazine in 1918 than it had been in 1911 when Lorimer wrote to Albert J. Beveridge: "We have had to pull the first [Curtis] issue of Country Gentleman out of the air, and that is where the second, and third, and fourth numbers are now all reposing. I am keeping at it till midnight every night and making a very rotten little country weekly at that."[20] The circulation then was about 30,000. Now it was nearing 500,000 copies weekly; five cents per copy, $1.00 per year, for a magazine that averaged eighty outsize pages in the autumn and winter months; thirty-two pages in the summer doldrums. Reaching 1,600,000 monthly circulation in 1930, when a three-year subscription cost but $1.00, it would boast the largest distribution of any farm magazine in the world to that time. It achieved this eminence by the simple formula of fighting the farmer's battles for him and making him feel important; the last legatee of the old, rural individualistic and humanistic America that was fast crumbling before the onslaughts of industrialization and the "hideous rise of the alien city." The inefficiency of the U.S. Department of Agriculture was a favorite editorial target.

The magazine has been overlooked by students of the outdoor-action school of American fiction, probably because they did not think of it in this context or, if they did, dreaded the drudgery of mining its pages. The fact that it was the means whereby Zane Grey was elevated from the pulp magazines and into the pages of *Ladies Home Journal, Collier's, McCall's,* and *American,* but never the *Saturday Evening Post,* should have called this to their attention. Under the editorship of Barton W. Currie in these years, it used a higher proportion, almost 40 per cent, of outdoor-action material in its fiction offerings than any other of the magazines examined.[21] This was accentuated when the magazine (12/6/1919) began the first of a series of outdoor-action serials for boys, thus hoping to wean them away from dependence upon such as *Boy's Life* and *American Boy* for this fare. The first serial was titled "The Ring-necked Grizzly," and was written by Warren H. Miller, the editor of *Field and Stream.* It was illustrated, appropriately enough, by Frank Stick.

Currie's general format was one serial installment, one short story, often a rural romance or a collie story by Albert Payson Terhune, and ten articles. Most of the articles, were of the "how-to-do-it-better" or more easily or more profitably when dealing with farm crops and chores and livestock and machinery. He used more wide-ranging articles as well: David Lawrence on "The Farm Outlook for 1918," William Jennings Bryan on "Prohibition and the Farmer," and Harry S. Stabler on "Draining the South of Labor," when the lure of higher wages began drawing Negro field hands into northern factories. Articles dealing with wildlife and natural-resource conservation were contributed by Hal G. Evarts, who later played a prominent part in Koerner's career. An eight-page gravure section appeared from time to time, and often carried photographs of exotic foreign lands, thus bringing rural America glimpses of the world beyond the oceans that had made its moats for more than three centuries.

Covers for the magazine were about equally divided between photographic reproductions and the wildlife of Charles Livingston Bull and Paul Bransom. An occasional wholesome pretty girl by J. Knowles Hare or an athlete by F. X. Leyendecker or a Norman Rockwell slice of Americana provided variety. It paid well for illustrations, if Koerner's records are any guide, and Harrison Cady, then on the staff of *Life,*

regularly contributed a full page of human characters that closely resembled the zoological extravaganzas he did for Thornton Burgess's "Peter Rabbit" and "Old Mother West Wind" stories. Its other illustrators all were prominent in the magazine field, and included Charles D. Mitchell, Ernest Fuhr, Frank Schoonover, Edward Penfield, Henry J. Soulen, Anton Otto Fischer, Arthur G. Dove, Ralph Pallen Coleman, and Harold Brett. Walter J. Enright did the editorial cartooning chores, that Herbert Johnson performed for *Saturday Evening Post,* and three of the Stick-Koerner students—James H. Crank, Frank Spradling,[22] James E. Allen—appeared in its pages. It had three art editors in this three-year period—Arthur N. Hosking, Guernsey Moore, Loring A. Schuler—which was unusual for the normally stable Curtis organizations. This turnover was due in part to a seismic disturbance generated by William Randolph Hearst.

Its first tremors were felt in late November, 1918, when *Cosmopolitan* lured Ray Long away from *Red Book,* which he had been editing since 1913 when Karl Harriman went to *Ladies Home Journal.* Harriman promptly returned to the editorship of *Red Book,* thus causing some rearrangements in the Curtis organization, and just as promptly (12/17/1918) wrote his old *Pilgrim* associate, "Dear Bill" Koerner:

What do you think about me being back on this job? One of the most delightful features of it is that I am back among old friends, of whom you and I both know you are indeed one.

I am more pleased than I can express that you are going to do the Blue Book covers, but want you to relieve the distress I feel on being told by Ray that you can't do any more stories for the Red Book for the time being. You simply must not be out of the magazine, Bill. Do tell me that you are going to reconsider.

Koerner's reply brought this rejoinder (1/3/1919):

Thanks for your good letter!

Won't you give me the advantage of every doubt in the way of illustration, for I want you to be in the Red Book as nearly continuously as possible. I have two or three stories which are not Boyle stories but that I know you would like to do.

In point of fact, I would prefer for two or

three months to slide the Blue Book cover over to someone else, and retain you for [Red Book] illustrations for that period. Couldn't you work in two stories within the next three months if you did not have the Blue Book cover to do?

Koerner had done work for Ray Long during his tenure at *Red Book,* notably a "series" of short stories by Jack Boyle featuring "Boston Blacky,"[23] who combined the skills of a safe-cracker, the wiles of a confidence man, and the impulses of an avenging angel. He continued to do work for Harriman, including a new series by Jack Boyle which was laid in San Francisco's Chinatown and involved opium dens, smuggling Chinese from Mexico, and warfare between the "Hop Sing" and "Four Brothers" tongs. Harriman billed these stories as "The most remarkable series this magazine has ever published." His other major work for Harriman's magazine was a three-part serial by Ben Ames Williams, whom Harriman introduced to his readers as a man destined "to be one of the truly great writing men of this New America of ours."[24] After this serial, the professional relationship between Koerner and *Red Book* became attenuated, although his personal friendship with Harriman remained.

This decline in his *Red Book* appearances was not due to compensation; Harriman matched what *Saturday Evening Post* paid him, and the *Post* in this period was increasing Koerner's rate per story with regularity. It seems due more to the fact that Harriman accentuated what Long had begun. Where Long had blazoned boldly that *Red Book* was "The Largest Illustrated Fiction Magazine in the World," Harriman had its cover proclaim it to be "The Magazine of a Remade World." Without any unbecoming modesty, his table of contents proclaimed its offerings in each issue to be "The *Best* Serial Novels of the Year," and "The *Best* Short Stories of the Month." Whether they were the "best" does not disguise the fact that he used good writers: serials by Rupert Hughes, Peter B. Kyne, George Gibbs, Clarence Budington Kelland, Mary Robert Rinehart, for examples; short stories by Robert Benchley, Earl Derr Biggers, Albert Payson Terhune, Beatrice Grimshaw, James Oliver Curwood, P. G. Wodehouse, Arthur Somers Roche, and others, including some of the first "slick" appearances by C. E. Scoggins, later a *Post* regular.

The magazine's expanded page size, 8½ × 12 inches, provided more room for illustrators to spread themselves, although never in color save on the "pretty girl" covers by Edna Crompton, J. K. Hare, and Haskell Coffin. Established illustrators such as Gustavus C. Widney, who had illustrated for it virtually since its inception, Charles Sarka, Henry Raleigh, F. R. Gruger, Arthur William Brown, and James M. Flagg appeared regularly. So did comparative newcomers to the "slick" magazines' pages, such as Frank Street, Rea Irvin, John Held, Jr., W. B. King, Clark Fay, and Dean Cornwell. The shift in *Red Book's* emphasis, a shift characteristic of the post-war years, was epitomized in its issue for March, 1926. Trumpeted as "Something Entirely New—The First Time in Any Magazine," this was a serial "Story in Pictures" by Robert W. Chambers,[25] long noted for his earthy historical fiction, who supplied long captions, no text as such, for the illustrations by George Wright. These contained acres of exposed female legs, a nubile, half-nude female on horseback, and one voluptuous female in the all-together. It was a sex sensation and reflected Harriman's drive to bring his 162-page magazine within hailing distance of Ray Long's bubbling sex pot.

Cosmopolitan had reached the one million mark in 1916, the first non-women's monthly magazine to do so. Its then editor's explanation for this success was set forth by Herbert Kaufman (3/1916) when it went to a 8-1/2 × 11-5/8 inch page:

Cosmopolitan by its far-sighted policy of contracting, wherever possible, for the exclusive services of its distinguished writers and illustrators, enables them to limit their expression, and provides an abundance of leisure for the production of vital, masterly works. An artist without a definite market must necessarily speculate and turn out an excess amount of promiscuous material, much of which is inferior to his possibilities.

Cosmopolitan is publishing more of the finished, brilliant, forceful literature of our day than any dozen of its contemporaries—work that will stand on tomorrow's book-shelves. It has a mission—that's why it has a million.

Regardless of what he thought of his predecessor's self-serving prose, Long continued the contract policy wherever he could, and he could not with Koerner who had learned the Hearstian lesson well while in Chicago. If he could not contract the authors and illustrators that he wanted, Long simply offered them more money than they were receiving elsewhere. Edwin Balmer,[26] for example, was receiving $600 per short story from *Saturday Evening Post* and Long gave him $800. Over the next five years, the Hearst-financed "raids," so other editors viewed them, lured Irvin S. Cobb, Montague Glass, and Clarence Budington Kelland away from the *Post's* stable of regulars, and deprived *Red Book* of the services of Peter B. Kyne and James Oliver Curwood. In the course of his acquisitions, Long dropped such previous standbys of *Cosmopolitan's* pages as John Galsworthy's "Forsyth" stories and George R. Chester's amusing confidence man, "Get-Rich-Quick Wallingford,"[27] as well as Samuel Merwin, Gouverneur Morris, Arthur B. Reeve, and Charles G. D. Roberts, whose specialty was the Canadian "bush" without the sex Curwood found in it.

His average issue contained two serial installments, with work by such as Rupert Hughes, Robert W. Chambers, Arthur Somers Roche, Robert Hichens, and Louis Joseph Vance, whose "Lone Wolf" mystery yarns were extremely popular; seven short stories, from such as Fannie Hurst, Dana Gatlin, E. Phillips Oppenheim, Courtney Riley Cooper, P. G. Wodehouse, Sir Phillip Gibbs, Zona Gale, and Don Marquis, and three articles guaranteed not to strain the thought processes of their readers. He also threw in a poem by Edgar Guest upon occasion. Harrison Fisher's "pretty girls" had a stranglehold on his covers, which made the magazine's only color pages until 1925, when *Hearst's International Magazine* was merged into it. James M. Flagg and Howard Chandler Christy long had been regular illustrators for the Hearst publications, as had John T. McCutcheon. Paul Bransom was inseparable from Curwood's stories, no matter where they appeared, and Long used the work of such established artists as F. X. Leyendecker, W. T. Benda, Dalton Stevens, John Alonzo Williams, and Thomas D. Skidmore. Relative newcomers to the mass-circulation field included such later well-known illustrators as Herbert M. Stoops, John La Gatta, Gordon Ross, Forrest C. Crooks, Marshall Frantz, and Pruett A. Carter.

The result of Long's efforts was a slow growth to about 1,200,000 copies of a magazine averaging close to two hundred sexy pages, but with less advertising proportionately than such a circulation and content warranted.[28] It jumped to 1,500,000 copies monthly, after its merger with *Hearst's* in 1925, and by this time Koerner's sporadic association with it had ended. Long consistently paid Koerner 25 per cent more per story than he received from *Saturday Evening Post*, up to 15 per cent more than he received from other magazines, but Koerner illustrated no more than twelve stories for him between 1920–22. Of these, only seven have been identified as to type: one adventure-romance in Mexico by Royal Brown, one Kentucky mountaineer story by Jay Gelzer, one slightly macabre zoo story with a gorilla for menace by Courtney R. Cooper, two outdoor-action, oil-field yarns, which were popular in this period,[29] by William MacHarg, and two African adventure stories by Perceval Gibbon and R. G. Kirk.

The African thread in the tapestry of Koerner's career brought him his first assignment from *Woman's Home Companion,*[30] the keystone of the Crowell Publishing Company's magazines, which then included *American* and would include *Collier's* in 1919 to rival the Curtis group in their cumulative impact. Ahead of *Delineator* in circulation at 1,000,000 copies, but behind *Ladies Home Journal, McCall's,* and *Pictorial Review,* it sold for twenty cents the copy, $2.00 per year, which was appreciably more than any of the others. It also brought him the friendship of its managing editor, Sophie Kerr Underwood, who, even as Willa Cather, is best remembered today for her writings as Sophie Kerr, her maiden name, than she is for her editorial abilities as Mrs. Underwood.[31] Her first surviving letter to him (6/8/1918) shows some of the hazards that faced both editor and illustrator in wartime.

Will you not make us one picture for the enclosed story ["The Substitute" by Harrison Rhodes] and let us have it almost right away? We should like very much to have you do it and it can, of course, take precedence over the [African] serial. And please don't get the picture too dark, as we are having a dreadful time both with paper and ink. It is impossible to get decent paper and the ink we get seems specially designed for the worst possible printing. Therefore our drawings have got to be pretty clear and not too dark else they become nothing but smudges.

This was followed quickly by another letter which led to the second time that Koerner's picture had been used in a major magazine:

We should like very much to have a picture of you for use in our announcement pages this fall, as the illustrator of the [African] novel. Won't you have one specially taken for us? If possible, have a photographer come in and make a picture of you in your studio. We will gladly defray the expense of it.

We are not going to use any pictures that are not new and that are not exclusive for the Woman's Home Companion. We could, however, use a snapshot, provided it is not too small and is very clear, but we should much prefer a larger picture and one taken specially for us.[32]

Another letter (7/11/1919) brought him the opportunity to have his work reproduced in the colors with which he painted it, the third such magazine to pay him this honor, the others being *Harper's* and *Ladies Home Journal,* and it made the first of his western scenes, a mining-camp story, to have color reproduction.

It gives me great pleasure to tell you that the Companion is giving out some illustrations in full color and we have quite a wonderful story which we would like to have you illustrate for us—the pictures to be reproduced, as I say, in four colors. When do you suppose you could take it on? I am not sending it with this because I thought I would rather hear from you about it first, but I hope you will consider it, because it will give you a chance to pull off something quite spectacular.

We will make one of the pictures practically full page size and another in big vignette, or two small vignettes—all full color. I hope that this glowing description will entice you to write to me and say that I may send the story ["The Boy in the Corner" by M.L.C. Pickthall] on to you at once.

Her format was one or two installments of "novels," they were not labeled "continued stories" in *Companion;* four short stories; three or four articles; and regular "departments" dealing with art, music, verse, fashions, and cooking;

plus short fillers of the "Helpful Hints to Harried Housewives" variety. The resultant magazine averaged 112 pages, about what *Ladies Home Journal* contained in this period, and textual material was carried over into the advertising pages. Novels were contributed by Fannie Heaslip Lea, Mary Hastings Bradley, Mark Lee Luther, Frederick Orrin Bartlett, and Sophie Kerr, the writer. Short stories came from Georgia Wood Pangborn, Ellis Parker Butler, of "Pigs Is Pigs" fame, Mary Heaton Vorse, Abbie Carter Goodloe, Zoe Akins, Margaret Deland,[33] and Elsie Singmaster, many of whom also were regular contributors to *Harper's.*

The covers she used ran very heavily to children and mother-child combinations, with occasionally a pretty miss, not the "pretty girl" that graced such as *Cosmopolitan* and *Red Book.* Her cover illustrators included C. Coles Phillips, Katherine R. Wireman, and Adolph Triedler; her story illustrators, by and large, were well-established artists, including Herman Pfeifer, W. B. King, E. F. Ward, Denman Fink, F. Walter Taylor, T. K. Hanna, Orson Lowell, May Wilson Preston, Frederick Dorr Steele, and the ubiquitous James M. Flagg. She also used the work of Fanny Munsell and Frances Rogers, who had entered the magazine field in the immediate pre-war years. As with her authors during her editorship of *Companion,* very few of her illustrators appeared in *Ladies Home Journal.* Koerner was one of the few who did, illustrating an eight-part circus story, "The Moreton Mystery," by Elizabeth DeJeans, for which he composed twenty-three illustrations. He continued to do work intermittently for *Companion* for several years after Sophie Kerr resigned in November, 1920, to devote full time to her writing,[34] but it was not the same. It is known that Sophie Kerr asked that Koerner illustrate the stories she did later for *Saturday Evening Post* and was disappointed that his schedule permitted him to do only one of them.[35] She was a fine writer and a congenial editor, a combination not often encountered then or now.

His work for another Crowell magazine, *American,* began in 1919, the year Crowell acquired *Collier's.* It became his only outlet, other than the *Saturday Evening Post,* in the last half of the 1920's when he gave Zane Grey the best illustrations he had had to date with sixteen for "Sunset Pass" and sixteen more, plus twelve pen-and-ink drawings, for "Drift Fence."[36] Even though the color reproduction of many of these illustrations did no justice to their creator's palette, they made a startling contrast in their clarity, line, and characterization with those done by Stockton Mulford for Grey's first *American* appearance, "Nevada" (11/1926–5/1927). His illustrations brought Koerner a letter (2/24/1928) from Thomas B. Stanley, the magazine's art editor:

Zane Grey was in the office yesterday and was greatly pleased with your illustrations for Sunset Pass. In fact he was so delighted that he wants that square-up of "True Rock" [hero] on the white horse with the pack horse grazing [nearby]. We were telling him how much we like them—the illustrations—and he said, "You don't need to tell me; I know good pictures when I see them." I know that you said that the waiting line had already formed for that picture, but I said I would write you and see what could be done. Don't bother to answer by letter, but just tell us when you come up the next time.

Founded in 1876 as *Frank Leslie's Popular Monthly*, it became *The American Magazine* in October, 1906, when it was acquired by several of *McClure's* muckrakers—Ida M. Tarbell, Ray S. Baker, Lincoln Steffens among them—who wanted a magazine of their own with which to rake more vigorously.[37] Crowell had purchased it in July, 1916, when its monthly circulation hovered around 500,000 copies, averaging eighty-eight pages, and moved its physical production to Springfield, Ohio, although the editorial offices remained in New York at 250 Park Avenue. In 1919, its editor was John M. Siddall and the magazine was on an almost vertical climb towards 2,300,000 copies in 1930,[38] when its size ranged from 180–204 pages per issue; each one heavy with advertising and especially that for automobiles, their tires, and accessories.[39] It made this surge despite raising its price from fifteen cents per copy, $1.50 per year, to twenty cents and $2.00 and then to twenty-five cents and $2.50 in 1923. That it flourished in a time that saw the death or absorption of such once giants of the monthlies as *Everybody's*, *Hearst's*, *McClure's*, *Metropolitan*, and *Munsey's* was not happenstance.

It bucked the high-life-and-loose-living trend of *Cosmopolitan* and *Red Book* and took dead aim at the prosperous, or soon-to-be prosperous, *urban* segment of the nation's expanding middle classes. It published the first novels of Kathleen Norris and Edna Ferber, as well as Olive Higgins Prouty's famous "Stella Dallas" (10/1922). It was an early and consistent user of "murder," "mystery," and "detective" stories,[40] labeling them as such in its table of contents, and used serials in this genre by Carolyn Wells and then by S. S. Van Dine. Serials of other types were by such as Booth Tarkington and Bruce Barton. One serial installment per issue was standard, with five to seven short fiction pieces. Lincoln Colcord's sea stories, Bess Streeter Aldrich's homey stories of small-town life, and Octavus Roy Cohen's vaudeville sketches appeared regularly. Other short fiction contributors included Conrad Richter, Everett Rhodes Castle, Sinclair Lewis, H. G. Wells, Edwin Balmer, and Fannie Kilbourne. Lots of "dog" and "boy-dog" stories filled its pages, while William Dudley Pelley and Frank Richardson Pierce contributed outdoor-action yarns.

Feature articles became increasingly important during its steady climb in circulation, with Douglas Fairbanks's "own story," Mary Robert Rinehart's "personal creed," F. Scott Fitzgerald's article about himself at age twenty-five, Harry Emerson Fosdick's "Sermon for a New Year," Emerson Hough's "There is No Dead Line at Forty," and the first magazine article by Harold Bell Wright ever published, "The Sword of Jesus." Lincoln Steffens contributed "Becoming a Father at Sixty Is No Fun" and Albert Payson Terhune and Harold Bell Wright debated the question of the youth of the day in a manner that would smack of "relevance" to even the most "with it" member of today's society.[41]

A strong business emphasis permeated its other articles, by such as B. C. Forbes and Irving Bacheller, while Neil M. Clark contributed a steady stream of sketches, forerunner of today's "profile," about successful businessmen, including J. C. Penney, which often were enhanced by portraits of their subjects. Clarence Budington Kelland brought "Scattergood Baines" to *American* (9/1919) after launching him in *Saturday Evening Post*.[42] He contributed more than one hundred "Scattergood" stories to its pages over the ensuing years, stories that were the quintessence of solid, practical, small-town mores and values, with a strong business flavor. In so doing, he gave Paul J. Meylan the equivalent of a guaranteed annual wage for illustrating them. It used more humorous material than its contemporaries—Irvin S. Cobb, Don Marquis, O. O. McIntyre, J. P. McEvoy—and it used poems by Grantland Rice and verses by Edgar Guest. For many years it had a standing department with three reader-written reports on "The Best Idea I Ever Had," and another such of "Interesting People," apparently culled from reader submissions.

Its covers contained the magazine's only color pages, until the middle-twenties, and ran heavily to winsome misses, puppy dogs, and miss-with-puppy. C. W. Anderson, Clarence F. Underwood, Neysa McMein, J. Knowles Hare, Lou Mayer, and Walter Beach Humphrey were regular cover artists, while Norman Rockwell contributed at least one.[43] Their story illustrators made up a galaxy of good ones: Frank Schoonover, A. B. Frost, E. F. Ward, Douglas Duer, Charles Sarka, George Wright, Lejaren A. Hiller, Gayle Hoskins, Henry J. Soulen, Harry E. Townsend, Arthur Little, W. T. Benda, Hanson Booth, and F. Graham Cootes, the last named doing work most reminiscent of that by James M. Flagg and Howard Chandler Christy. Gerald Leake, J. Clinton Shepherd, and Mead Schaeffer appeared in the middle-twenties, with the latter two doing many of the outdoor-action stories, including westerns, after Koerner left its pages.[44]

His first *American* assignment was two illustrations for "The Bag of Black Diamonds" by Herman H. Matteson, a sea mystery-action-romance yarn, for which he received $100 each. He would make thirty more appearances in its pages over the next decade, illustrating Lincoln Colcord's China Coast stories and Frank Richardson Pierce's Alaskan action yarns. One of these (8/1923) had a twist in that the heroes were Chinese and Aleut salmon cannery workers, while the villain of deepest dye was a brutish white man. He also did a Navy story, "Yeller as Deck Paint," by Eugene Jones; a Mississippi River steamboat adventure, "The Texas Queen," by Gordon H. Hillman; and a five-part serial, "Scotch Valley," about homesteading in the modern West by Mildred Cram, the wife of a Navy officer stationed at Mare Island, California.[45] His work for this serial brought *American's* editor the following letter from the author: "I have

wanted for a long time to write to you about the splendid illustrations for "Scotch Valley." I have been delighted but neglectful! The drawings [*sic*] are simply stunning and I am proud that you thought the story worthy of such a talented illustrator."

His *American* years brought Koerner the longest "series" assignment of his career; fourteen stories (1926–30) featuring "Colonel Braxton," the creation of Melville Davisson Post, a West Virginia lawyer and a distinctive contributor to the detective-story genre. His first character had been created about 1906 in the person of "Randolph Mason," a lawyer of tremendous talents and a morality given to magnetic deviations:

Post made a variation of the Sherlock Holmes detective tale and set more bells to ringing than he realized. He was a lawyer, as Conan Doyle was not, and his criminals were not hunted down by means of clues impossible save to the superman detective. The criminals were caught red-handed and they were allowed to slip through the intricate loopholes in the law to undeserved freedom. Uncannily skilled . . . most fecund in the invention of plot and crime . . .[46]

About 1909, Post put "Mason" on the right side of the law and thereafter is said to have abandoned writing for some years; the title of an article by him in *Saturday Evening Post*, "The Immorality of Chance," provides insight into his view of equitable due process. In 1918, he is said to have created a second legal character, "Uncle Abner," who appears to have been the forerunner of "Colonel Braxton."[47]

"Colonel Braxton" would have been quite at home in *Saturday Evening Post*, but its pages already contained a similar lawyer-based character created by Arthur Train,[48] and he dwelled therein for years and years. Thus "Colonel Braxton" became *American's* counterpoint to "Ephraim Tutt." As his creator conceived him, "Colonel Braxton" was a courtly, lawyer-squire of Virginia's back country, a man of rock-hard character and formidable physique, who knew the punctilio of the code duello as well as he knew the subtleties and nuances and shadings of the statutes made and provided. He used all his qualities to unravel crimes heinous and deeds malignant in the interests of simple justice for wronged individuals and in the interests of the integrity of the law. As Koerner depicted him, he was a massive figure of a man, with ruggedly masculine features, who seemed to loom out of every picture in which he appeared. He would have been at ease in any of the great colonial paintings by Howard Pyle and Stanley M. Arthurs. When the last of his adventures appeared in *American*, Koerner's work for it came to an end.

He found time during these wartime and immediate post-war years to illustrate "The White Threshold," a north-woods-type serial, with sled dogs, snowshoes, and action scenes for *The Ladies World*, a McClure magazine that was losing the struggle for survival in its field, although it paid him well. Written by George Van Schaick, it appeared in book form as *The Peace of Roaring River* with a frontispiece and three illustrations by Koerner. He did other book work in these years for Harper and Brothers and for Bobbs-Merrill in Indianapolis. In a full-page advertisement (11/1920) Harper's listed him among "America's most distinguished artists" who would make its pages "more beautiful than ever before" in 1921. He also did a fishing scene for Forbes Lithograph Company of Boston, presumably for calendar use. Most of all in these years, he executed assignments from *Saturday Evening Post*, illustrating one hundred stories and serial installments with 281 drawings and paintings between arriving at Interlaken and the end of 1922.[49]

A sampling of what he illustrated in these years demonstrates his versatility; a harness-horse short story by John Taintor Foote and one of Harry Leon Wilson's many stories about "Ma Pettingill," who ruled her ranching roost in the West with salty zest; an oil field story by Wilbur Hall and "Venetian Lovers" by Sir Philip Gibbs; a South Seas adventure story by John Russell and a South American adventure-romance by Lloyd Osbourne. Selected serials from this period reflect the same versatility. Harold MacGrath's "The Pagan Madonna" had its opening in the curio shop of Ling Foo on Woosung Road in Shanghai and overlapped several installments of Eugene Manlove Rhodes's "Stepsons of Light." Richard Matthews Hallett's "The Canyon of Fools" dealt with an aging prospector, a true rainbow-chaser all of his life, whose youngest daughter stayed beside him to care for him as he pursued his dream, while Henry Milner Ride-out's "Fern Seed" was a foreign travel-adventure-romance.

His work on Hallett's serial brought him his first cover for the *Saturday Evening Post* when one of its illustrations so impressed Lorimer that he asked Koerner to re-do it in colors expressly suitable to the magazine's two-color process used for covers. It is well to note again that it was not until 1926 that the *Post* printed its covers in four colors and that its covers before this date were made to look like more than two-color work through the skill of the production staff. Germane as well is the fact that many artists did little work for magazines other than covers. The names of Norman Rockwell, Joseph C. Leyendecker, Neysa McMein, and Harrison Fisher probably are the best known of these, but other well-known artists of the Golden Age of American Popular Fiction who did cover work primarily were Robert Robinson, J. Knowles Hare, Henry Hutt, and Edna Crompton. Koerner painted six more covers for the *Post*, all but one of which "stood alone."

It was during these years that he did his first illustrations for stories by two of the *Post's* most noteworthy writers, Ben Ames Williams and Mary Roberts Rinehart. Mrs. Rinehart should need no introduction even to a present-day audience, but it will bear repeating that her *The Circular Staircase* (1908) was the only detective novel between the *Adventures of Sherlock Holmes* (1892) and Ellery Queen's *Dutch Shoe Mystery* (1931) to reach the top rank in sales.[50] Also worth noting is the fact that she made the best-seller list more times, eleven, than any of her contemporaries, being followed in placements there by Zane Grey, Booth Tarkington, and Sinclair Lewis.[51] She sold her autobiography to *Good Housekeeping* without letting Lorimer, whom she called "George," see it, because she did not think he would be interested in it. This evoked his comment, next time they met, "Mary, I wish to God you'd let *me* edit the *Post*."[52] Her piece that Koerner illustrated was "Pirates of the Caribbean," a dissection of the Havana tourist-mulcting trade that she had experienced after returning from covering the Allied front for Lorimer, a feat she had accomplished by joining the Belgian Red Cross. Their association in the serial "Lost Ecstasy" came during Koerner's later years and is discussed hereafter.

Ben Ames Williams came to rank next to Mrs.

Rinehart as the highest paid writer for the *Saturday Evening Post* and more than 160 of his short stories and serials appeared therein between 1917–35. Koerner illustrated thirty-two of these, including twelve serials, which was many more than any other illustrator handled. Many of these were the Maine-village stories Williams did so well, and which certainly Koerner knew firsthand. Koerner illustrated all of Williams's four best-known contributions to the *Post*—"Jubilo," "No Thoroughfare," "Jepthah's Daughter," "Money Musk"—except the last.[53] A correlation of the dates on which Koerner completed his illustrations for many of Williams's stories and the dates that they appeared in the *Post* leads to the conclusion that Lorimer bought them, had them illustrated, and then kept stories and illustrations in inventory until a slot appeared in the magazine's schedule where they would fit, or when their inclusion would "balance" the magazine's fiction contents. This appears very clearly in his five-part serial "Son of Anak," for which Koerner completed the first three of eleven illustrations on November 15, 1927, delivering the last on January 25, 1928, while its first installment did not appear until October 13, 1928. This policy undoubtedly was due to the fact that Williams was guaranteed "box office" with the *Post's* readers, and it also served to keep Williams aloof from the blandishments of other magazine editors who knew and were interested in his popular appeal.

The amount of work that Koerner did for other magazines in this period and its excellence did not escape Lorimer's attention. Neither did the fact, because business espionage is of almost geologic origin, that other magazines, including both the other Curtis publications, were paying Koerner more in 1918 than was *Saturday Evening Post*. Ergo, Koerner's payment from the *Post* went from $50 per painting to $60 late in 1918; to $75 in April, 1919, with the request that he keep the increase "confidential!"; to $100 in December, 1919, with the guarantee that he would receive a minimum of two stories per month, each with three illustrations; and to $125 per painting in May, 1922, again with the request that this rate be "kept in confidence." Even at this rate, *American, Woman's Home Companion,* and *Harper's* were paying him more per painting for anything they could get him to do for them, and it only matched what *Cos-*

mopolitan already was paying him. Not until 1927 would the *Post* meet *American's* payment of $300 per painting and not until 1928 that it surpassed it at $350 and then $400. It remained at this last figure until the full impact of the Great Depression smote the *Post* in March, 1932, when Koerner's rate dropped to $350 and then to $300 in April, 1933.

There was more than money to Koerner's long association with and ultimate concentration on work for the *Post,* and there was more than the prestige that came with being one of its outstanding regular contributors. It sent him stories of the type he liked to illustrate, whether they were action stories or challenging characterizations, such as William Faulkner's "Red Leaves," and its Art Department did not pester him with nit-picking suggestions about illustration size, technique to be used, or story incidents he *should* illustrate. He admired the values and traditions the magazine upheld and cherished the deep friendships that he formed with members of the *Post's* staff: Guernsey Moore, typographer, art consultant, art editor in emergencies, and artist in his own right; Herbert Johnson, now its editorial cartoonist, who had given him his first assignment from the *Post* when he had been its art editor; Adelaide Neall, the right-bower of George Horace Lorimer, "long a sort of unofficial Managing Editor;"[54] Arthur McKeogh, a World War I hero of the famous "Lost Battalion," and Bess Riddell, its art editor until 1931.

These friends visited them at Interlaken and they in turn made social affairs out of their frequent visits to Philadelphia to deliver paintings. Lillian early learned to drive and often delivered the paintings by herself. When Koerner could get away, they went together and made a day of it, lunching with their *Post* friends in the Curtis dining room or taking them to lunch at Wanamaker's, visiting whatever art galleries had exhibitions going, shopping, and generally taking a break from Interlaken's domestic and artistic daily rounds. They occasionally took trips together to New York and one of these junkets was to see an exhibition of some of his color paintings for *Ladies Home Journal* that had been touring the country for a year and were now on display in a leading department store in that city. This is how Lillian Koerner recalled their venture:

1932

Jan 8.	②	Ranchero – Hacienda Post	800	00
" 20	②	" – Fiesta Post	700	00
Jan 29	②	Ranchero – Merienda Post	800	00
Feb 18	②	Ranchero – Monteroy Post	800	00
Mar. 2.	②	Ranchero – & Politics "	800	00
" 16	②	" "	800	00
Mar. 26	③	Short grass Post	1050	00
April 4	②	" "	700	00
" 12	②	" "	700	00
" 21	②	" "	700	00
April 25	①	" "	700	00
May 15	②	" "	700	00
" 12	②	" "	700	00
June 1	③	The Proud Sheriff Post	1050	00
" 14	②	" "	700	00
" 24	②	" "	700	00
July 12	②	Folded Hills Post	1050	00
	②	" "	700	00
	②	" "	700	00
Aug 15	②	Way, Ponicles! Post	700	00
Sept 6	③	Tycoon Post	1050	00
" 15	③	Let Ober Hurricane Room "	1050	00 · 21250 0
" 22	②	" "	700	00
" 29	①	Tycoon "	700	00
Oct 6	②	" "	700	00
" 15	②	" "	700	00
" 27	②	" "	700	00

1916

Jan 4	①	The Water Man. Harpers.	100 Pd.
" 12	②	Stepping Momento (J. Hendry)	150 Pd.
" 19	③	The Flight. Post	125 Pd.
Feb 1	②	His Heart's Desire, Post.	250 Pd.
" 14	③	The Cuckoo. Post.	150 Pd.
" 29	①	Standing in His Fires (Post)	150 Pd.
Mar. 6	②	The Dumb Patience (Harper)	200 Pd. Apr 19/16
Mar. 16	④	The Cow Belt. Post	150 Pd.
" 29	①	Coming Jim (Goldbeck)	275 Pd.
April 3	②	The Lark in the Hedge. Post.	150 Pd.
" 17	②	Nicholas Woodman (Harper)	200 Pd.
May	④	Snifter Trigen Post	150 Pd.
" 15	④	Trail-cut – (North House K)	275 Pd.
June 17	④	Leopard Woman Post	150 Pd.
July 1	④	" "	150 "
" 1	⑥	" "	150 "
" 8	①	The Cabin Bride. Harper.	200 " Oct 17
" 10	①	Leopard Woman. Post.	150 "
" 15	③	"Home" Lusty. Good H.K.	150 Pd.
" 15	④	The Leopard Woman	150 " 4787
" 22	④	" "	150 " 675
" 29	④	" "	150 " 6668
Aug 5	④	" "	150 "
Sept 1	②	The Back Beyond (Harper)	200 " Mar 13
Sept 13	③	In a Shadow Land. Sing. g.H.	187.30
" 19	②	Robert. Harper.	200.00
"	④	Volume & Parade, Post	175 Pd.
Oct 7	②	Linking for Value Received.	150 Pd.

These two pages from Koerner's "Record of Work Produced," page 109 for 1916 and page 146 for 1932, show the productivity and compensation rate over the years

We would go and see how they [the paintings] looked, go somewhere for lunch, see a matinee, have a quick dinner, go to a play that evening, then go dinner-dancing, and stay overnight at a hotel. But, the play we saw in the evening was morbid and sad. That finished us! We did not feel like dancing after that. We skipped the hotel idea and took the 12:01 train for home. "We should have gone to the matinee in the evening," said William. "This is a Hell of a lark"! Like two spoiled youngsters, we pouted for awhile and then saw how ridiculous we were and laughed as we walked home from the Allenhurst depot.[55]

There was time for golf, too, a game to which Koerner had been introduced years earlier by "Pop" Hines of Street and Smith, and which he then had dismissed as an aberration. Now he began to play in earnest and even when the Depression struck, he made it a practice, if possible, to paint but half of each day and play thirty-six holes of golf in the afternoon, covering the course in long, swinging strides that made his companions remonstrate at his pace, and generally in vain. Frank Stick had a fishing camp amidst the dunes at Barnegat Bay and woe betide any unwary wight who walked to windward of Stick's fire when he was cooking the catch. Koerner was a frequent companion of Stick on these fishing trips, and a photograph of him playing a channel bass appeared in the book Stick wrote and illustrated on surf fishing.[56]

Stick also introduced Koerner to a part of America entirely new to him when he induced him to make one of the foursome to go fishing in the Florida Everglades and Keys. By-products of this expedition were to be motion pictures for *Field and Stream* and specimens, if possible, for the American Museum of Natural History. The party was gone for a month, the first time that the Koerners had been truly apart since their marriage. He returned with a distaste for the other two men Stick had asked to compose the party and with vivid memories of wonderful fishing, of being chased up a tree by an irate bull alligator, and of the stentorian snores of William Jennings Bryan, who occupied a berth in the same sleeping car on the homeward journey. He filled several sketch books on the trip and kept a detailed diary, from which the following excerpts have been taken: "beautiful sunrise coloring on the water—light green, purples, rose and greys"; "the coloring in the water very light green with purple shadows"; "sky is very beautiful—always full of clouds, the sunsets are immense." He put these impressions to good use in the serials by Nordhoff and Hall that made his last major illustrations.

Lillian cleaned his studio during his absence, which caused him to grumble good-naturedly for some months that he could not find anything where it belonged. She also prepared to surprise him when she met him at the depot on his return. This surprise had its origin with Charles Abels, the interior decorator who was their neighbor.

He said I could be much better looking if I would think more about myself and my make-up. That sounded hopeful to me. Then he said he would "do my face" the day William returned, if I would get some new clothes, and his sister would make my hat for my costume. "You don't think about yourself," he finished his offer, "if you were my wife, you would be beautiful."

The day William was to arrive, I was in a quiver to prepare to be beautiful. I was prompt to be dressed and "made up" and finally I was off for Asbury Park. As the train pulled in slowly, I was held up by a policeman at Main and Cookman, who said I was trying to pass a red light. There I sat! The day was hot and my face began to smear. My whole body was perspiring. Then the light changed. As William stepped off the train, tanned brown in rumpled clothes, I rushed into his arms. As he kissed me, he saw the runny mascara and the make-up base oozing through the powder. He held me at arm's length. "My God, what have you been doing? You're not Dick!"

John Held, Jr.'s flask-swigging flapper, who bobbed her hair and her skirts and rolled her stockings below her knees, has come to symbolize the changes that made the "Jazz Age" after World War I.[57] These changes were reflected in the six-part serial "Hooch" by Charles Francis "Socker" Coe that Koerner illustrated with an impact that still was felt more than forty years later. "Every time I see a large truck with a tarpaulin, I think of a Koerner illustration he did of some rum-runner hi-jackers."[58] John La Gatta's women became famous for the swing

Koerner's snowshoes were more than just studio models

of their torsos and the long lines of backs and shoulders, with their decolletage stopping a bare millimeter short. These changes became all too apparent to Bill and Lillian when they attended an exhibition and ball at the Grand Central Art Galleries in New York, where several of his paintings had been hung.

Dean Cornwell and his wife and James Montgomery Flagg and his model seemed quite exclusive. I got a distinct shock to look over on the far wall and see that the gorgeous, full-sized nude in the painting there, lying on a couch, perfectly relaxed, was the self-same girl dancing with Flagg. The painting was the center of attraction and so was she. William's girls were sometimes beautiful but they were always real girls, such as you would meet, admire, know and like. Flagg's model was his mistress and he tried to vindicate her tragic death in his autobiography. Typical of him![59]

This was a far cry from the antic revels of the Fakirs at the Art Students League, from the teaching and example of Howard Pyle, and from the gay, gladsome, innocent times at Naaman's-on-Delaware.

There were other changes as well. More than thirty illustrators made their first appearances in *Saturday Evening Post* during the 1920's, including such as Matt and Benton Clark, Raeburn Van Buren, Albin Henning, Henrietta McCaig Starrett, McClelland Barclay, Corinne Dillon, J. Clinton Shepherd, R. M. Crosby, Donald Teague, and H. R. Ballinger, while Harold Von Schmidt, later famous for his western illustrations, broke into *American, Collier's,* and *Cosmopolitan* during this decade. H. R. Ballinger outlined the figures in his illustrations to give them better definition and used a slick, almost glaze-like technique. Lejaren A. Hiller and Martin Justice continued their work in photographing models posed in the scenes they had envisioned. The lighting captured highlights and shadows very well, but the scenes obviously were posed and the reproduced work had an air-brushed appearance. There were other changes, too, and these came home to Koerner in a very personal way.

Even as did many of Howard Pyle's pupils, Koerner felt an obligation to his profession and to those who had helped him when he needed it. He set aside eight to nine o'clock each morning, before he got into *his* day's work, for criticism and advice to four younger artists, two of whom had been Frank Stick's students in Chicago and had followed him to Interlaken. Koerner hammered at dependability in delivering work as the *sine qua non* for success as an illustrator, and he hammered even more at the formula he knew so well—study and paint, study and paint, and paint and paint and paint! He stressed, too, the fact that making large canvasses greatly enhanced the sharpness of the illustration's necessary details when it was pulled down for magazine reproduction. This did not jibe with the new trends, as his students saw them, and they argued with him interminably. In Koerner's view, they should take and absorb what he offered, or reject it out of hand, but not waste his time in argumentation. "They are sapping me and giving nothing in return," he once told Lillian wearily. The climax came when one of them decided to study under Harvey Dunn at his Grand Central School of Art in New York and thereafter told Koerner that his paintings were out-of-date. The fashion in illustration now was patterns, not figures and details; black-and-white work was adequate for black-and-white reproduction, while color painting was reserved for easel work, true Art, not commercial work. Also, Koerner's paintings lacked undertone and were too thin. This brought Koerner's teaching to an end, but it is worth noting that three of the students won recognition for themselves as illustrators, while the fourth married a Rockefeller heiress.

If his wife's recollections are accurate, the cumulative effect of the changes wrought in the post-war years was to bring her husband to a personal crisis in his career. It passed, but for a brief period he seriously contemplated abandoning illustration. Her explanation of why he did not was simply that he looked at all the artists in New York and elsewhere who were having a hard time selling enough easel work to exist in minimal comfort, and his decided practical streak came to the fore with the flat statement, "We must eat." There can be no question of Koerner's practicality; he was a working artist, not a showman or self-aggrandizing personality. There also can be no question that he was not money-hungry and that throughout his long career, he accepted with relish the challenge of giving an author's characters the dimen-

Surf fishing from Frank Stick's camp, Barnegat, New Jersey

Ruth Ann and her father on the wharf at Gloucester, Massachusetts, 1923

sions and the dignity of humanness, as he "lived" the lives the stories gave them.

In keeping with what has come to be sensed as his personal creed, Koerner went back to school himself in his early forties. Beginning in 1919, he and Lillian had begun to snatch brief summer interludes, from a few days to two weeks as his schedule and their childrens' needs permitted, at Gloucester, Massachusetts. There he became aware of the work of Hugh Breckenridge, a faculty member at the Pennsylvania Academy of the Fine Arts, who conducted his own summer school at Gloucester in the use of "broken color." Breckenridge had been nourished on Late French Impressionism, and his "broken color" utilized the so-called "rainbow colors"—red, orange, yellow, green, blue, and

violet, plus white—while eschewing brown and black. What he sought was to capture the way light hit on objects and reflected color off of these objects onto other objects, while imprisoning the artist's private interpretation of a particular mood at a particular time of day.

The technique was to use little strokes to lay the colors side by side, not on top of the other, and thus utilize the complementary colors to best advantage. These are colors that are opposite on the color wheel, or spectrum, and are the colors that show the others off to the best advantage. The particular groupings of these complementary colors are: yellow and violet, or purple; blue and orange; and red and green. As Breckenridge used them and taught their use, they gave an optical mixture of pulsating, vibrant color to a painting, and his "Breckenridge reds," made up of many colors, were not easily forgotten.[60]

With his personal crisis passed Koerner took the 1-2-3-4 Koerners to Gloucester, where he rented a red cottage on the hill at the head of Rocky Neck, above the wharf where, amidst the sea tang and the smell of drying fish, Breckenridge conducted his classes. They spent two whole months there, while Koerner, eager as any schoolboy, drove himself to grasp what Breckenridge had to give. When he came to apply what he had learned in his own work, he found that "broken color" did not reproduce well in value. He then tried outlining it with a thin, black line but found that he lost his sense of depth thereby. He continued to work on this problem, because the color excited him tremendously, and evolved his own technique, which still was "broken color" to a certain extent, be-

cause it was colors side-by-side, but much more reproducible. He got this reproduction value by using tinted glass through which to view his color paintings. One was a smoked yellow, or amber glass, which turned all of his colors monochromatic, so that he saw, through a yellow tint, what the colors would look like in black-and-white reproduction. He also used a purplish blue glass which achieved the same effect.[61] By putting the two together for viewing, he got even more of a gray effect, and grays are to a painter what sauces are to a French chef. He now had his own palette, and no other illustrator of the West in this century has had one so distinctive.

His rocks and grass became a kaleidoscope of color, ranging from corals and greens to blues, purples, and orange. He used cobalt blue and ultra-marine—the active darks—to get his darkest effects that move both in and out of the picture plane. He painted a "scientific" sky—

The shaded areas on this double-page layout for Saturday Evening Post *indicate where the artist placed the illustrations he conceived for the story, and show why Koerner's use of vignette technique was so effective in giving visual impact to the text*

white for atmosphere, pink for strata-dust, and blue — and the level of clouds nearest the horizon were tinged with creme, oranges, and pinks from dirt in the atmosphere. Brown to him became a lower state of orange; that is, orange with blue highlights. His colors were strong and clear, never muddy, and he rarely used colors straight from their tubes, which in some cases are rather raw. By subtle mixing, he made his colors seem to have come directly from the tube, and he rarely used additives to speed the drying process. He was confident enough, "courageous" perhaps is a better word, to clean his palette every night, and return the next day to squeeze out new paints and mix new colors and have them be the exact value or tint or shade, whatever term is preferred, of the tones he had used the day before.[62] In between, Ruth Ann and Bill, Jr. had the task of cleaning his brushes in warm water and Ivory soap.

Unlike many artists, Koerner used no appliances, appurtenances, or tracings for his composition sketch work. After he had read the story and had gotten "into" its setting, time, and characters, he would do his research, both in his own "morgue" and wherever else he felt it necessary. Then he would compose what might be termed a "thumbnail sketch," perhaps 4 × 5 inches or slightly larger, and he might make four or more of these, often in color, until he came upon the perfect composition for the particular painting he had in mind. Once he had his composition, and remember that he already had worked out his color scheme on it, he transferred this freehand in charcoal to his canvas or to the "Thistle Brand" of Strathmore illustration board, that

his granddaughter, an artist in her own right, stoutly asserts was much superior to the cheap illustration board of today. With his charcoal outline in place, he painted over it with Prussian blue, so that the outline was distinct, and was ready to paint in earnest, literally to attack the canvas.

He painted *"a la prima,"* or freely and spontaneously, and he hit his mark the first time around. In none of the hundred or more canvasses that have been cleaned, not restored mind you, by O. H. Ericson has any sign been found of overpainting — scraping out and repainting.[63] His strokes were bold and strong, and he never spared the paint, sometimes using a palette knife or a wide brush, well worn down, to obtain a "rich impasto" approach, which lent excitement to his strokes. His colors, however, always were sensitive and, at times, even delicate. Another point that O. H. Ericson has noted, probably because it has caused him some problems in their cleaning, is that in his vignette work, Koerner was apt to combine any, many, or all of various media — charcoal, wax crayon, colored pencil, oils, water colors, and the hard "Mon Ami" pastels — to get the effect he wanted. Finally, it should be noted that the painter's lexicon is line, color, space, texture, and shading. Even as the great poet says a great deal without wasting words, so Koerner said his say with what John Ayres has called "a splendid economy of means."[64]

Koerner's last years were his best years, in which he painted at the height of function as an artist. This was his great good fortune, one denied many men, be they creative or not.

1. Irritation over taxes, of which Asbury Park was the major beneficiary, caused Frank Stick to lead a successful move, 6/20/1922, to make Interlaken a separate and independent borough, of which he became the first mayor and Koerner one of the first councilmen. Council meetings appear to have been short and succinct, due perhaps to Koerner's great willingness to move for adjournment when the proceedings dragged out beyond a reasonable time.

2. Koerner, *Narrative.*

3. Anon., *Interlaken 50th Anniversary,* (n.p.) 1972. Koerner's children were among the sponsors of this booklet.

4. Koerner soon acquired two 200-foot vacant lots, one

on each side of the house, to ensure privacy, a play area for the children, and ample space for his long-contemplated personal studio.

5. A six-cylinder Buick roadster cost $1,175, f.o.b. factory. Other makes were: Overland five-passenger touring car, $985; Hudson Six, $1,550; Ford Model T, $950; Hupmobile, $1,050; and Cadillacs came in six models from $1,975 to $3,250.

6. His studio operating expenses for 1919 totaled $1,635.64, including $687.92 for art supplies, $200.75 for trips to Philadelphia and New York, $120.00 for photographic supplies, $40.00 for fireplace wood, and $124.00

for the flowers and shrubs planted outside its Dutch door with a brass eagle knocker. His income for this year was at least $10,325.

7. Mott, *American Journalism*, 626.

8. Julian Street, "Our Fighting Posters," *McClure's*, 7/1918, deals briefly with this work.

9. *Collier's*, 6/23/1917, 12.

10. Brown did women after the fashion of Flagg and his precursors, but achieved his greatest fame with his creations for the "Mr. Tutt" stories by Arthur Train which ran endlessly in *Saturday Evening Post* after World War I.

11. Mott, *Magazines*, IV, 589–607, *passim*.

12. A letter from Towne to Koerner, 3/1/1918, indicates that Koerner suffered a protracted illness in the winter of 1917–18 for which no other evidence has been found.

13. Discovery of this fact led to the checking of other charges for illustrations against the actual number of illustrations contained in the stories when they appeared in print. This revealed that from 1917 until his career was over, Koerner often put characters' heads, which were reproduced as one-column by two-inch "spots," into stories whenever he felt the story needed such and without regard to whether he received extra compensation for them. Visual enhancement of the author's characters was his goal.

Most of these were done in oils or other color media. More than thirty such added attractions were tallied during a spot check of his work. The total such remains unverified.

14. Mott, *Magazines*, IV, V, has but a few scattered references to this magazine.

15. While best known for his "Wolfville" stories in the western genre, Lewis was a political writer of some standing and contributed such pieces to major magazines, especially those of the Hearst organization.

16. Mott, *American Journalism*, 622, states that her American visit was covered in a "pool" operation by Rheta Child Dorr, New York *Mail*, and Bessie Beatty, San Francisco *Bulletin*. Beatty also wrote "We Fight for Russia," *Woman's Home Companion*, 3/1918, about Maria. The New York *Times*, 7/11/1918, 2:1, refers to her reception by President Wilson and spells her name Butchkareff. Her book *Yashka: My Life as Peasant, Exile and Soldier* was taken largely from the magazine version and was published in 1919 by Constable and Company in London and by Frederick A. Stokes Company in New York.

17. A fairly common plot in the immediate post-war fiction offerings was the fiery, revolutionary girl pitted against the son of oppressive capitalists, or the intense, visionary young male Marxist falling in love with a decadent daughter of the idle rich. These idealistic young revolutionaries were the "counter culture" of their times, or so they thought.

18. "Grey treated the Wobblies as a corrupt labor union at best, as spies for the Germans at worst." Carlton Jackson, *Zane Grey*, 72. Grey's "Wildfire" had begun in *Country Gentleman*, 4/8/1916, with illustration by Frank Tenney Johnson, his first appearance in a major magazine.

19. The same fate befell a cover illustration by N. C. Wyeth, 1/26/1918.

20. Tebbel, 174.

21. If the outdoor-action story, of which the western was a sub-genre, appealed to the victim of urban claustrophobia and industrialized monotony, it would appear from this incidence in *Country Gentleman* that the rural resident also needed vicarious release from his own daily round.

22. Spradling illustrated Grey's "To The Last Man," beginning 5/29/1921.

23. His name, at least, seems to have derived from the old folksong "The Boston Burglar."

24. Harriman was right, but *Saturday Evening Post* became Williams's major vehicle.

25. Rupert Hughes did an article on Chambers in *Cosmopolitan*, 6/1918.

26. Balmer's sea-action fiction had appeared in *Saturday Evening Post* as early as 7/6/1907. He became editor of *Red Book* about 1927.

27. "Wallingford" had appeared in *Saturday Evening Post* as early as 10/5/1907. His creator had been lured away to *Cosmopolitan* earlier and now was dropped.

28. Long resigned from *Cosmopolitan* in 1931 and later committed suicide.

29. Rex Beach, never one to miss the trend in outdoor-action demand, did an oil-field novel, *Flowing Gold*, for which Koerner provided the dust-wrapper and interior illustrations.

30. Mott, *Magazines*, 763–72.

31. Honoré Willsie Morrow is another better remembered for her writings than for her stint as editor of *Delineator*, 1914–19.

32. The first had been in *Metropolitan* during the Maria Botchkareva serial.

33. Deland had gone overseas for *Companion* during World War I. Koerner had illustrated two of her pre-war books published by Harper and Brothers.

34. Kerr to Koerner, 10/13/1920.

35. *Ibid.*, 3/17/1921.

36. He received $5,400 for illustrating "Sunset Pass," and $6,400 for "Drift Fence." Grey had other good illustrators in this period—F. B. Hoffman, H. M. Stoops, Frank Schoonover, Harold Von Schmidt among them—but the remark stands. After 1929, Koerner illustrated exclusively for *Saturday Evening Post*.

37. They did some international muckraking as well. John K. Turner's series of articles, "Barbarous Mexico," was an excoriation of Porfirio Díaz and began to appear 10/1909.

38. Merle Crowell became editor in 1923, with Mary B. Millett as managing editor; James C. Derieux held the latter title in 1926.

39. In its issue for 7/1923, Dodge Brothers offered their touring car for $880 and boasted of "over 700,000 owners"; Overland's "Red Bird" touring car cost $750, and Maxwell, the car beloved of the late Jack Benny, priced its touring model at $885.

40. It did not label "western" stories as such until 1920.

41. The number of articles per issue increased from seven to ten in 1919 to twelve to fifteen in 1923. Referred to feature articles were in the following issues: Fairbanks 7/1917, Rinehart 10/1917, Fitzgerald 9/1922, Fosdick 1/1924, Hough 6/1918, Wright 2/1918, Steffens 8/1928, Terhune-Wright debate 6/1928.

In the Terhune-Wright debate, Terhune took the position that youth was hell bent for destruction, while Wright just as stoutly opposed this notion; the root of Terhune's argument was alcohol, equal to today's concern over marijuana.

42. Kelland later returned to the *Post's* pages but not with "Scattergood," who remained a fixture in *American*. Tebbel, 101–102, says that an intangible, mutual antipathy existed between Lorimer and Kelland.

43. In 5/1921. Rockwell also illustrated a Booth Tarkington serial that began 11/1918. His covers were better than his inside work.

44. It did not list illustrators in the table of contents until the middle-1920s, when it began to hawk its authors on its covers.

45. He received $300 each for the illustrations, and Bill, Jr. posed for the young boy in the serial.

46. Nye, 249–54, *passim.*

47. Nye, *op. cit.*, indicates that Post's work influenced Earle S. Gardner's depiction of "Perry Mason." The *Post* article appeared 11/16/1912. Where the "Uncle Abner" stories appeared was not discerned in the course of this study.

48. Illustrated by Arthur William Brown.

49. Tebbel, 79, says that the *Post's* low point came in 1918 when it had a net paid circulation of 1,976,161 copies weekly; each issue averaging 152 pages and yielding advertising revenue of $466,982. New editorial blood, including Thomas B. Costain, later famous as a writer of historical romances, and Wesley Stout, helped it climb in circulation to 2,264,000 copies per issue by 1922, and aided it withstanding the weekly advertising competition provided by the founding of *Time* in 1923 and *Liberty* in 1924.

The painting for Forbes Lithograph was priced at $500, sent prepaid express, and never seen or heard of officially thereafter. Koerner painted it again, but whether he salvaged any compensation from the express company for the lost original remains unknown.

50. Mott, *Golden Multitudes,* 265.

51. Nye, 40.

52. Tebbel, 63. She received $4,500 per short story and perhaps $60,000 per serial at the peak of her association with the *Post.*

53. Tebbel, 88.

54. Mott, *Magazines,* IV, 708.

55. Koerner, *Narrative.*

56. *The Call of the Surf,* 254.

57. Furnas, 894, believes that the flapper's lack of angularity, let alone curves, can be traced to the heroine of Frank Norris's *The Pit* (1900) with the line of descent coming through Maxfield Parrish's "innocently naked young pagans," the nymphs indistinguishable from the boys. He sees the flapper as an important step down from the Diana-like Gibson Girl, being neither goddess nor lady.

58. Kidd to W.H.H., 6/15/1970.

59. Koerner, *Narrative.* Flagg's autobiography was *Roses and Buckshot* (N.Y., Putnam's) 1946. Koerner once judged a beauty contest at Asbury Park; "I selected a sweet, wholesome miss. Everybody else preferred a very professional-looking model. They never asked me to judge again. And—that suits me perfectly." Koerner Papers.

60. Diane Koerner Schwartz, typescript concerning her grandfather's technique and use of color, prepared for W.H.H., 1972.

61. *Ibid.*

62. W.H.D. Koerner, Jr. to W.H.H., 8/1974.

63. O. H. Ericson, various interviews by W.H.H., April and August, 1971.

64. Professor of art, California State University, Chico, and an easel painter in his own right. This work has benefitted from extensive critical appraisal of Koerner's art by Professor Ayres.

Chapter VIII
PUTTING THE COVER ON "THE COVERED WAGON"

ONE OF this nation's few native art forms, the western story was flourishing atop a deep tap root long before "The Covered Wagon" gave it a new dimension. Its literary antecedents have been discussed beyond any need for repetition.[1] Long before such scholarly attention, an anonymous author in *Saturday Evening Post* had said much the same about the cowboy in the western story: "Perhaps we have always admired the cowboy because he represented typically our own American youth and self-confidence. . . . He exists as a sort of Leatherstocking figure, which will perhaps go down to the future as a definite and permanent conception."[2]

In the closing decade of the last century, the triumvirate of Theodore Roosevelt, Owen Wister, and Frederic Remington was foremost in the literary upgrading of the West and its denizens in the taste-making magazines—*Atlantic, Century, Harper's, Scribner's.*[3] Their offerings from pen and palette in essence hymned the praises of the nation's successful conquest of the last great segment of its frontier experience, that continental expanse of grasslands, deserts, basins, and mountains between the Missouri River and the crests of the Sierra Nevada–Cascade Range complex that still demark the Pacific Coast from the West. In this same decade, the buckskin extravaganzas of William F. "Buffalo Bill" Cody and his imitators—the so-called "Bill Shows"—supplied tangible, superbly visual presentations of this same theme, the Winning of the West, and their audiences were solid evidence that their symbolism fit the nation's mood.[4]

Wallace Stegner has noted recently that exam-ining the collaboration between Wister and Remington reveals the ontogeny of the cowboy as a literary figure.[5] Before their efforts and those of Roosevelt, the cowboy's image in literature had been akin to that held by colonial New Yorkers fighting for independence from England, who used "cow-boys" as an epithet for marauding Tories who sanctified their cattle thefts by professing loyalty to George III.[6] There can be no argument that cattle were a part of the frontier's inexorable advance from Atlantic tidewater through trans-Appalachia to the Mississippi River. But, and a very big but it is indeed, these cattle were adjuncts and only adjuncts of the basic agricultural frontier.

It was not until this frontier ventured onto the almost oceanic expanse of grasslands, where "the Mariner's Star once singed the nose of Coronado,"[7] there to encounter an already established Hispanic tradition of working cattle from horseback through illimitable distances, that our frontier experience produced the nation's contribution to the horsemen of the world, the American Theseus-in-leather-leggin's, the cowboy. He was the last of our frontier types to be molded by the land in which he worked and the work that he did, and the efforts of Wister, Remington, and Roosevelt prepared the way for appreciation and then distortion of this salient fact.

Such redoubtable students of the Cattle Kingdom as Bernard DeVoto, J. Frank Dobie, and Walter Prescott Webb, as well as Stegner, have attested their belief that Wister's *The Virginian* (1902) clothed the cowboy with literary respectability. It is not intended here to dispute these investigations of the storied splendors of America's vanished Papyrus Age. Neither is it intended to question the fact that *The Virginian* was an instantaneous success as a book and as a stage play,[8] nor that its stage success spawned others which had an impact on the popular fancy quite comparable to that of later cinematic offerings. It is intended here to note firmly that *The Virginian* caused no upsurge in the incidence of western stories in the quality, mass-circulation magazines between 1900–10. Neither did it alter in any significant way the image of the cowboy presented weekly and monthly to millions of readers of these magazines.

The *Saturday Evening Post* is regarded as the most representative of these magazines for good reasons. Its appeal was not urban oriented, as was *American's*; the motif of its offerings was not limited, as *Cosmopolitan's* was aimed at the woman seeking psuedo-sophistication after its acquisition by Hearst in 1905; it did not descend into the lurid exposé, as did *Everybody's*; and it eschewed the virulent muckraking that distinguished *Collier's* and *McClure's*. Its appeal to the expanding, upward-bound middle segment of the populace was demonstrated unequivocally by its increase in weekly circulation from about 100,000 to more than 1,500,000 copies between 1900–10, while the nation's population rose from 76,000,000 to 92,000,000. Lorimer claimed with reason that each copy of each issue of his *Post* had at least three readers, which gave it a most substantial audience. By contrast, *Collier's* in this period increased from 300,000 to 521,000 copies weekly, a rate of growth probably due to the relative lack of fiction in its pages during its muckraking emphasis.

In common with its competitors, the *Post's* story offerings included a substantial number that belonged to what may be called the outdoor-action school of American popular fiction.[9] Components of this school were the north-woods story—set in Maine, Michigan, Canada, Alaska, the Arctic in general—which can be dubbed the moose-and-snowshoe genre;[10] the sea story, long a staple of American fiction; the exotic action yarn, wherein the exotic element was provided by the locale—Africa, Asia, Latin America, the South Seas—and the peoples thereof; and the western, in which the cowboy began to submerge its other types—prospectors, railroaders,[11] loggers, Indians, cavalrymen, for examples—during this decade.

The "Strenuous Decade"—perhaps so called because Theodore Roosevelt was elected president in his own right in 1904—was the decade of that yeasty social and political ferment, exemplified by muckraking, which culminated in the Progressive movement. The relationship between this movement and the cowboy's emergence was shown clearly by Herbert Johnson's editorial cartoon in the *Post* (9/28/1912) which showed six western states, each garbed in full cowboy regalia, including woolly chaps and two six-guns apiece, shooting a hat labeled "Special Privilege" from off the head of a corpulent, cutaway-clad figure labeled "Big Business." Both the Progressives and the emergence of the cowboy reflected the nation's schizophrenia: torn between fascination with the material blessings provided by a burgeoning industrialization and a communal longing for what appeared to have been the unfettered, unconventional freedom of that simpler, cleaner, purer time before the rise of the cities and the loss of Thomas Jefferson's world of independent, rural yeoman.

Examination of more than four hundred issues of the *Post* published during this decade makes it possible to note that the western story comprised only 7 per cent of its short fiction and a minuscule proportion of its serial offerings.[12] These figures parallel the ratio of similar stories in the fiction contents of the other mass-circulation magazines studied for the same time span. Of the *Post's* western stories, about one-third belonged to what here is termed the "Wolfville genre," which dominated the art form in this decade.[13] The most prolific producers of such stories, those whose output gave the anecdotal Wolfville genre its place in the evolution of the cowboy western, were Emerson Hough, Henry Wallace Phillips, Alfred Henry Lewis, William R. Lighton, Kennett Harris, Rex Beach, and John Haslette.[14] Some of O. Henry's southwestern stories fall into this category, as do Thomas Janvier's prose sketches concerning "Santa Fe Charley," while many of Owen Wister's "Scipio Le Moyne" incidents, which were significant forerunners of *The Virginian*, meet the Wolfville criteria.[15]

These comprised a thoroughly masculine society, in which women, by and large, were stage properties stuffed with sawdust; a picturesque setting quite distinct from the confining urban East, such as Hough's "Heart's Desire," based on White Oaks, New Mexico, and Lewis's "Wolf-ville," based largely on Tombstone, Arizona, and often a continuing central character, such as Phillips's "Red Saunders," Lighton's "Billy Fortune," and Harris's "Ricky Raymond." A plot was not essential, but if there was one, it bordered on "mellerdraymah." A tinge of heart-of-gold knight-errantry was useful; there was explosive action, not necessarily with pistols, and the cowboys and other characters were given such tags of dialect, mannerism, and costume as would positively distinguish them from their more combed and curried and convention-bound fellows. Finally, humor in these stories was broad and masculine, often verging on adolescent, locker-room, low comedy, but, and it should be remembered well, *this humor was equal to the action in both story content and flavor.*[16] These stories took the Harte-Twain legacy—self-reliance, individualism, disregard for danger, disdain for class distinctions, pride in country, and a self-imposed obligation to aid those in distress—and began their expansion into what later became "The Code of the West," the stereotyped characteristics of the fictional cowboy.[17]

The characters created by writers in the Wolf-ville genre did not lend themselves to visual images that would engender immediate reader identification. Thus their illustrators by and large were not those who left a mark in creating the iconography of the cowboy. Men skilled in free pen-and-ink work, such as A. B. Frost, Will Crawford, F. R. Gruger, and Arthur I. Keller, drew many a western story assignment. Charcoal and black-and-white wash drawings were the other media in vogue at this time, and for the first half of the decade, others such as George Gibbs, Martin Justice, and J. N. Marchand did the bulk of the illustrative work for the western story. The second half of the decade saw the emergence of N. C. Wyeth, Harvey Dunn, and Allen Tupper True, all Pyle pupils, as major western illustrators, while W. H. "Buck" Dunton was widely used in the field.[18]

Even though Frederic Remington illustrated relatively few magazine stories in these years, his influence on the visual images of the West is considered to be as dominant as it had been in the last decade of the previous century. This was due primarily to his work in *Collier's,* for which he did covers, inside double pages in color, and full-page black-and-white composi-

tions, with a dozen or more such appearances in many years, until his death in 1909.[19]

This was the decade, too, in which the West and its characters were discovered by advertisers. Omar Turkish Cigarettes offered a miniature Navajo blanket with each package; Cudahay Packing Company offered a portrait in full color of an Indian "chief" for the metal cap from a two-ounce jar of its beef tea and four cents postage; while Pendleton Woolen Mills proclaimed that its blankets were made by genuine Indians and priced them between $4.00 and $15.00 each. Winchester used a mountain man to promote its rifles, and Smith & Wesson used Dan Smith's drawings of cavalry-Indian skirmishes to extoll its revolvers. Koerner drew a prospector with burdened burro for Postum, "Red Top" Rye showed two western types bellied up to a bar, and the Santa Fe Railway used a cowgirl on horseback to drive home its message "A Pullman to the Grand Canyon."

The two most widely used cowboy advertisements were full-page paintings by N. C. Wyeth for Cream of Wheat. The first depicted a cowboy atop a bucking horse, all hooves and muscles, and the second showed a cowboy depositing a letter in an isolated mailbox made from a Cream of Wheat wooden packing case, with the legend "Where the Mail Goes Cream of Wheat Goes." These appeared in at least twelve leading magazines, beginning in 1907, and were used for many years on the back-cover pages in two colors.[20] It is believed that Wyeth received $250 each for them.

This inquiry into the evolution of the western story would be incomplete if it did not notice some of the New York stage versions of the western-*cum*-cowboy that both preceded and followed the theatrical success of *The Virginian's* dramatic adaptation. Many of these were similarly derived from literary works and while they did not add a cubit to the western's stature, they did make the flesh-and-blood transition from the "Bill Shows" to the "reel" life of cinema.[21] In 1900, Maxine Elliott was featured in *The Cowboy and the Lady* at the Knickerbocker Theater, while in this same year, Eleanor Robson and Vincent Serrano starred in *Arizona* and later took the play to London. Dustin Farnum was going strong in *The Virginian* in 1904 and Guy Bates Post played the part of "Steve," the cowboy who erred a trifle and was hanged for his mistake. In 1905, William Faversham starred in *The Squaw Man,* in which William S. Hart played a part, at Wallack's Theater, and David Belasco's production of *Girl of the Golden West,* starring Blanche Bates, was getting rave reviews at the same time. In this year, too, an adaptation of *Wolfville* flopped in Philadelphia and never made it to New York. Belasco's success sparked a burlesque of the stage western in 1906, *The Squaw Man's Girl of the Golden West,* and on August 13, 1906, Walter Woods's version of *Billy the Kid* opened at the New Star Theater for a long run. On the road until 1918, it was seen by an estimated six million persons.

A bumper crop of western plays graced the New York boards in 1907: Frances Starr and Charles Richman in *Rose of the Rancho;* H. B. Warner and Eleanor Robson in *Salomy Jane;* Florence Rockwell as heroine of *The Round-Up,* while Professor William Vaughan Moody's *The Great Divide* appears to have been the first pistol-and-psychology drama. This may explain why N. C. Wyeth said that it was pronounced "the first American classic" by New York's "big critics."[22] Edgar Selwyn was the lead in *Pierre of the Plains* in 1908 and Mabel Van Buren, a grandniece of the former president, now was playing "Molly" as *The Virginian* went on and on.[23] The decade came to a close, fittingly enough, with Enrico Caruso singing the male lead in the opera version of *Girl of the Golden West,* for which Puccini was the composer, Toscanini the conductor, and Gatti-Casazza the producer. The stage western never would reach such heights again.[24] Nor would they be approached until *The Covered Wagon* in either fiction or film.

As the Strenuous Decade closed, there were signs and portents in the writings of Eugene Manlove Rhodes and George Pattullo that the cowboy might become a full-bodied, four-dimensional, literary figure who would truly reflect and represent the frontier experience that had forged and shaped and tempered him.[25] Rhodes's novella "The Little Eohippus" was the first, *the very first,* cowboy-and-the-lady romance to grace the pages of any major magazine,[26] which makes it mandatory to recall that *The Virginian* was not serialized as such, but was reworked and refined by Wister from prior short stories and two-part episodes, dropping much of their humor in the process.

A Canadian-born Scot, George Pattullo was editor of the *Boston Herald,* after newspaper experience in Montreal and London, when he spent the first of three consecutive summers, 1908–10, roaming the Southwest with Erwin Smith, one of the truly great photographers of the Cattle Kingdom's declining years.[27] Pattullo saw with a reporter's eye and he wrote of what he saw with a deep awareness of the foibles of mankind, the idiosyncracies of livestock, and the vagaries of chance. 'Gene Rhodes, a horseman from who laid the chunk, believed until he died that Pattullo's "Corazón" *(McClure's,* 7/1910) was the finest horse story ever written. Between 1907–17, Pattullo's short stories and articles, as well as his reportage of the border troubles incident to the Mexican Revolution, appeared in the leading magazines, where Koerner illustrated at least eleven of them.

A long developing literary groundswell became the wave of the future that inundated the work of Rhodes and obliterated that of Pattullo. An almost imperceptible surge of this groundswell was felt during Theodore Roosevelt's presidency when Street and Smith launched *Rough Rider Weekly,* which featured the exploits of "Ned Strong, King of the Wild West," and a cowgirl named "Stella." Clarence E. Mulford's now famous "Hopalong Cassidy" stories, anecdotal in form, raucous with action, and haloed by gunplay, were launched in 1905 by *Outing,* a limited-circulation monthly travel magazine. The Outing Company published two collections of these stories in book form, 1907–1908, and when the Chicago house of A. C. McClurg & Co. found an audience for another collection, *Hopalong Cassidy* in 1910, that required six quick printings, they reprinted the earlier volumes, as well as the new *Bar-20 Days,* in 1911, giving them illustrations by Wyeth, Schoonover, Allen True, and Maynard Dixon.

In 1904, Street and Smith's *Popular* published Bertha M. Bower's "Chip of the Flying U," the first of almost sixty short stories, novels, and serial installments she would contribute to that magazine over the next six years.[28] Street and Smith then published it in book form and the publisher's blurbs for this first of the sixty-eight Bower novels are worth attention: "A Comedy With Dramatic Touches" in which "Pathos and Humor Are Adroitly Commingled" to make "A Wholesome and Delightful Story." Bower knew the land and the people of Big Sandy, Montana, and the "contagious vicinity" and her retention of humor and her homespun characterizations separate her from Mulford and those who followed him.

Beginning with *Wyoming, A Story of the Outdoor West* in 1908, William MacLeod Raine, whose western fiction was found but rarely in the magazines examined for this work, began his long career of writing one or more western novels a year for thirty years. That his work was popular abroad, as well as at home, was attested during World War I when His Majesty's Government purchased some 500,000 copies of his various titles for distribution to the "Tommies" at the front. Before book illustrations, save for a frontispiece, largely were supplanted by the gaudy dust wrapper as an eye-catching inducement to purchase, Raine's visual images were supplied by Clarence Rowe, D. C. Hutchison, and "Buck" Dunton.

Charles Alden Seltzer,[29] another volumetric producer of westerns, whose cowboy protagonists were distinctive for their hard-bitten qualities, added impetus to the groundswell with such titles as *The Range Riders* and *The Two-Gun Man* in 1911. The first had inside illustrations by Clarence Rowe, the next had only a frontispiece by Robert W. Amick, a friend of Koerner at the Art Students League. Seltzer produced at least thirty more westerns over the next twenty years, of which six had frontispieces by Percy V. E. Ivory, who had made one of the Naaman's-on-Delaware group with Koerner.[30]

The groundswell became a towering comber in 1912 that crashed onto the literary sands with a roar that sent reverberations into the present. The roar was made by Zane Grey's *Riders of the Purple Sage*, with illustrations by Douglas Duer, which "More than any other book determined the universal stereotype of the West."[31] Grey had been discovered, as it were, by *Popular* in 1910 when it serialized his first successful western story, "The Heritage of the Desert." The venerable publishing house of Harper and Brothers, which would not sully the pages of its monthly magazine with such offerings, read the nation's tastes correctly and published it in book form with such success that they did the same with *Riders of the Purple Sage*, which had been serialized in *Field and Stream*, and remained Grey's book publishers for many years.[32]

With this book, Grey became foremost among the first of the Formula Fabulists—Mulford, Raine, Seltzer being the others—and he became the only one of the four to leave a deep imprint in the pages of the major mass-circulation magazines, an imprint made and left in those pages after World War I.[33]

The climate of opinion in the year of Theodore Roosevelt's "Bull Moose" attempt to regain the White House may explain the instantaneous success of *Riders of the Purple Sage*.[34] Whereas the raffish, unconventional characters of the Wolfville genre had given vicarious expression to a growing distaste for the constricting social conventions of a rapidly maturing, urban milieu, the cowboy of the fabulists reflected a deep desire to find personal solutions to increasingly complex political and economic problems through direct, individual action which would produce positive and immediate and beneficial results.

The cowboy of the fabulists became Galahad in a morality play for Everyman; the clearly and cleanly limned proponent of good over evil; protecting the weak from the rapacious; bringing benefit to others through his courage and self-sacrifice; displaying excellence in craft and hard-twisted moral fiber. He became in short the Sun God produced by all peoples in all ages in time of need—blood brother to Taras Bulba, El Cid Campeador, and Robin Hood—and the humor that had marked his forerunners became a virtuous solemnity made necessary by the tensions and the conflicts of his righteous errands into the wilderness of what became for the fabulists a timeless and unchanging West.

In this West, the inhabitants partook quite logically of the West's positive influence in creating basic nobility of character. If this nobility had eroded, the West had a regenerative effect upon it, and in extreme cases could cause it to appear in those who had not shown it before. This and related themes were used by others than the fabulists. Long before he wrote *The Shame of the Cities*, Lincoln Steffens reported on a bronco-busting contest at Denver, Colorado,[35] wherein he made it clear that he found a nobility of character among the contestants, fresh from the range, that he found lacking among eastern urbanities. The cowboy as symbol was never so plain as in Herbert Johnson's editorial cartoon showing Uncle Sam in cowboy garb applying his LIBERTY brand to the Kaiser Wilhelm bull.[36]

The end of the *jihad* to save the world for democracy marked the end of the Age of American Innocence; certainly the end of its self-confident adolescence. The growing disillusionment of the Progressive Era became a creeping, crippling cynicism, as the nation faced the fact that the orderly, secure society of the pre-war years had vanished into the maw of international involvement. These things were reflected in the writings of John Dos Passos, the birth of *Black Mask* magazine and its espousal of the hard-boiled detective story, the assaults on the values of the "boo-boisie" of H. L. Mencken, the disillusionment of Sherwood Anderson, and the anti-Babbitry of Sinclair Lewis. They were reflected, too, in a political neo-isolationism and a passionate desire for a "return to normalcy" that placed Warren G. Harding in the White House. These in and of themselves bespoke a deep national desire to escape the impact of accelerating change and its erosion of traditional values deeply felt and strongly held. As a bulwark against the inchoate present, the nation turned inward and homeward to the most American of all American experiences, the frontier, and the formula western story burgeoned accordingly.

The *Ladies Home Journal* used its first western short stories in 1920 and began serialization of its first Zane Grey offering, "The Call of the Cañon," the following year (11/1921). One attempt to gauge the popularity of American authors in the immediate post-war period placed Grey at the top of the list, based on sales of his nine books published between 1919–26.[37] He and his fellow fabulists were joined by such as J. Allan Dunn, Eugene Cunningham, W. C. Tuttle, and, with blare of trumpet and ruffle of drum, the Old Master of Thud-and-Blunder, Frederich Schiller Faust, who reserved three of his many pen names, the best known of which became Max Brand, for his western output.[38] While only Grey found his major market in the quality, mass-circulation magazines, the "big slicks," the others found prominent publishing houses for book versions of their offerings.

Despite the proliferation of the formula western, its "slick" appeal was not evident when a Chicago-born weekly magazine was launched (5/10/1924) to compete with *Saturday Evening Post* and *Collier's*. This was *Liberty — The Magazine for Everyone*, a name selected by a contest in which the first prize was $25,000.[39] It used authors unknown to the other "slicks" and seasoned them with well-known names, such as Burns Mantle, Kathleen Norris, Rupert Hughes, Dorothy Parker, George K. Turner, Albert Payson Terhune, and Hugh Fullerton for baseball stories.[40] Its illustrators, too, were largely newcomers to the mass-circulation magazines, with again a stiffening of well-known artists: Neysa McMein, Coles Phillips, and Penryhn Stanlaws did its "pretty girl" covers, with such as C. L. Bull, J. J. Gould, Guernsey Moore, Arthur William Brown, James M. Flagg, John T. McCutcheon, and Anton Otto Fischer on the inside.

In thirty-five of its first fifty-two issues, it used a very small proportion of outdoor-action fiction, including five western short stories that were illustrated by Harold Von Schmidt, R. W. Stewart, Frank B. Hoffman, and C. J. McCarthy. One of these was a "modern" western by Beatrice Blackmar, better known as half of the husband-and-wife team that became editor of *Ladies Home Journal* in 1935. Of the other four western-story authors, only W. C. Tuttle carved a pulp niche for himself with his "Hashknife Hartley" and "Sad Sontag" characters.

It has been said of the *Saturday Evening Post* that "Lorimer . . . kept before his readers the cowboy as a symbol of the rugged individualism that had made America great."[41] Careful analysis of the *Post's* fiction offerings during Koerner's long career in illustration does not support this statement. It does show that in the post-war years Lorimer strove to give his readers renewed pride in their country and in their countrymen's accomplishments which would help them face the uncertain future with their traditional values unimpaired. One means towards this end was to make the nineteenth century's culmination of the unique American experience, the Westward Movement, the equivalent of the historical romance of the turn of the century, for which *When Knighthood Was in Flower* may stand as exemplar. He was helped immeasureably in this effort by a fruitful and significant collaboration between Koerner and Emerson Hough.

Hough's first appearance in the *Post* was "The Dinner at Heart's Desire" (12/6/1902), which was illustrated by Howard Giles in such fashion as to make its cowboy protagonist resemble a male Gibson Girl with big hat and pistol. In this same year, *The Mississippi Bubble* reached fourth on the best-seller list and established Hough's national reputation. His association with the *Post* had continued steadily thereafter, and his stream of articles on wildlife and other natural-resource conservation in its pages, coupled with Lorimer's sustained editorial support, had much to do with getting the National Park concept accepted and established.[42]

In 1919, Hough wrote a series of articles for the *Post*, "Travelling the Old Trails," which Koerner illustrated, their first association since the Chicago *Tribune* days. Upon completion of this series, Hough almost called it quits. He was then in his sixty-second year and had written steadily and voluminously for most of them. Deep inside, he felt that he was through as a writer, that the wellspring of his creativity had gone dry. He personally conveyed these feelings to Lorimer early in 1920 and Lorimer eventually persuaded him that he could take material from the "Trails" series and turn it into fiction. It was fortunate all around that he succeeded.

Hough holed up in Yellowstone Park to write the first draft of "The Covered Wagon" in longhand and then rewrote it at least twice, following Lorimer's suggestions,[43] to make it what Lorimer wanted—a true epic of the Great Migration to Oregon in 1843. By October, 1921, Hough had the final manuscript well in hand with more than 90,000 words completed. Lorimer was pleased with it and willingly acceded to Hough's request that Koerner do the illustrations. Just when Koerner received the galley proofs of the first installment is unknown, but he delivered the first three of twenty-four magnificent paintings on December 15, 1921, and the last three on February 5, 1922, many of which were canvasses 36 × 30 inches. Among the first paintings was one of the heroine, "Molly Wingate," on a wagon seat, framed by the background of the wagon sheet and given a halo effect by the opening in it, a veritable Madonna of the Prairies.[44] This painting made the *Post's* cover for April 1, 1922, when the serial began its eight-part appearance.

Hough had seen this painting before it was published and wrote of it to the *Post's* art editor,[45] who promptly forwarded the letter to Koerner with the comment that it contained "about the highest compliment any writer could pay an illustrator. I am pretty sure it won't go to your head."[46]

Out Where the West Begins

There, seventy years ago, the romance of Molly Wingate and Will Banion unfolds, amid scenes of thrilling adventure and ghastly peril. A novel of pioneer days, intensely interesting and throbbingly alive with the daring and the courage of the brave men and women who staked everything on faith and won.

THE COVERED WAGON
By EMERSON HOUGH, Author of "THE MISSISSIPPI BUBBLE"

$2.00 at all bookstores   This Is An Appleton Book

D. APPLETON & COMPANY   New York and London

Window display card for The Covered Wagon, *using Koerner's painting of Molly Wingate, its heroine*

When I saw that girl on the wagon seat I exclaimed aloud "Oh Boy! Dar she!" I don't know when an illustration has hit me in the face that way that one has. Tell Koerner that this is the first time in my career that an artist has really pleased me with his work. Here we have imagination and fidelity both. I use to know Koerner in Chicago. Tell him that his old boss Bill Wells is still around and is spending the winter at Magnolia Springs, Alabama.

It was my understanding all along that Appletons [D. Appleton & Co.] were to use at least four of these illustrations. It was after our contract was signed, in fact only a few days ago, that I learned that only one was to be used and that they were going to use a horrible thing for the [book] cover. There would be a difference of fifty thousand copies in a well-pushed book between their [proposed] jacket and one on which this cover girl of yours [Koerner's] would appear.

I want to thank you for the very splendid work on the illustrations of "The Covered Wagon" and I want to assure you that I have never put more work and more heart into any book that I have ever written.

Hough's concern over the dust-wrapper illustration was resolved in favor of his wishes and Appleton also used "Molly" for their bookstore advertising which brought Koerner this letter (5/17/1922) from Hough.

I am sending you today one of the little window display placards of The Covered Wagon, *showing your girl on the wagon seat. I am as crazy as ever about that picture—and indeed all the other pictures—and think this is the best window display card I ever had. Thank you very much for doing the work in the* Saturday Evening Post *serial which they tell me is very much of a success.*

When the book version appeared, a copy came to the Interlaken studio inscribed "To W.H.D. Koerner, who put the cover on 'The Covered Wagon,' with sincere gratitude from Emerson Hough."

Its tremendous success with "The Covered Wagon" was capitalized upon by the *Post,* a matter discussed more fully hereinafter. Its impact on other magazines was exemplified in the pages of one of the Big Four of the women's magazines, which had reached this eminence with little or no attention to the outdoor-action school and less than that to its western component. It began (12/1924) a serial, "The Splendid Road," in "four large installments" by Vingie Roe. That it was clearly derived, to use a euphemism, from "The Covered Wagon" is shown in its illustrations by Robert W. Stewart and in *McCall's* blurb for its impending appearance:

Forever westward has moved the course of empire. . . . And of all the chapters in this recital none is more thrilling, more resounding with the clash and clamor of human destiny, than that concerning the two thousand mile trip made by the '49ers in their covered Wagons across a hostile, Indian-infested continent to the far shores of the blue Pacific. . . . This is the greatest story of the winning of the west yet written. In the character of Sandra Dehault, "the first woman to bring her outfit through," Miss Roe adds a wonderful portrait to the gallery of great American heroines. Sandra, a daughter of Cavaliers, could grace a silken drawing-room, but she could ride hard and shoot straight as well.[47]

The impact of the film version of *The Covered Wagon* on the popular conceptions of the people, events, and settings of the West-That-Was cannot be overemphasized. Famous Players–Lasky paid Hough $8,000 for the screen rights and intended it to be a five-reel picture for Mary Miles Minter, who was under contract as an established star at a large salary, whether she made a picture or not. The film's direction was allocated to James Cruze and he saw far more in the story than just another run-of-the-studio "star-series" picture. What he made from what he saw was the first "epic" western film—the first American film "epic" not directed by David Wark Griffith—and he made it with a lavish hand.[48] Virtually the entire film was shot on location in Snake Valley, athwart the Nevada-Utah boundary, where the panoramic shots of the vast distances put the human players and their efforts in perspective and where hundreds of horses and cattle were readily available. A buffalo hunt using genuine bison was a feature of the film.[49]

Colonel Tim McCoy, 1891–1978, began his long career in western films by assembling five hundred Indians of all ages and sexes from various tribes and became virtually a second-unit director because he was the only one who could communicate with them effectively.[50] Dedicated to Theodore Roosevelt, the film opened in the East at New York's Criterion Theater, the heart of The Great White Way, at 8:30 P.M., Friday, March 16, 1923, and ran there with two performances a day for fifty-nine weeks, thus eclipsing the record set by *Birth of a Nation.* Koerner and Hough were part of the throng—Will Hays, Lew Cody, and Betty Blythe among the film notables present—that attended the opening, and Koerner was gratified to note that his costuming of the story characters had been followed closely in the film,[51] especially in the case of "Molly," who was played by Lois Wilson. J. Warren Kerrigan was the hero; Alan Hale a villain of the deepest dye, and Ernest Torrence, formerly a musical-comedy player, gave a memorable portrayal of a frontier scout and guide. The drama critics of New York's leading newspapers—*Times, Herald, Tribune*—gave it rave reviews in next day's editions and followed these with lengthier disquisitions on the film's excellence and epic proportions in the Sunday editions (3/25/1925). The western film was almost moribund before *The Covered Wagon* was released,[52] with but fifty identifiable westerns having been made in the preceding year, and these of the "they went thattaway" variety. In the following year, almost 150 western films were made and this level was maintained into the 1950's, when the erosions of television began to take effect.

Renewed in spirit and in purse by his success, Hough plunged into writing "North of 36," an epic of the first trail herd to be driven from Texas to Abilene, Kansas.[53] On September 25, 1922, he sent Koerner a progress report.

Early in July I was taken sick. About August 1, I went to a hospital for a month. Am now located for the next month at above address and resume work on my novel,[54] which was so terribly delayed by my illness this summer. Inside of a week I shall have the first draft completed and will then begin on the revise. I ought to have the final draft by the end of the year, I hope much earlier. In October, Mr. Lorimer will begin to advertise this novel as one of the next year's serials and although no date has been set we shall all want the book [sic] finished at the first possible moment.

I hope that you are to do the pictures for this book and shall never cease to regret that Appleton used only one of your pictures for The Covered Wagon, *for they are the best I ever had from any artist. I think there is a great field for you in the sincere and actual and faithful depiction of the real West, not the grotesque, motion picture West done by many writers who never fail to disgust me.*

I have not sent you any material for your own studies on this book, because I have not been sure I was going to live to finish it. Before long, I hope to send you a very precious old book of mine printed in 1874.[55] In these very crude wood cuts . . . you will find no hint of the cowboy as we since have come to accept him. By reading some of the curious old pages you will get the feel of the [cattle] industry at that day—and that is what we are going to have in our novel. I will help you with other data. I think you will make a killing.

Three months elapsed, with another siege of illness, before the promised data from Hough arrived, and a sampling of his comments shows his intensity of purpose.

Beware of chaps! *The boy "Cinquo Centavos" is its only cavalier who may wear chaps.*

Only character who can have a steeplecrown Mex hat is "Sanchez." The rest wear just hats— mostly widest brim, crown not too high, no fancy hats.

Pants in boots; not knee high.

Coats—not many. They usually rode in shirt and waistcoat and pants only.

Neckerchiefs—for God's sake, go careful. None of this deep wide neck handkerchief stuff you see in cowboy pictures today always. Those men wore bandanas, not so large, tied around neck—not all *did. Shirt often open at collar. They looked a lot of sloven dressers—no two dressed alike—though black-and-white checked pants were quite common then.*

Study the old *Texas saddle, low, wide horn; two cinches, deep tree; always with taps on stirrups. This is* not *the cow saddle of today.*

Carts, no wagons; *ropes, hide reatas; all wore six shooters, old, long, Army type.* Not fancy.

He supplemented these nuggets two days later with a letter (12/28/1922) to the *Post's* art editor, from what he termed the "Presbyterian Morgue" in Chicago.

Please tell Koerner to look up Civil War uniform. . . . Officers in Civil War wore black, wideawake hat, with cord—I remember seeing that. They may have worn that on the Indian frontier in 1867. The Bureau of Ethnology, Washington, can supply Koerner with Comanche portraits and he should have them. Also he must study the Comanche moccasin and leggins of that date . . .

The conventional Indians, or soldiers or cowboys will not do us at all—we've got a chance to put out the real West, not the false West. The latter I have always fought. . . . In short, there's a whole series of big stunning new *canvases for Koerner in this. No one is doing that now— we've only the foolish fake cowboy pictures of today. There must be no "good enough" in this book for either author or artist. We must have it right, both of us, all of us. Here's a chance to do something for the country. Please pardon my scribble—I can't always get a stenographer.*

On February 20, 1923, he sent Koerner a succinct telegram: "Thirty Six is scheduled. [You]

"North of 36" was written by the author of "The Covered Wagon" as the sequel to that great tale of pioneer days and is equally enthralling and rich in adventure

There are many flashes of wholesome humor as well as tense dramatic action in "North of 36"

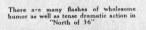

In riding breeches Lois is twice the peach she always has been

First aid on the wilderness "location," a hundred miles from civilization

Adolph Zukor and Jesse L. Lasky
present
An Irvin Willat Production
"NORTH OF 36"
with
Jack Holt, Ernest Torrence, Lois Wilson and Noah Beery
From the famous novel by Emerson Hough
Screen play by James Hamilton

A Paramount Picture

THE CAST

Taisie Lockhart..................Lois Wilson
Dan McMasters...................Jack Holt
Jim Nabours....................Ernest Torrence
Sim Rudabaugh..................Noah Beery
Cinquo Centaves................Stephen Carr
Dell Williams..................David Dunbar
Major McCoyne..................Guy Oliver
Sanchez.......................William Carroll
Colonel Griswold...............Clarence Geldart
Milly.........................Ella Miller
Pattison......................George Irving

Indians, cowboys, bronchos, longhorn cattle, etc.

"If we're both alive—which I doubt—when we get to Abilene, I'll marry you," "Taisie" promises "Dan"

Just before the start of the scene in which thousands of infuriated longhorn cattle stampede across a river

Irvin Willat, producer of "North of 36," and his assistant on "location" during the filming of the cattle stampede scenes

(Below) The clash between "Rudabaugh" (Noah Beery) and "McMasters" (Jack Holt) is one you'll long remember

"Jim Nabours" (Ernest Torrence) senses dirty work afloat

Promotional material on the movie North of 36

The heart of every American will thrill at "North of 36", a spectacular epic photo-play and exciting romance of the olden, golden West of the cattle ranges

Lois Wilson and Ernest Torrence give even better performances than they did in "The Covered Wagon"

Lovely Lois Wilson as "Taisie Lockhart," brave heroine of "North of 36"

Just one company of the army of 3,500 longhorn cattle that play prominent rôles in the picture

(Below) Ernest Torrence, as "Jim Nabours," which reminds you of his "Bill Jackson" in "The Covered Wagon"

Noah Beery has a marvelous part in "Rudabaugh," Texas land-shark and killer

"NORTH OF 36"

WHAT "The Covered Wagon" did for the romantic pioneer days of '49, "North of 36" does on the same sweeping scale for the rollicking, turbulent after-the-war period of the '70's. It is the time when the great republic, having weathered the storm of war, is setting sail for further adventures.

Irvin Willat, producer of "Wanderer of the Wasteland," has caught the glamour and fascination of his remarkable period of our history perfectly in "North of 36," the Hough, who wrote both the novels "North of 36" and "The Covered Wagon." On the same wide-flung plan on which "The Covered Wagon" was produced, Willat has picturized the story of "Taisie Lockhart" (Lois Wilson), girl rancher, who has inherited the greatest herd of cattle in Texas. How "Taisie," to avert poverty, drives her gigantic herd North, aided by her ranch foreman "Jim Nabours" (Ernest Torrence) and a certain handsome mysterious stranger "Dan McMasters" (Jack Holt), is harassed at every turn by the villainous "Rudabaugh" (Noah Beery) and his cohorts, by Indians, stampedes, raging rivers, and all sorts of perils, and finally fights through to victory, is unfolded in a picture that will thrill Americans to the very marrow!

(Right) Handsome Jack Holt never had a better rôle than as hard-fighting "Dan McMasters"

(Below) "North of 36" was filmed on the site of the story, the burning alkali plains, canyons and ranches of Texas

A sweet love story is told amid the stirring adventures

Will have to hustle. I was very successful in New York. Sold 36 [film rights] for thirty thousand. Closed that and five other books and have made a little fortune all at once."[56] Hough did not live to enjoy his "little fortune" that had stemmed from the success of "The Covered Wagon." Neither did he live to see "North of 36" appear in the *Post*, with twenty-four stunning illustrations by Koerner.[57] The story made another film epic, with Lois Wilson again playing the heroine, "Taisie Lockhart," for whom Lillian Koerner had been her husband's model, dyeing her hair red for verisimilitude. Ernest Torrence, and Jack Holt played the male leads and Noah Beery was cast as the villain, a role he played many times.

Hough's death did not affect posthumous six-part serialization of his last work, "The Ship of Souls," which brought Koerner his major assignment from *McCall's*.[58] Its function for many years had been to sell the patterns designed by James McCall, a Scottish journeyman tailor; towards this end, it had begun using fashion plates in chromolithography by 1899. Costing but fifty cents per year for twelve 100-page issues, three years for just $1.25, it climbed steadily to 1,000,000 circulation per month by 1910, with its emphasis still on styles and patterns for women. It had the features usual to such magazines—cooking, care of the complection, needlework—with little fiction among its offerings. Its authors and illustrators were those who made no appearances to speak of in the other magazines, and its editors between 1910–20 had been Alice Manning, Myra G. Reed, and Bessie Beatty.

The New York investment banking firm of White, Weld, & Company purchased *McCall's* in 1913 with the plan of making it a magazine similar to the giants in its field. It did not achieve this status until Harry Payne Burton was installed as editor in 1921 with a mandate to bring famous and popular authors into its pages. This he did, with such as E. Phillips Oppenheim, Robert W. Chambers, Louis Joseph Vance, Arthur Somers Roche, Booth Tarkington, Mary Roberts Rinehart, Ethel M. Dell, Fannie Heaslip Lea, Jeffrey Farnol, and Coningsby Dawson. Gene Stratton Porter contributed a column for several years, and the magazine boasted the equivalent of today's "Dear Abby" in Winona Wilcox, while advertising itself as "The Happy Magazine" for $1.00 per year.

Its 100–132 pages usually contained three serial installments and three or four short stories, plus twenty or more special articles and features, including such titivating titles as "Does a Moment of Revolt Come to Every Married Man?" Neysa McMein's "Types of American Beauties" held a virtual monopoly on its covers,[59] and its inside illustrations were done by well-established artists—James M. Flagg, John La Gatta, Thomas D. Skidmore, H. R. Ballinger, W. T. Benda, Pruett A. Carter, C. E. Chambers, Charles D. Mitchell, and Gerald Leake, while one of Koerner's former pupils, James H. Crank, broke into its pages in the middle-twenties. It did not give its illustrators credit in its table of contents during Koerner's work for it and may never have done so. By 1924, it had reached 2,000,000 copies per month, thus crowding hard on the heels of *Ladies Home Journal*, and running slightly ahead of *Pictorial Review* and *Woman's Home Companion*. It survived the Great Depression with less damage than most of its competitors.

Why Hough's last work appeared in *McCall's* can be explained by an educated guess. Its plot revolved around an aging and widowed fur trader in the well-frozen North whose two daughters lived with him: one legitimate by his long-dead white wife, the other the natural result of a dalliance with an Indian beauty of the vicinity. One of the two males in the plot was a stalwart young man "from below," who was escaping the clutches of an avaricious and heartless wife without benefit of divorce; the other was a "Mountie" who turned out to be a lover of the other man's wife while competing with him for the affections of one or both of the fur trader's daughters. This plot with its adulterous overtones was too much for Lorimer.

It was acceptable to *McCall's*, which blazoned its cover with the bold legend "The Author of *The Covered Wagon* Begins His Last Novel." Inside the cover it said, "Here it is—the swansong of big-hearted Emerson Hough. Only two weeks before his tragic death, Mr. Hough brought the manuscript to *McCall's*. 'This is my best,' he said to the editor. 'Yes, even better than 'The Covered Wagon'! for behind it lies an idea vital to all humanity.'"[60] Koerner's sixteen illustrations spoke eloquently of the snow and ice and numbing cold of the sub-Arctic; they were dramatic with conflict, and they were distinguished

(text continues on page 181)

Lillian and Ruth Ann, 30-inch diameter, oil on canvas, 1914

Lillian, 27 × 20, pastel, 1904

Haying Time, oil on canvas, 35 × 28, for "Miching Mallecho" by Ben Ames Williams, Saturday Evening Post, *4/9/1921*

Haying Time #2, oil on canvas, for "The Balking of Christopher" by Mary E. Wilkins Freeman, Harper's Monthly Magazine, *9/1921*

The Heat of Battle, oil on canvas, 33 × 24, for "Decoration Day" by Eugene Wood, Good Housekeeping, *5/1914 (Collection of Hal du Pont)*

Before the Railroad Came, oil on canvas, 36 × 26, for "Ann Eliza Wetherby's Trip to Town" by Muriel C. Dyar, Harper's Monthly Magazine, *3/1916*

Prairie Sun, oil on canvas, 30 × 32, for "A Corn Belt Pioneer" by Herbert Quick, Saturday Evening Post, *4/15/1916*

For "The Ships Must Sail" by J. P. Marquand, Saturday Evening Post, 11/26/1929 (Collection of W.H.D. Koerner, Jr.)

Fourth of July Street Scene, oil on board, 14 × 16, Gloucester, Massachusetts, 1922, painted for Koerner's own relaxation

Wharf Scene, oil on board, 14 × 16, Gloucester, Massachusetts, 1922, painted for Koerner's own relaxation

The Madonna of the Prairies, oil on canvas, 36 × 30, Saturday Evening Post *cover, 4/1/1922, for opening installment of "The Covered Wagon" by Emerson Hough*

Indian Territory Demand for Tribute, oil on canvas, 30 × 36, for "North of 36" by Emerson Hough, Saturday Evening Post, 5/5/1923 *(Collection of W.H.D. Koerner, Jr.)*

Pitcairn People, oil on canvas, 36 × 33, for "Pitcairn's Island" by Nordhoff and Hall, Saturday Evening Post, *10/13/1934*

The Homesteaders, oil on canvas, 28 × 40, for "Let the Hurricane Roar" by Rose Wilder Lane, Saturday Evening Post, *10/22/1932*

Prairie Storm, oil on canvas, 28 × 36, for "North of 36" by Emerson Hough, Saturday Evening Post, 5/12/1923

The Price of the Old Northwest, oil on canvas, 28 × 40, for "Tomahawk Rights" by Hal G. Evarts,
Saturday Evening Post, 4/6/1929

Primal Woman, oil on canvas, 34 × 34, for "The Music Box" by Arthur Stringer, Saturday Evening Post, *4/17/1937*

Lumberjack Brawl, oil on canvas, 28 × 40, for "Winner Take All" by J. P. Marquand, Saturday Evening Post, *2/3/1934*

Composition for possible Saturday Evening Post *cover*

Composition for possible Saturday Evening Post *cover*

Composition for possible Saturday Evening Post *cover*

Composition for possible Saturday Evening Post *cover*

Main Street, Cooke City, Montana, 1924, oil on canvas, 20 × 24, painted for Koerner's own amusement

Vaqueros, oil on canvas, 28 × 40, for "Ranchero: Matanza" by Stewart Edward White, Saturday Evening Post, *3/12/1932*

Crow Chief and Warriors, oil on canvas, 28 × 40, for "The Shaggy Legion" by Hal G. Evarts, Saturday Evening Post, *11/30/1929*

When a Saddle Is No Obstacle, oil on canvas, 32 × 30, for "Why, Pericles!" by Henry Herbert Knibbs, Saturday Evening Post, *4/1/1933*

On the Alert, oil on board, vignette technique, 30 × 40, for "Wolf Dog" by Hal G. Evarts, Saturday Evening Post, 7/28/1934

Alcalde's Welcome to Taos, oil on canvas, 30 × 40, for "The Long Rifle: Senorita" by Stewart Edward White, Saturday Evening Post, *3/7/1931 (Collection of Robert Rockwell)*

Arapaho Attack, oil on canvas, 28 × 40, for "The Long Rifle: Indian Country" by Steward Edward White, Saturday Evening Post, *3/14/1931*

Comin' Home, oil on canvas, 28 × 40, for "Pasó por Aquí" by Eugene Manlove Rhodes, Saturday Evening Post, *2/27/1926*

Lost Ecstasy, oil on canvas, 28 × 40, for "Lost Ecstasy" by Mary Roberts Rinehart, Saturday Evening Post, 5/28/1927

High Country Rider, oil on canvas, 28 × 40, for "Lost Ecstasy" by Mary Roberts Rinehart, Saturday Evening Post, *4/23/1927*

Pursuit, oil on board, 33 × 50, for "Ranchero: Reata" by Stewart Edward White, Saturday Evening Post, *2/27/1932*

Hard Winter, oil on canvas, 28 × 40, for "Shortgrass" by Hal G. Evarts, Saturday Evening Post, 6/4/1932

as always by the fact that the story's characters became individually realizable as human beings. It was not the last work in the north-woods genre that he would do in the decade left to him.[61]

The last installment of "The Covered Wagon" scarcely had made its appearance when Koerner received the galley proofs of the first installment of another epic-type western from the *Post.* This was "Tumbleweeds" by Hal G. Evarts,[62] a story of the mad rush for land when the Cherokee Strip, a tract of 12,000 square miles in Oklahoma Territory, was thrown open to white settlement. Koerner's fifteen illustrations captured perfectly the drama and high adventure of the rush,[63] and Evarts became another author who asked for Koerner to illustrate his work. This was not always possible, owing to prior commitments on Koerner's part, but he did illustrate most of Evarts' major serials in the *Post* thereafter. These included "Tomahawk Rights," a story of the settling of the Old Northwest; "Fur Brigade," a forerunner of later stories about the fur trade of the early Far West; "Short-grass," which dealt with the final open range, glory days of the Cattle Kingdom; and "The Shaggy Legion," which dealt with the virtual extermination of the buffalo by the commercial hide hunters.

This last named story brought Koerner a letter from its author (1/17/1930) that explains what happened to many of Koerner's paintings after they were returned to him by the publishers:[64]

Many thanks for the picture of the 'Dobe Walls fight.[65] It's a marvellous picture and will have the place of honor in my den right over my desk. I want to take this opportunity to express my admiration for all of your illustrations. They're great. Many people have congratulated me on my good fortune in having you illustrate my stories.

Raoul Walsh, one of the great directors of both silent and talking westerns, transformed "The Shaggy Legion" into a film entitled *The Big Trail.*[66]

Of all the epic westerns that the *Post* published and Koerner illustrated, the one with the greatest sweep and scope was written in a series of forty-three related stories, for which Koerner supplied more than ninety illustrations (that appeared in the *Post* between 7/5/1930 and 3/23/

1935). Collectively these comprised Stewart Edward White's saga of "Andy Burnet" and his long rifle,[67] the veritable "Boone gun," from the Ohio River to California, via the fur trade of the mountain man days, and his successful life as a ranchero thereafter, despite the coming of the *gringos* with the Gold Rush.[68]

A minor ripple from the success of Koerner's work on Hough's last two serials in the *Post* was his first appearance (8/22/1925) in that magazine's "Who's Who and Why" page which made a regular feature in its issues. This page was devoted to "Frivolous Facts" about its authors and illustrators, and Koerner's great contribution to self-puffery was to suggest that people look at his work to know what he was about. Another effect was to bring him the first serial by Earl Derr Biggers that truly featured his calm and logical Chinese detective "Charley Chan."[69] Entitled "The Chinese Parrot," its setting primarily was in the high desert of southeastern California. Most of Koerner's illustrations reflected this western setting, while his depiction of "Charley Chan" bore little resemblance to that image given him by Warner Oland in film which became a part of American folklore.[70] Koerner's work and generosity therewith brought him the following letter (11/27/1926) from the author.

I was quite overwhelmed to receive that illustration of "The Chinese Parrot" which arrived in perfect condition. It was never my intention that you should be put to the trouble and expense of shipping it. I thought that perhaps it was kicking around the Post *office, and I asked [Thomas B.] Costain to send it on if it was.[71] In any case the* Post *should have attended to the shipping. I have no way of knowing how much you paid in express charges . . . but I would be very happy to reimburse you.*

I was abroad at the time the story appeared, otherwise I should surely have written you about the illustrations, which as I told Costain were the best and most satisfying I ever got in the Post. *Usually I expect [sic] them of trying to economize a bit on my illustrations, but in this case they couldn't have picked anybody who could have done a better job. So you see I was feeling grateful towards you even before you sent the illustration.*

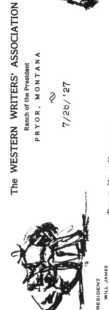

The WESTERN WRITERS' ASSOCIATION
Ranch of the President
PRYOR, MONTANA

7/28/'27

PRESIDENT
WILL JAMES
VICE-PRESIDENT
KARL E. HARRIMAN
SECRETARY
CLEM YORE
DIRECTORS
WALTER NOBLE BURNS
WILLIAM H. HAMBY
KENNETH HARRIS
WILLIAM MACHARG
ROSS SANTEE
OWEN P. WHITE

Dear Mr. Koerner,

The Western Writers' Association, on behalf of the Chicago Association of Commerce, invites you to be our guest at the Third Annual Chicago Rodeo, to be held in Soldier Field, Chicago, August 20th to 28th.

We were so impressed with the earnest desire of The Chicago Association of Commerce to keep alive the ideals and traditions of the real West and to encourage and perpetuate the sports of the cow country that, aside from the many attendant pleasures, we feel it to be almost a duty to be present at the Chicago Rodeo.

We who have seen what they are doing in Chicago urge you to attend this year as a guest. Your expenses from and to your home and while you are in Chicago will be defrayed. Our Association will have charge of the arrangements, so please answer as soon as possible and tell us that you will be there.

The above answers all it says and then some. There'll be many an old timer writers or artists who'll be there to sell to meet. It'll be a great gathering I think, so put'm your store clothes, bring your hat and look and be on hand by August 19th. We'll sure be looking for you and also

Sincerely
WILL JAMES.

W. H. D. KOERNER
1616 RODNEY STREET
WILMINGTON, DELAWARE

November 16th 1916

Dear Miss Mitchell

The enclosed letter from Harper's will explain why I was so long in answering your very appreciative letter. I was mighty glad to get it I assure you, for I have tried hard to express in the pictures just what you feel I get. I enjoy illustrating your stories because they have the human interest in them that so many of the writers fail to get.

I am about to illustrate your Miss Barry story "The Smaller Craft" which is a gem.

Thanking you for your letter I am

Sincerely yours
W. H. D. Koerner

Miss Mary Esther Mitchell
Arlington, Ohio.

Examples of Koerner correspondence: The Koerner letter to Mary Esther Mitchell is one of the few outgoing letters to be found in his papers; he illustrated eleven of Miss Mitchell's New England stories in Harper's between November 1915 and January 1919. The Will James letter concerns an event that occurred when Koerner was on a pack trip in the Big Horn Mountains. (Although the letter is

NEW YORK UNIVERSITY
SCHOOL OF COMMERCE
ACCOUNTS AND FINANCE
WASHINGTON SQUARE EAST, NEW YORK

DEPARTMENT OF MARKETING

October 20 1931

Dear Mr Koerner:

I am sending this in care of the Post, because I am writing at the office & my receipt never would leave me nor your address to write taken, as I think it is. Everytime I see your work I feel as though I had a message & greeting from a friend; but the Clark Co. on this week's Post has galvanized me into telling you so. I have of the remarkable three way — crayon sketches you used to bring back from the West are their to Red that you were doing some of them; for to their maximum effect with a minimum means strikes me as an artistic achievement. I remember Gibson's advice to beginners exercises about their tools: "The paper should be white & the ink black." This is a whole ga cora — a startling example. The fact that the simplest tools are all that a real artist needs, with all for wishes to Eva self & Mrs Koerner. I am

Faithfully yours
Thos. B. Stanley

La Veta, Colo.
Feb - 11 -1932

Mr. W. H. D. Koerner.
℅ The Saturday Evening Post.

Dear Mr. Koerner.

I have no doubt, but that you are pestered by many such as I.

Anyway, I wonder how much you ask for one of those Horse illustrations that is on page 16 of the Post for Feb 13-1932, — the story "Ranchero".

I am a poor man, but if your price is not too high, I would try and scrape up the money to pay for it. I hate to take your time, but would appreciate a word, in case you do dispose of your such illustrations in this manner.

If you do not wish to be bothered you will not reply to this letter, for my feeling will not be hurt. Anyway I'm enclosing a stamped and addressed envelope.

I have admired your illustrations in the Post for a long time, so even tho I cannot secure one, I wish you to know they will always give me pleasure in reproductions.

Respectfully
A. W. Hale

from Will James, the printed artwork on the letter is by Ross Santee.) Thomas B. Stanley had been the art editor of American when Koerner illustrated Zane Grey's work for it. The A. W. Hale letter was one of many fan letters

Perhaps George Cruikshank's watercolors in 1828 of the London performances of an Italian street puppeteer, Giovanni Puccini, made the classic models for all future "Punches." Even so were today's images and habiliments and icons of the West-That-Was fixed by the illustrators of the western story—enhanced by that story's cinema derivatives—in the years that followed "The Covered Wagon." Of all the illustrators who contributed to this fixation, none made a greater contribution than Koerner. In the last fifteen years of his active career, he illustrated more than two hundred western short stories and serial installments with more than five hundred paintings and drawings in many media. He brought to these his creative imagination, his fidelity in characterization, his tremendous color sense, and that vitality which is the one thing needful to all creative work. And to most of them he brought a firsthand knowledge of the West that he had loved at a distance for many years.

1. Henry Nash Smith, *Virgin Land;* Russell Nye, *The Unembarrassed Muse;* James K. Folsom, *The American Western Novel.*

2. "Out-of-Doors" column, 4/1/1911.

3. Emerson Hough, "The West and Certain Literary Discoveries," *Century,* 2/1900, did not like Frederic Remington, among other portrayers and purveyors of the West.

4. Don Russell, *The Lives and Legends of Buffalo Bill* remains the best work on the man and his shows.

5. Benjamin M. Vorpahl, *My Dear Wister . . . ,* vii–xiii, *passim.*

6. *Century* insisted on using the hyphenated word until 1911.

7. The phrase is Tom Lea's.

8. It sold 300,000 copies in its first two years, ran *ad infinitum* on the New York stage and in road companies, was made into a motion picture four times, and became a television serial in the 1960s.

9. "Virgins, Villains, and Varmints," *Huntington Library Quarterly,* 8/1953.

10. The Klondike-Yukon gold rush in 1898 and after gave his story an added impetus, as well as spawning the poems of Robert W. Service.

11. Frank Spearman and Cy Warman were foremost in the railroad story in this period.

12. About 5 per cent of its articles concerned the West, which was a higher proportion than found among the other magazines.

13. *Wolfville* was published in 1897. See also *Wolfville Yarns of Alfred Henry Lewis* by Rolfe and John Humphries.

14. Harry Leon Wilson's "Ma" Pettengill stories in the 1920s and Kennett Harris's "Sam Stegg" stories in the 1930s carried on this genre in attenuated form as did the "Buffalo Bend" stories of Michael Foster in *Saturday Evening Post* even later.

15. Edward Bulfin's *gaucho* stories in *Everybody's* had the *caballero* mystique.

16. Marie Manning's *Judith of the Plains* (Harper and Bros., 1903) was "A romance . . . throbbing with the life and vigor of the West as it is, and abounding with robust humor."

17. Harte's "Colonel Starbottle," a "Perry Mason" of the Mother Lode, still was appearing in *Harper's* in 1901–1902.

18. Dunton's horses had their heads in the stars and Wyeth's horses had hooves the size of wash tubs.

19. *Collier's* was using Remington's works to which they held copyright as late as 1934.

20. A reproduction of this advertisement, suitable for framing, was obtained in 1973 for thirty-five cents and one "purchase seal" from a package of Cream of Wheat.

21. *Munsey's,* 1/1906, in "The Stage" department, mentions two other western plays, "Sunday" and "The Heir to the Hoorah," for which other data were not accumulated.

22. *The Wyeths,* 207. Another stage play of this year was "The Ranger" for which other data are lacking.

23. Emerson Hough, "Wild West Faking," *Collier's,* 12/19/1908, is fairly virulent on the subject, including the sins of Mr. Remington.

24. Motion pictures eroded the stage play, even as television eroded the motion picture western.

25. This writer's *A Bar Cross Man* is a biography of Rhodes; no major study of Pattullo exists.

26. *Saturday Evening Post,* 11/30–12/28/1912, with illustrations by Harvey T. Dunn. Its latest reprinting in book form is by the University of Oklahoma Press, 1975, under the title *Bransford in Arcadia: or, the Little Eohippus.* Rhodes died at La Jolla, California, in 1934, Dunn's illustrations for the serial appearance emphasized the romance rather than the action.

27. J. Evetts Haley, *Life on the Texas Range,* 22–27, has information concerning Pattullo's wanderings with Smith. A collection of Pattullo's short stories appeared as *Untamed* (1911) and he wrote one novel of the West, *The Sheriff of Badger Hole.*

28. Orrin A. Engen, *Writer of the Plains . . . B. M. Bower,* presents a capsule sketch of B. M. Bower-Sinclair-Cowan's life and has a useful bibliography. Both Bertrand William Sinclair, "The Fiddleback Kid," and Bud Cowan wrote about the West in their own right, Sinclair being the most prolific.

29. His son, Louis B. Seltzer became the distinguished editor of the Cleveland *Press* and his *son,* Chester, became "Amado Jesus Muro" of recent Chicano literature fame.

30. Ivory's career as an illustrator diminished markedly after 1915.

31. Lawrence Clark Powell, *Southwest Classics,* 211.

32. Grey's seventy-eight books are estimated to have sold thirty million copies at home and four million abroad.

33. Of his forty-one major magazine serials, fourteen appeared in *Country Gentleman,* eight in *Ladies Home*

Journal, four each in *Collier's* and *McCall's*, and three in *American*.

34. Its villainous Mormons benefitted from the polygamy propaganda that had attended the seating of Reed Smoot as Senator from Utah, and the claustrophobia that the ending of the frontier induced also helped its success.

35. *McClure's*, 12/1902, "The American Man on Horseback," illustrated by photographs.

36. *Saturday Evening Post*, 6/2/1917.

37. Irving Harlow Hart, *Publisher's Weekly*, 2/21/1925, 619–22.

38. Robert Easton, *Max Brand: The Big "Westerner,"* covers Faust's life in detail.

39. Harold W. Ryan to W.H.H., 1/15/1974.

40. *Liberty* is said to have lured P. G. Wodehouse away from *Saturday Evening Post* by offering him $1,000 more per short story than the $2,500 that was his standard fee from Lorimer. This may explain why the *Post* raised F. Scott Fitzgerald to $3,500.

41. Mody C. Boatright, *Southwest Review*, Summer, 1951.

42. Hough had been in and around White Oaks, New Mexico in 1883–84. Lorimer sent him West in 1904 to gather materials for magazine articles, and Hough had been a steady visitor to the West thereafter.

43. Frederick S. Bigelow, *A Short History of the Saturday Evening Post*, 23; Tebbel, 75–76.

44. Maud Stick had been Koerner's model for this painting.

45. Hough to Arthur McKeogh, 2/4/1922.

46. McKeogh to Koerner, 2/7/1922.

47. Stewart was one of several younger artists who began illustrating western stories in the early 1920s.

48. William A. Johnston, "The Box Office Verdict," *Saturday Evening Post*, 11/10/1923; Mody C. Boatright, "The Formula in Cowboy Fiction and Drama," *Western Folklore*, April, 1969, 136–37. Such western "epic" films as *The Iron Horse* and *Pony Express* followed immediately.

49. This hunt was staged on Antelope Island in Great Salt Lake.

50. George E. Virgines, "Colonel Tim McCoy—Westerner All-Star," 81–82. McCoy took an Indian contingent to London for the film's opening there. Also, Tim McCoy to W.H.H., 8/12/1975, and *Tim McCoy Remembers the West*.

51. Koerner, *Narrative*, which also states that the usherettes were costumed exactly as had been "Molly" in the magazine serial. It has not been feasible to confirm this statement.

52. Owing to a surfeit of "Broncho Billy" Anderson two-reelers and their imitators. The more honest films of William S. Hart also had run their course by this time, while Tom Mix and his horse were just emerging as a staple of the trade.

53. Hutchinson, *A Bar Cross Man*, 187–206, deals with the literary grass fire Hough's novel ignited.

54. 630 Franklin Street, Denver, Colorado.

55. Joseph McCoy, *Historic Sketches of the Cattle Trade of the West and Southwest*. The image of the cowboy in this work was that of a creature without redeeming qualities, evil and degenerate.

56. It is believed that Hough's total receipts from these sales exceeded $80,000.

57. McCracken, 140, says that Frank Tenney Johnson's income in 1923 of $8,003.29 was his highest to date; Koerner's income in this year exceeded $12,000.

58. Mott, *Magazines*, IV, 580–88.

59. They also sold Colgate's Ribbon Dental Cream on its back cover.

60. This "vital" idea appears to have been that true love and pure would conquer. Marconi's "wireless" made the plot's *deus ex machina*.

61. Arthur Stringer's "The Music Box" was conspicuous among these.

62. It made William S. Hart's farewell to films. Evarts deserves to be better known today than he is, not alone for his historical westerns but for his numerous conservation writings as well.

63. One of these was sold to an admirer in Texas for an unknown sum.

64. Others were given away by his editors, Lorimer chief among them, with Koerner's consent.

65. Now in the possession of Hal G. Evarts, Jr., La Jolla, California.

66. And cast a sidelight on motion picture history thereby: Evarts was hired to do the screenplay, something he had not done before, and Walsh drove him wild by writing and re-writing the script as they went along. In the end about all that was left from "The Shaggy Legion" was the villain, who kept chewing on a stick of willow and spitting out the masticated pieces. Walsh wanted a brand new face to play the male lead and finally spotted a studio laborer who had played football in college and who fit Walsh's idea of fresh and rugged masculinity. When the picture was released, it was such a box office "turkey" that it brought John Wayne's screen career to a virtual halt, until John Ford made him the Ringo Kid in the first film version of *Stagecoach* a decade later. This account is based upon an interview with Mr. Evarts, 3/14/1970.

67. Koerner had illustrated another African serial by White, "Back of Beyond," in 1927.

68. A knowledgeable *aficionado* of western films, one who had no prior acquaintance with Koerner's work, saw his painting from this series of four *vaqueros* riding *paso sobre* through the California night and exclaimed "Why that's *High Noon!* Those are the four men riding into town to meet Jack Palance when he gets off the train to kill Gary Cooper." Inasmuch as *High Noon* was not made until many years after Koerner's death, this reaction speaks eloquently of the enduring legacy of his work. Mary Ormsby to W.H.H., March, 1970, during filming of a pilot film for educational television that used this and other illustrations by Koerner among its visual effects.

69. His first appearance was in "The House Without a Key," *Saturday Evening Post*, 1/24–3/7/1925, with illustrations by William Liepse, a newcomer to that magazine.

70. Nye, 250. When Biggers died, "Charley Chan" was succeeded by J. P. Marquand's Oriental detective "Mr. Moto."

71. Costain was an important factor in the *Post's* ability to recruit and develop and retain popular authors in this period.

Chapter IX
MONTANA AND "LOST ECSTASY"

In the context of the nation's post-war years, when the number of automobiles almost trebled to 23,000,000, Koerner's first visit to the trans-Missouri West was a part of the increased emphasis to "See America First," itself a part of the inward-homeward turning that so affected the western story in fiction and on film. The increased post-war popularity of the dude ranch and its proliferation also reflects this feeling and the western railroads added impetus by their advertising: the Burlington (CB&Q) was the "National Park Line"; the Northern Pacific was the "Yellowstone Park Line"; the Great Northern used a Mountain Goat as its insignia and extolled the wonders of Glacier National Park, while the Santa Fe (AT&SF) added the "Indian Detour" to its well-publicized and permanent attraction of the Grand Canyon.[1] In terms of Koerner's personal life, the fact that he took himself and family for a four-month vacation adds credence to the belief that he was no more money-hungry than he was addicted to self-puffery.[2]

The initial impulse for this trip came during the winter of 1923–24 when the Koerner and Stick families attended a lecture at the Asbury Park Fishing Club by Walter Shaw, who praised what he called "the eighth wonder of the world." This was Grasshopper Glacier in which down eons of time the bodies of millions of grasshoppers had been entombed by downdraft winds during their seasonal migrations across the Beartooth Plateau and Range. The glacier was located just outside the extreme northeastern corner of Yellowstone Park in the Goose Neck Lake country. Access to this natural marvel was from the semi-ghost town of Cooke City, Montana, where Walter Shaw maintained a string of pack and riding animals that could negotiate the twelve long and almost vertical miles to the glacier.[3] Frank Stick added impetus to impulse by the fact that he had visited the northern Rockies some years before in search of fishing and wildlife materials and was eager to re-visit them. Additionally, a cousin of his had gone to Montana to teach school and there had found her husband and her future as a rancher's wife. She had urged Stick and his family to visit them and extended this invitation to the Koerners.

The two families made their plans and gathered their equipment, for this was to be a round-trip tour of some five thousand miles by automobile, in a day when "tourist cabins" were few and far between beyond the Missouri. In late May, after the two men had delivered the last of their scheduled illustrations and after Lillian had "bobbed" her hair for the journey, the two families, with two children each, set forth.[4] Their initial destination was Don Howard's ranch on Sarpy Creek, south of Hysham, Montana. Lillian later recalled the manner of their going:

On the running boards of our seven-passenger, open Buick, we carried a Brooks Umbrella Tent for four people; four "blowbeds" [air mattresses] that were pumped up by a device attached to the engine which saved William from blowing his lungs out, and on the front bumper we carried a two-burner gasoline stove, that was filled each night from our gas tank to cook dinner and breakfast. Pots and pans and bedding were wrapped in tarpaulins on the running boards

The way West, 1924. From left to right: Maud Stick, Ruth Ann Koerner, Bill, Jr., Charlotte Stick, David Stick, Frank Stick, and Lillian Koerner. Bill took the picture, which explains his absence from it

and back bumper. A set of three cans went on one running board: one gallon of oil, one of water, one of gasoline for emergency use. Gas stations were far apart. Inside the car, made out of khaki cloth and fastened to the back of the front seat, was a car-wide deep bag with separate places for clothing. The four side pockets on the doors and the dashboard were filled. We never hunted where to find what, for the children saw to it that everything was perfectly packed where it belonged. Canvas bags filled with water hung on the outside door handles and we carried canteens inside the car for drinking water, which we had to use carefully, not wasting a drop. We had agreed before we left home that neither car would travel over thirty-five miles per hour; that we would never look at the other family when discipline was in progress, and that we would never interfere or argue with each other — almost![5]

They camped their way to Chicago where Koerner's sister gave them a taste of luxury. Taking her butler, a former railroad dining-car chef, they spent several days at her lakeside cottage in Wisconsin. The butler did all the cooking and arose early to catch and cook fish for their breakfast. Fortified by this experience, they took to the road again:

Up through Minnesota with its dairy herds and innumerable beautiful lakes. Then came Dakota's strange Bad Lands, with now and then wranglers taking a bunch of horses through or cowboys a herd of cattle, but mostly just the eerie alkali bluffs that took on queer forms and shapes, that intensified the heat and dust and the dread of what the next turn might bring. Then into wheat fields with grain elevators waiting along the railroad tracks; more sandy dirt roads with deep ruts and high centers, and over in the fields were sod houses with rounded half-dome dirt-and-grass roofs and sunken low entrances. We made our camp [one night] near a sod house with its dirt floor which fascinated the children. The door was half open and they looked in at its sparse furnishings. No one was home. The mosquitos were there though and

Main Street, Cooke City, 1924

unrelenting. This, too, was a dry camp! William was keenly alive to all the new experiences; the day-by-day travel in our cars; the stopping at dusk along the road or some place near by; pitching our tents; undoing our duffle; getting our dinner, and to bed.[6]

They saw a wildfire raging through the ripe wheat beside the road and Koerner coaxed the Buick up to more than thirty-five miles per hour to shove the danger zone behind them. Then came Miles City, Montana, with the annual rodeo in progress and the town alive with real cowboys, horses, genuine Indians, and excitement. They pushed on towards their destination the next day.

The Howards met the two-car caravan and guided it to their ranch on Sarpy Creek, where a spare house was placed at the disposal of the visitors. Don Howard ran a working cattle ranch but Koerner had too much common sense to play at being a cowboy. He sketched and photo-

graphed as he rode and, most of all, he absorbed what he saw and sensed—cattle and horses and riders and ranchers' wives, buttes and coulees and rimrocks, the earth colors and the light of the semi-arid western country that were so different from what he had known before save through his research, the thunderheads that boiled up out of the west almost every afternoon, often trailing filmy veils of moisture that seldom reached the thirsty land below. Sarpy Creek was not too alkaline for livestock use, but the only cooking and drinking water came from blocks of ice that Howard cut each winter and stored away well insulated in sawdust against the sere and summer months. The days spent there provided a legacy of contrast when they encountered the Alpine and sub-Alpine zones that had cradled Cooke City in splendid isolation for all of its existence.

They reached this final destination via Gardiner, Montana, the northern gateway to Yellowstone Park. The dusty forerunner of today's

Grand Loop Highway took them to Camp Roose-velt, where they turned left up Lamar River to its confluence with Soda Butte Creek. There Walter Shaw met them and there they sampled the sulphurous waters from bubbling springs that gave the creek its name. Then it was up the creek on a one-car road through Icebox Canyon to Cooke City, nestled in a narrow valley at more than 7,000 feet.[7]

Spring was heralded in Cooke City by the smell of frying onions when the first pack strings broke their way through the surrounding drifts. It awakened briefly each fleeting summer when its resident knot of tenacious miners was augmented by hardy fishermen, visitors to Grass-hopper Glacier, and riders who moved cattle up for summer grazing from lower ranges in Montana and adjoining Wyoming. For these brief weeks, Cooke City became a microcosm of Old West and New, and the human beings who gave this commingling its reality were not wasted on Koerner's acute sense of characterization.

The two families found unused log cabins that could be occupied by dispossessing their resident rodents, and the Koerners moved into a two-story affair with a kitchen and living room downstairs and a loft that was reached by a ladder. The loft became their sleeping quarters, and the aging and weather-warped shingles let the frequent summer showers through without diminution. The living room became Koerner's studio and boasted the only green, roll-down window shades in town. Its logs were chinked with strips of oil cloth that broke some of the force of the winds that washed down the valley each morning and surged up it each afternoon. A mountain stream for water supply brawled beside the cabin, a family of bluebirds had a nest under the eaves until early August, and marmots whistled from the rocky slopes that led up and up to Daisy Pass that loomed outside the kitchen door.

Once when I entered the kitchen from the studio, the only milk cow in Cooke City was half-way through the back door, calmly chewing her cud. At night we could hear the soft-toned bells of horses that gathered around our cabin kicking and squealing or just sniffing and snorting at the playthings left outside by our children. In August a heavy snowstorn swept through in a straight line, leaving our part of Cooke City, Daisy Pass, Mt. Baldy and Old Silver [another

Koerner sketching in the West

peak] in a blanket of white, while the General Store and Mt. Republic were in sunlight. Then at twilight, the sky softened to purple and gold and then glowed in full moonlight. It was inspiring!

William was continually sketching and painting. His oils and paint box with a stretched canvas inside, his colored crayons and water colors, and his book in which he drew his compositions for his illustrations were always with him, ready for notes or scenes or people who wanted to pose. An old army scout who remembered Jim Bridger had his log cabin lined with William's illustrations, especially those from "The Covered Wagon." He followed William wherever he went and swore his approval.[8]

Leaving the children with the Sticks, the Koerners made the first of their visits to Grasshopper Glacier; two days for the upward trip with an overnight stop for humans and horses at Shaw's sub-camp on Goose Neck Lake and just one day

Koerner en route to Grasshopper Glacier, 1925

coming down. Their delight was such that a bevy of the *Saturday Evening Post's* editorial staff made the trip with them in 1925; when they took the children along in 1926, a newsreel camera crew recorded the junket for movie-going audiences throughout the land.[9] Perhaps even more useful to Koerner's store of impressions was his first experience with Cooke City's annual Fish Fry, for which the nearby lakes and streams supplied ample fare.

This event was Cooke City's Fourth of July and Christmas and Easter and *Oktoberfest* and class reunion compressed into one hectic twenty-four-hour day. Miners came out of their holes, prospectors descended from the higher country of their seekings, cowboys came from near and far—Pete Schultz riding the high country all the way from Red Lodge, Montana—park rangers and dudes were in attendance, sheepherders were tolerated, and joy was unconfined.[10]

Koerner and Stick renewed the signs on the one-time A(ss). O(ut). Saloon and the (U. B. Damned) Dance Hall after the fashion of their original legends, and spruced up the town in general. Walter Shaw purchased a new pair of white chaps for the occasion, and each artist took a leg and went to work with such good effect that Shaw became the only ambulatory art gallery in Cooke City's history.[11] A whole steer was barbecued on a slowly turning spit, more trout were fried than seemed possible even to Frank Stick, ice cream was turned out from hand-cranked freezers, and barrels of beer reposed under a sign that proclaimed "Soft Drinks." There were horse races and other contests and Lillian was dumfounded to see her two children pelting by bareback in a mule race organized by Bill Rowland. "He was a handsome, wild kind of fellow; daredevil cowboy enough but out of hand completely when he got into liquor. Best

At Grasshopper Glacier, 1925, left to right: Johnny Eacret, one of Walter Shaw's dude wranglers; Bess Riddell, Art Editor of Saturday Evening Post; *and Koerner*

Koerner completed his first post-vacation illustrations early in October and his experiences during that vacation were put to good use in his major illustrative assignment from *Pictorial Review.*[13]

Founded in 1899 as a house organ for Albert McDowell's System of Dressmaking and Tailor-

Walter Shaw and his illustrated chaps, showing the leg done by Koerner; the wineglass shown was Shaw's brand

and worst of all, he liked William and posed for him by the hour." A parlor organ was imported to augment the local fiddler for the dancing that night and Lillian and Maud Stick were kept busy dancing with all and sun-dried, including their husbands, at ten cents a couple until the two families retired, long before the organist and fiddler called it quits from too much exertion and too many free beers.

Next morning the human wreckage from the festivities was plainly visible around Cooke City and the Stick and Koerner children were overjoyed when Charlotte Stick found a crumpled five-dollar bill beneath the overturned soft drink counter. The thin film of ice that began to appear each morning in the water bucket beside the wash basin on the bench outside the Koerners' kitchen door grew thicker with each passing day and it was time to retrace the long, long miles to Interlaken and the waiting studio and school.[12]

Northern Pacific Railway photograph of Grasshopper Glacier, 1925: the dark strata are the bodies of 'hoppers (more properly locusts) which crumbled quickly on exposure to the air

ing, *Pictorial Review* had grown steadily and without fanfare from 150,000 copies per month in 1906 to 2,100,000 copies in 1925, despite increasing its price from $1.00 per year to fifteen cents per copy, $1.50 per year. Its editor was Arthur T. Vance, who presided over a magazine that reached 140 pages of text, each 10 3/4 × 13 3/4 inches, in the spring and fall advertising peaks and dropped to an 80-page average in summer and winter doldrums. His usual format was one serial installment, with occasionally a complete novel, by such as Gertrude Atherton, Donn Byrne, Edith Wharton, Henry K. Webster, and Frances Marion; five short stories by the likes of Elsie Singmaster, Agnes Laut, Beatrice Blackmar, Theodore Dreiser, and Konrad Bercovici—with an occasional "modern" western by William Dudley Pelley or a sea story by Wilbur Daniel Steele—and six feature articles, using

a series of them on Mark Twain and another series on Lincoln by Carl Sandburg, together with such as "How to Stay Married" by George Gibbs, "Woman's Place Is at the Polls" by Ida C. Clarke, and "Do Women Really Like One Another" by Zona Gale.

Earl Christy did virtually all of its covers in this period, and its inside pages were brightened by color, including "stand alone" plates depicting each of the Ten Commandments by M. Leone Bracker and seascapes by Gordon Grant. Two of the Koerner-Stick students, James E. Allen and James H. Crank, appeared in its pages in the 1920s, as did such other newcomers to major magazine illustration as Hubert Mathieu, John R. Flanagan, Hibberd V. B. Kline, and Nancy Fay. Among the established illustrators who enlivened its wares were John La Gatta, Remington Schuyler, Arthur G. Dove,[14] Arthur D. Fuller, Charles D. Mitchell, George Wright, Harold M. Brett, and Charles Livingston Bull. Koerner had illustrated several stories for Vance's magazine, before a story contest staged jointly by *Pictorial Review*, the publishing house of Dodd, Mead & Co., and Famous Players–Lasky brought him the winning manuscript, which made one of the great magazine successes of its decade.

The contest rules called for book-length fiction that had originality, strong character development, a "feeling" that was different, modern, and alive, with no artificial ordering of events to make a suitable culmination at the end. The treatment must be realistic, with everywhere the thrill of actuality, life as it was really lived by men and women, unidealized and untinted.[15] More than 1,100 manuscripts were submitted in the $13,500 contest and the first prize went to Martha Ostenso—a Norwegian-born, South Dakota-reared poet and author—for "Wild Geese." It was she who asked that Koerner do the illustrations for the first and most famous of her ten novels.

Set in a small Scandanavian farming community in the Dakota grain belt, the story concerned a family dominated by its husband and father "Caleb Gare," whom Ostenso saw as "a spiritual counterpart of the land, as harsh, as demanding, as tyrannical as the very soil from which he draws his existence." That she depicted him in prose as she had envisioned him is borne out by the comments of a scholar of the West and its manifestations, "the fearful product of pioneering days . . . a merciless archfiend with an insatiable lust for land and power and with no grand desires to redeem it."[16] Only his daughter Judith dared to withstand her father's brutality and Ostenso created her with murder in her heart and the will to attempt it with an axe. The "wild geese" in the story epitomized her loneliness and her yearning for the freedom their gabbling, honking passages drove home with a poignancy almost beyond enduring.[17] There was a suitable love interest, not overdone, and the domineering father got his just deserts by means of a raging wildfire in his ripe and standing grain; just such a demonic event as Koerner had driven through on his way West the summer before.

He combined his deep sense of rural life and his feeling for it with the newer experiences with prairies and plains and the different light

to compose fifteen illustrations that many said were his best work to date.[18]

He labored with "Wild Geese." He tried too hard to excell himself and, if the truth were told, to please the author who had asked for him. He knew that reserve had crept in, inadequacy, self-criticism, and hatred toward the tyrant father, a brutal man. He did not let himself go, let his deep impulses be unrestrained, when he did that he just drew and painted and lived the picture.

When the Koerners headed West in May, 1925, for another four-month sojourn, they went by train and the children were left behind with Grandmother Lusk. After a stopover in Chicago, while Lillian visited friends in Battle Creek and Bill visited his mother in Clinton, they resumed their journey with the only daughter of old friends from their Chicago courtship days in tow. Attractive, lissome, convent-educated, and an accomplished equestrienne in the English manner, she was almost seventeen and filled with the eagerness, willfulness, and emotional intensity of metabolic ferment. Her recently widowed mother never forgave Koerner for her daughter's ill-starred mésalliance with a dude-wrangling cowboy that this summer brought her. Lillian always believed that this short-lived and pregnancy-shadowed romance was the inspiration for the most famous fiction story about the dude west ever written, which made one of the longest serials ever to appear in the *Saturday Evening Post*. This was Mary Roberts Rinehart's "Lost Ecstasy," for which she sought and received illustrations by Koerner.[19]

The "1-2-3-4 Koerners" paid their last visit to Cooke City's environs in 1926. The next summer's vacation was to be different.

After the children had recovered from whooping cough and before Koerner had delivered the last of twenty-one illustrations for "Lost Ecstasy," he received a letter from its author after the first installment had appeared:[20]

I am delighted with the illustrations for "Lost Ecstasy." It seems to me that you have caught the feeling of the West and of the principal characters extraordinarily well. It is so seldom that an author finds the illustrations conform to the characters he had in mind that I want you

Lon Carpenter catching-up horses for the day's work, while Bill, Jr. and Ruth Ann watch from the safety of the corral fence

Bill, Jr. and his mount on the pack trip in 1927

to know how very happy I am about these. I have heard very fine comments elsewhere also, and [because] I know that illustrating, like writing, is a good deal like shooting in the dark, I want you to know how well your splendid work is being received. The horses were simply wonderful, true ranch types, full of action. When I saw them I wondered how you could do them without models to hand. You must have worked very hard and very fast, too, for I was incredibly late in getting the manuscript to the Post. *I am one of those writers who can keep on polishing and reworking indefinitely, and I daresay I would still have the manuscript had not Lorimer rushed me so.*

With my grateful thanks and deep appreciation, please believe me . . .

When the last illustration for "Lost Ecstasy" was finished, the family began a three-month tour by rail of a West that was new to them all.

En route to California via the Santa Fe Railway, they detrained in Las Vegas, New Mexico on June 20, to take an early version of the railroad's later expanded "Indian Detour" side trips through the "Land of Enchantment" and the Painted Desert. Their escort was Erna Fergusson, who just had sold her own Koshare Tours to a railroad subsidiary. Descendant of a family long active in New Mexico's political and legal affairs, sister of the well-known novelist Harvey Fergusson, and a distinguished writer and lecturer in her own right, she showed her charges Puye and Taos and Santa Fe before seeing them aboard the westbound Limited in Albuquerque on June 26. She procured Navajo rugs and other artifacts for Koerner's growing collection of authentic western materials, and remained Lillian's friend long after her husband's death.

The light and the colorings, the scenes and the people of the Southwest he visited, including four days at the Grand Canyon, left impressions on Koerner that he put to good use in illustrating stories by Oliver LaFarge and others. But his first love in the West remained the northern ranges and he returned to them on this trip, after five weeks spent touring California's scenic wonders by automobile. A pack trip into the Big Horn Mountains along the Montana-Wyoming boundary was followed by a visit to Mary Roberts Rinehart and her family at the Eaton Ranch near Sheridan, Wyoming.[21] She intro-

duced him to Joe DeYong, who spent his summers working at the ranch while studying to be an artist with the West as his forte. In 1962, DeYong recalled that meeting in a letter to Koerner's daughter.

I still have several pages of technical advice and encouragement that were written by your father at that time. Due to my being totally deaf, it was necessary that he write *them to me. I was Charlie Russell's pupil during the last ten years of his life but moved to Santa Barbara the fall he died, where I lived for the next ten years. As a result, I am fairly familiar with the artists of your father's time and I clearly recall the masterful illustrations that appeared above the signature of W.H.D. Koerner.*

The pack trip into the Big Horn Mountains was conducted by Phillip Torrey Spear and in him, twenty years his junior, Koerner found a lifelong friend.[22] Phil's father, Willis M. Spear, was semi-retired when Koerner first met him, in Sheridan, Wyoming, a state he had served as state senator for fourteen years, and confined his active interests to his camp for hunters, fishermen, and just plain dudes in the Big Horn Mountains at an elevation of 8,500 feet. Its main building was the locally famous "Spear-O Wigwam,"[23] a tipi made of logs that boasted a concrete floor forty-feet in diameter, which the Koerners visited in the course of their pack trip.

In the middle-twenties, Phil Spear and his wife Jessie, a onetime Montana schoolteacher from Pennsylvania, ran 1,000 or more head of cattle in the P-Spear and Rafter-Cross-Bar brands twenty-six miles west of Lodge Grass, Montana, which was in the valley of the Little (Big) Horn River and the heart of the Crow Reservation.[24] Among the horse-buffalo tribes of the Plains, the Crow were notable in many ways. They were blessed with an earthy humor and possessed remarkable expertise in lifting enemy horses and scalps; their women were noted for their skills in tanning and dressing hides into garments and artifacts that were the envy of friends and enemies alike; the trailing bonnet of eagle feathers probably originated with the Crow; and they were valiant and seasoned fighting men from the constant necessity of resisting the expansion-minded Blackfoot and Sioux. This may explain,

Rambler
W. H D
Koerner

Koerner crayon sketches made at Spear Ranch

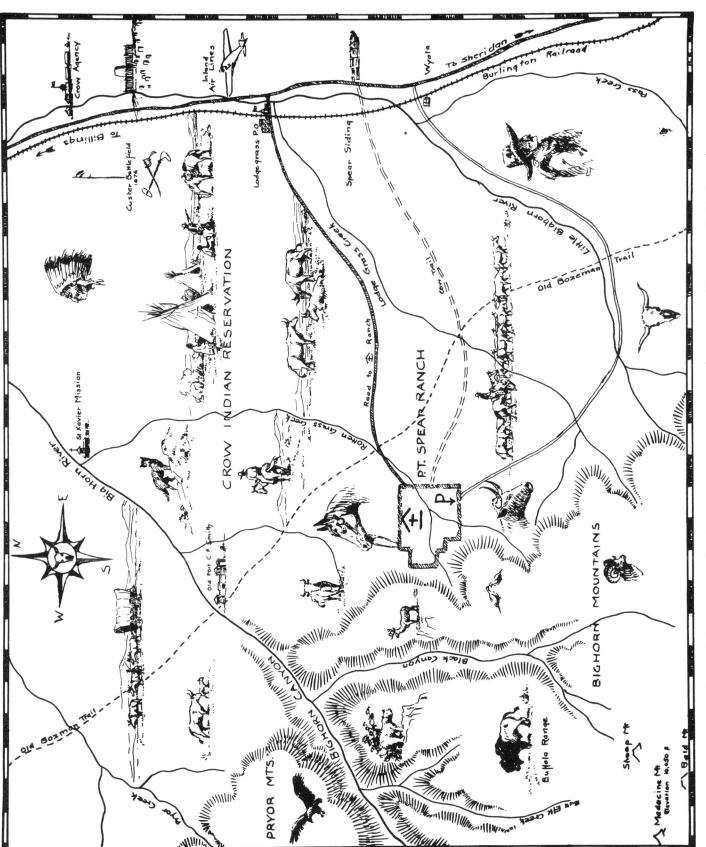

Map of the Phil Spear Ranch where Koerner spent several summers (Courtesy P. T. Spear)

Preparing to lead the parade through town for the annual Crow Rodeo at Lodge Grass, Montana, these Crow standard bearers posed for Koerner's camera, 1928

in part, their generally friendly attitude towards the American trappers and traders of the fur-trade days. Plenty Coups, perhaps their most notable leader in war and peace, had fought with General George C. Crook in 1876 against Crazy Horse and the Sioux. He was in his early eighties when Koerner first visited his people, but a magnificent figure of a man nonetheless. Alive, too, was White-Man-Runs-Him, who had made one of Custer's six Crow scouts before the debacle in the valley of the Little Horn, just forty miles north and east of Lodge Grass.

The P-Spear log ranch buildings initially had very limited accommodations for dudes and were set amidst ruggedly beautiful surroundings, where the plains rolled up into the mountain foothills, located on the east bank of Rotten Grass Creek. This was one of several streams

that gave northward drainage into the Bighorn River between the headwaters of the Little Horn and Black Canyon Creek flowing west into the Bighorn from the eastern slopes of the Big Horn Mountains. Towering red rimrocks loomed over the ranch to north and east, while Rattlesnake Butte at 4,300 feet dominated the western rim across the creek. Spear's range rolled upwards south and west onto the lower slopes of the Big Horns and had been traversed by the "bloody Bozeman" Trail on its way toward ill-starred Fort C. F. Smith before Red Cloud and the Sioux had closed it in the 1860s. Land along Rotten Grass Creek was plowed and planted to hay each year against the needs of winter feeding, and a cold and constant, spring-fed brook flowed through the ranch premises. Its water was bucketed into a fifty-gallon oil drum perched atop a

The Spear outfit moves camp: the chuck wagon shown here had been in continuous use by the Spear family since 1893

Phil Spear at the chuck wagon, with Bill, Jr. observing from beyond the end-gate

corral near the dipping chute to provide a summer-season shower bath for hardy visitors—often the prospective bather had to fill it before using; if it already had been filled, the summer sun often made it too hot for comfort, and it had a habit of running dry before the bather had finished rinsing off the soap.

This modern touch was offset by Phil Spear's functional chuck wagon, which dated from 1893 and had been his father's. And a living link with the trail herds surging up from Texas to stock the northern ranges was present in the person of Charlie Binion, who had ridden for Phil's father and whom Phil kept on his own payroll until the year he died. Born near Uvalde, Texas, before the Mexican War broke out, Binion had gone on "cow hunts" before he reached his teens. Thereafter, he had ridden for cattle in Texas and Old Mexico, before coming up the trail to the northern ranges that held his life thereafter. Now in his eighties, he remained what he long had been, one of the best ropers who ever sat a horse. In one working afternoon during his earlier years, he never missed a throw in bringing more than four hundred head to the brand-

Koerner's camera portrait of Charlie Binion, 1927

Charlie Binion doing what he did best—bringing another calf to the branding fire

ing fires, "He never used his arm, but with a twist of the wrist the loop shot out as if from the muzzle of a gun."[25]

His newspaper obituary summed up the breed he represented well: "Like most of his type, he spent his money freely as he went along and had made no provision for old age. When he died, Binion had little else except his saddle and bridle, a trunk of old clothes, and a host of friends, especially among the old cattlemen and cowboys. They took charge of the funeral rites which were held by the Catholic priest at Hardin [Montana]."[26]

For the rest of his productive years, Koerner visited Phil Spear as often as he could for as long as he could.[27] Whether his visits were made in late spring or summer or in early fall, he seemed to bring rain with him, which led Phil to give him the nickname of Rain-in-the-Face. One summer, the kids came with him, leaving Lillian at home, but the rest of his visits were made alone. Their story best is told by excerpts from the surviving correspondence among and between the families.[28] Koerner to "My Dear" (6/20/1928):

Well, we sure had a big day Monday. Had breakfast at 4 A.M., then rode seven miles over the mountains to a cattle Round-up of the Moss outfit. They were rounding up the cows and calves to take to summer pasture and Phil had a bunch of his own in there he wanted to get. Were there all day and had lunch (they call it dinner) at the wagon. Got home at 7 P.M.. We were in the saddle all day and sure were tired when we got home. Billy was so tired he says those darn cows drive him Ku-Ku, but Ruth Ann was full of pep when we got home.[29] There were about 20 cowboys there and about 1,500 to 2,000 head of cattle. Bawling so you couldn't hear yourself think. Rained off and on all day.

Took Billy out shooting today. Put up a target 100 feet away and told him I would give him a nickel every time he hit the bulls eye and he earned a dollar. Hope weather clears up so I can make or try to make a watercolor, but so far grey and rainy. Sure was glad to get your letters yesterday. Saw a Sheridan paper, I think it was Monday's, and saw General Motors didn't do a thing, 170 something. I hope we still are O.K.

Lon [Carpenter] is not riding lately as he has

a cracked rib. Horse threw him. Charlie Binion has been laid up for a couple of days with a cold but is feeling better again. He is quite a remarkable old man to ride and herd cattle. He is O.K. as long as he doesn't get any liquor. Billy tried to milk and calf sucking at the same time. I guess he got about a half-glass full. Well, must close and look up children as it is getting our bed time. Good night dear heart, I love you.

Jessie Spear to Lillian (6/16/1928):

William was awfully tired and worn out when he got here, and it took him a couple of days to let down and relax but he looks and feels better every day and I believe his stay out here will do him a world of good, for from what he has been telling us, he has been going at high tension.

We all miss you so, it just doesn't seem right without you here. Your Big Bill gets pretty homesick for you. I can understand now how dependent he is upon you, and that you are his booster and the real mainstay for him. He has taken a world of pictures.

Phil Spear to "Dear Bill" (5/21/1929):

Rec'd your letter and the pictures sometime ago but have delayed answering 'til spring arrived so I could figure something about the work. Snowed every day until about ten days ago and the grass now is just getting good. I will make a short trip across Black Canyon to see how the feed is and can then plan when to take my cows over. Figure on taking 500 cows across Black Canyon and then brand the calves after we get there.[30] It will take about four days to drive them across there and a couple days to brand and scatter them.

The Dana outfit will be dipping at Spear Siding all thru June. They will dip about 10,000 cattle, putting them thru the dip twice about 10 days apart, and will then trail about 3,000 cows and calves across to his lease on the west side of the Big Horn River. This would be a mighty good chance to see some large herds of cattle handled.

If you would want to try June in this country again, I'll see the weather man and try and fix it up for better weather than we had last year.

Phil Spear, left, and Koerner above Rottengrass Creek at the rimrocks that gave the ranch its name; the spot is one Koerner used for sketching

Then you can pack up the entire *family this time and come out and we'll throw an outfit together and follow the Dana herds around as long as you wish and make the trip across Black Canyon with ours. Bring a movie camera and thousands of films and we'll do the thing right.*

A few minutes after we got the April American and looked over your pictures everyone at once remarked that the cow that was in one of them was out in the corral. Have had several come along who when looking thru my cattle say, "Why that cow there was in the American."[31] *Love from us to all the Koerners.*

Phil to Bill (5/5/1930):

We have had the best spring here that I have seen in fifteen years and everything is a good month ahead. Horses are fat and grass is big everywhere. Unless we get a lot of cold rainy weather now, I will start my spring work about the 15th. of this month and try and finish the most of it by June 1st. In this way I'll get my

cattle on the mountains before the "heel flies" bother us much, tho it will cause some extra work of branding later in the summer.

Do you remember the "buckskin" that wouldn't stand still for you to draw him? I had him broken last fall and rode him myself all winter and he is making one of the best horses I've ever ridden. Have had fifteen young horses broken since you were here and nearly every one is a real horse.

Jessie is raising a lot of chickens this year and has about 40 that will be large enough to fry in June and a lot more coming on for later use. Love to all the family.

Phil to Bill (8/5/1930):

We are gathering and branding a lot of calves now but do not expect to ship 'til sometime in September. We are building a corral on the bench above the Ranch now and will start training several young horses for contests. Calf roping mostly. Ruth Ann's pony will be one to get the training and I believe he will make a real one.

Now make a special effort to come out the latter part of September. You have seen this country spring and summer, now try it in the fall. We are needing rain bad! [*Koerner arrived in October and experienced "rain, hail, fog, snow and what else could I want?"*]

Phil to Bill (12/15/1930):

Rec'd the pictures some time ago and we all sure think they're great. The Boys [riders] *are more proud of theirs than they would be of a new saddle and Binion puts in most of his time admiring himself. We pack the pictures with us everywhere to show the Natives what a real photographer can do. The roads are dusty and people are beginning to worry about a dryer season next than last. So if you get a wire saying "Rain in the face come on!" you'll know we are in distress.*

Phil to Bill (3/10/1932):

Your telegram received yesterday afternoon, and last night I mailed you a book which was written at the time of or shortly after the Johnson County War [*1892*].[32] *This book is altogether one-sided but thought you would possibly get some information that would help.*

The settlers first started coming into Wyoming during the early '80s, and usually settled on the main river bottoms and the creeks running out of the different mountain ranges. The Buffalo [Wyoming] *country was settled up faster than any other portion except along the Union Pacific. There were very few fences away from the creeks until long after the Johnson County War, except on large state and railroad land leases. The range was held by stockmen, by buying water holes either from settlers or having cow-punchers homestead, or by buying soldier and railroad script and applying it on the different springs and other water. It was not until the 640-acre homestead law became effective after 1910 that the entire open range was fenced up.*

There were very few chaps in use among the cowpunchers in those days, and what there were, were of the double-barrel variety, tight laced along the seam usually with leather fringe. Most of the cow-punchers wore a pair of pants and a pair of overhauls [sic] *over them. The*

overhauls turned up with a wide cuff at the bottom, allowing 4 to 6 inches of the pants to show below. The saddles were double-rig, some of them with rolled cantle, very long trees and narrow fork.

Jessie was just telling me that you were wanting some Cheyenne Indian costumes and she has already located a lay-out and will forward them to you within a short time. Surely want to thank you and Lillian for the wonderful care and help you gave Jessie while she was back there.[33]

Koerner to "Dear 1, 2, 3" (6/19/1933):

Well, here I am. It doesn't seem possible. Last Monday I was trying to paint a Western cover and here I am where the real stuff is. My rain medicine has not worked so far, only two or three drops yesterday. So I'll have to get out old Medicine Bag and rub it some more for they sure need rain here for crops and the heel flies are so bad they can't work cattle in daytime. Phil and all the different reps left at 3 A.M. this morning, rounded up some cattle and were back by 8 A.M.[34] *I didn't go as I want to take it easy the first few days, until I get used to the altitude and get more rested up. I rode about a little this morning and met them coming in with cattle. Got some good pictures of riders and horses and of course cattle and some branding pictures. We go with chuck wagon in 3 or 4 days. Bell just rang for dinner so got to skip. It is now about 3:15 P.M. Love, Daddy.*

Jessie to Lillian (6/19/1933):

Yesterday was a nice quiet day here. William rested in his cabin all afternoon and towards evening the "Reps" from the different ranches near here started coming in with their strings of horses and their beds, so there was lots of activity around the corrals. We had fourteen men for supper and they will be here three or four days. Dinner is at ten this morning and supper at four this afternoon. I have a splendid cook and her daughter here doing the work, so I am relieved of lots of responsibility. I plan to ride with them this afternoon. The reason for all this early business and odd times for the meals, they have to work with the cattle during the cool of the day, early morning and late in the evening.

Dear Ruth Ann   Monday Eve.
Just a
note. Here are a few Indians
while listening to the
Radio. Just got another
dandy bunch of Indian
stuff and costumes
from out west. This
time Cheyanane
Indian stuff. Got a
belt you would like it is
like this. 🔲 big silver—

Love
Daddy.

A letter with watercolor sketches to Ruth Ann at boarding school in Saint Louis, 1932

Koerner to "My Dears" (6/29/1933):

Phil is going in town sometime in a day or so and I'll just drop you a note to let you know I'm getting along fine. I lay down every afternoon for a couple of hours to rest and it does me a world of good. Weather here has been a humdinger, hot and no rain at all.

Yesterday I got some fine photos of Crow Indians butchering a cow and jerking the meat. Was glad to get them and got some real close ups. I think so far I have gotten some very fine photos. Lots of fine new horse photos. Don't send any letters after you get this one, as I am going to start for home the 5th., right after the Wyola Rodeo,[35] as I feel I've gotten all I wanted to get and am anxious to get home. Would start sooner but I do want to see the Rodeo. Glad Billy didn't come as I am afraid he would have had a rather slow time of it. I miss my 1, 2, 3. Love, Daddy. Hope I'll have some work from the Post when I get home.

Jessie to "Dear William" (3/17/1934):

We have been so happy to see your pictures appearing more regularly and more often, and know by the looks of them that you must be feeling like your good old self, for they have all been great, and especially the [Post] cover with the horse and Indian.[36] Phil and I got a big kick out of the March 10th. [Post] number, with old "Lucky" and "Tommy Hawk" looking out of the picture so spry and smart.[37] We also noticed that the Post is lots "fatter" this time, which surely is a good omen that times are really picking up in the East and perhaps will be reflected out here before long. We hope so.

Phil is out in the corral handling some broncs. You ought to be here today, you might get some fast ones [photographs]. The boys have a dandy blue-grey saddle horse broken already and they are catching and tieing-up a bay now. They have also broken out three work horses and have been plowing with them already. Lots of excitement around here lately. Tell Lillian to please write to me.

Phil to "Dear Lillian and Bill" (4/25/1935):

You don't know how much I appreciate all the things you've done for Jessie, not only on

this trip but the one three years ago as well. Lillian, you do Jessie more good in a few days than anything I know of.

We are having a wonderful Spring here. Snow or rain every few days and the country is slowly getting soaked up so that it may get to be a good country again. If Bill was here with us I know it would rain all summer, even tho his "medicine" was mighty poor two years ago. Cow prices are booming, grass is growing, lots of white-face calves in the pasture and Jessie seems to be getting lots of dudes for July and August, so maybe Rimrocks is coming into its own finally.[38]

My wish is that the 1234 Koerners would come out for the month of June, not as dudes but as our guests. We could all have such a good time together. We would roundup and brand and if Bill's medicine works, we could sit by the new fireplace and tell stories. Please try and do this, not only because we would enjoy it so but also that we might return in a small way the many kindnesses you have shown Jessie.

Jessie Spear and her sister-in-law, Mrs. Robert T. (Jessamine Spear) Johnson, had found genuine Northern Cheyenne costumes for Koerner's collection. It was increased most measureably thereafter with Crow artifacts acquired through the agency of Ben Pease, one of Phil Spears' many friends among the Crow and their kindred.[39] Pease was half-Crow by blood and his letters to Koerner, 1930–32, contained far more than just the items and their prices that he offered for Koerner's purchase.[40] Many of these nuggets were in response to questions Koerner asked.

I received your letter with much pleasure but was too busy running around during the holidays [Christmas, 1930]. I am sending you a list of some of the stuff with prices. Indian cap'ot [capote] made of old [Hudson's Bay] blanket 8.00; Old beaded squaw saddle, 25.00; Indian chief shirt buckskin, 65.00; War bonnet—all eagle feathers, 20.00; red blanket leggings—beaded Crow, 12.00; Old tom-tom, 8.00; Old squaw dress, all buckskin, little beading on neck and sleeves, many fringes, 50.00; Indian tomahawk, 3.00; War bustle, 10.00; Old Indian war saddle covered with buffalo raw hide with stirrups, 20.00; Old Indian hunting coat, beaded, 20.00; Parflash [parfleche] trunks in pairs, 10.00; Crow quirt, 1.50; I could not locate my war saddle. Can find it later.[41]

. . . .

When the Indians went on a war path or on a horse stealing trip, they wore their most sacred medicine equipment. No, they did not use the eagle tail bonnet—so-called war bonnet—in time of war as in a battle. The war bonnet is used in time of making peace treaties and counsels, dances and other ceremonials.[42] *I want to say that when the Crows were getting ready to go on war path, they used all kinds of different medicines in head dresses, such as owl skin with the feathers on. Also swan skin with other medicine ornaments. They also painted their faces in streaks and also they would paint their horse with streaks and prints of hands on the hips of horses they ride. The swan skin and other medicine ornaments were tied on and medicine war shirt made of buffalo or buckskin. The old war shirt is a funny looking shirt. What I mean the real old medicine war shirt. It is about the size of a vest and slip over the head very short and covered with holes about the size of a nickle or a quarter. When the Crows go on a war path as a rule they don't braid their hair. They comb it back and tie it together in back.*

. . . .

Now I can tell you more about how the Indians in olden days went up on top of the mountain and fast and sleep 3 to 4 days, not a single thing to eat or drink, asking for wealth and being great medicine man. It comes to them in a dream, when they fast and sleep all alone they go to the highest mountain tops in the Big Horns. Clouds Peak was one of the most sacred places for them to go upon. Also Sheep Mountain. Many of the Indians do not believe in thunder and lightening. They do believe it is a big bird flying in the clouds roaring about and the fire coming from its wings. Some of the old Indians said they would see this great bird in the clouds beneath them as they would be high on a peak. No rain with sun shine. But it was those that fast[ed] that [had] seen the great bird [that] the white man calls the Thunder Bird. My wife's father went on top of Sheep Mountain and fasted.

. . . .

The camp and chiefs would call upon medicine man to go on top of mountain when it was hard times and no buffalo near and they were hungry. He would go on top of the mountain or

Koerner's sketch for a Saturday Evening Post *cover, inspired by Ben Pease's letter about the "buffalo caller"; Lorimer rejected the idea because of the skull*

a high hill and holds buffalo skull up toward the sun and prayers [prays] and sings to the sun or to the buffalo. He does it four times. Each time he holds the buffalo head up, he sings and prayers. Some times it is to the buffalo and sometimes it's to the sun. He also has a little buffalo manure in his medicine sack with him which is dry and fine. He would sprinkle small amounts of this about the snow near him where he stands. If he don't want more than 40 or 50 buffalos, he would scatter just a little upon the snow and if they wanted a 100 or more, he would then scatter more in proportion. And the next day or morning, all the men gets out on a buffalo hunt. They find the buffalo near and they are all sure of much meat. This was never known to fail in the olden days for there was lots of buffalo. This was only in winter time when it was storming and the snow is deep and they are out of

These drawings by Ben Pease accompanied his letter to Koerner explaining how the Crows marked their horses: the drawings, like the old ledger drawings of Indian artists, are on lined tablet paper

Koerner was ever pursuing details for accuracy in his art, as this drawing and letter attest on the evolution of the western saddle: this drawing of the type of saddle used on the Great Plains before the introduction of the swell-fork saddle in the 1890s came to Koerner from Paul Sturges, who was in the saddle and harness business with his father in Sioux City, Iowa. The letter (12/21/1935) describes the saddle and how Sturges found it:

"Yesterday I ran across one of these old Macheers in a harness shop at Schleswig, Iowa. The harness man is holding it for sale at $16.00. Outside of the rigging and girths, it is in a good state of preservation. It has that old-style bullhide covering, which is almost like amber, on the tree, and the horn is as big around as a saucer. The fork spreads slightly under the horn and then drops straight down, as the old straight-fork saddle did. The whole front of the saddle, outside the wraps around the horn, is of this clear amber bullhide. The cantle covering is skirting [leather] with a bullhide trim and the fenders and tie leathers are skirting. There is some carving but not near as much as in the modern saddles. It is carving, too—not stamping. You can see the cut in the leather on the fenders.

"J. D. Padgitt of Padgitt Brothers, Dallas, Texas, who started a saddle shop in Bryan, Texas in 1869, had this to say about early saddles: 'During the 1860s, Mexican saddle trees with broad, slanting flat horns were used. The cantle was low, the fork flat, with a diamond front rig, and half-seat. In 1870, Texas saddle trees came into use, the trees being made in New Braunfels, Mesquites, and Huntsville, Tex-

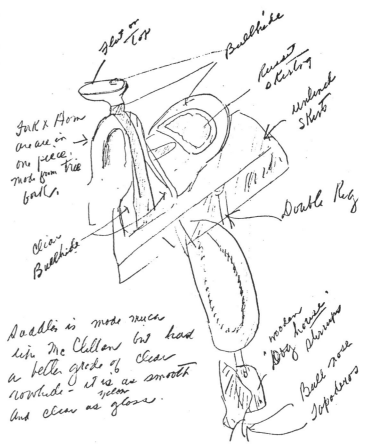

as. They followed the style of the original Mexican tree, sometimes called Macheer. Around 1880, the Texas saddle makers adopted the rigid or "corus" tree, the seat of the saddle being covered with one piece of leather. Later on, saddles changed to high horn, high cantle, and long seat.'"

meat and suffering hungry and can't move camp. Then they have to call upon the medicine man.

. . . .

I received your letter this morning with your check for $15 and now I take much pleasure in answering. Glad you like the Xmas gift. I will say on the sun sign painted on the horse, the Crow did not use this sign. It might be of some other tribe. But they use hand print. Also, sign of lightening. And sometimes round 2 circles. One on the back and one in front. Sometimes a circle around both eyes. The round circles on the back and in front on the breast of a horse indicates it make the owner lucky in owning the best and fastest horses for running and hunting buffalo. Sometimes they paint their horse with a highwater mark indicating he had swam the Missouri River in war time with the horse. In the old days, the horse was the Indian's treasure. He did not need any money. He always used his best horses to hunt buffalo, pack meat, move camp, go on war path, and horses were given away as most valuable present. Horses were used instead of money by the Indians.

. . . .

I want to say [when] a buck is courting a maiden playing on his love flute [he] wears an elk robe. Sometimes has a picture of a male & female elk facing each other on the back of his robe. He also should be painted and dressed, leggins and moccasins with hair done up nicely and put on all kinds of Indian perfume. The love flute is a medicine because it is something be-

yond words in courtship. As he is playing his flute, he swings himself and goes through all kinds of motions. He swings his whistle [flute] as he plays it so that the wind would catch it and make the tune soft or louder and sometimes drowned out by the motion and the wind for a moment and comes back again. I have seen them many times when I was a boy and more so has my wife. They would be swinging and twisting around and bending backward. They never hold the flute still when they are playing it. As a rule, he is always on foot unless he has a fellow companion and they are going to another camp a few miles away. Then they would ride double over to the other camp, probably tie their horse in the brush or somewhere out of sight and then approach the camp on foot with their flutes. They probably know where the prettiest maids are camped and sort of split up when approaching the camp. I have seen them swinging and twisting about in the moonlight and in the dark. I always liked to hear them play. I would lay awake and listen. Sometimes you barely can hear it and sometimes it sounds so lonesome you can just about cry.

Koerner composed three covers for the *Saturday Evening Post* that used his Indian collection and lore with striking effect. The last of these was completed September 3, 1935, but did not appear until the issue of April 4, 1936.[43] This caused the Spears to rejoice that he was active again and painting like his old self. He was not.

---

1. The Southern Pacific and Union Pacific roads added to this advertising spate.

2. In the eight months he painted commercially this year, he produced sixty-one illustrations for a gross return of $11,250.

3. Shaw and his family also operated a hotel and restaurant at Gardiner, Montana, the northern gateway to Yellowstone Park.

4. Charlotte Stick was fourteen, David Stick four, Ruth Ann Koerner ten, and Bill, Jr., nine.

5. Koerner, *Narrative.* Condensed and edited by W. H.H. Their average road speed was 18–25 m.p.h. W.H.D. Koerner, Jr. to W.H.H., 7/21/1975.

6. *Ibid.*

7. Cooke City was described as "a rough old hole" in the 1880s, when silver ore assaying $100 to the ton had brought it 135 log cabins, 13 saloons, hotels, general stores, livery stables, and a meat market, to say nothing of other

appurtenances of a hope-filled mining camp that soon would rival the famous Comstock Lode in Nevada or Leadville, Colorado. Its inaccessibility, coupled with a relatively small tonnage of high-grade ore, had aborted this first boom, and its population of rainbow chasers had pursued the dream elsewhere. This same lack of transportation, plus ore bodies that came in pockets, had doomed the revivification efforts of the Western Smelter and Power Co. in 1906. Thereafter Cooke City had slumbered down its years, as the dirt roofs of log cabins often became flower beds before they collapsed under the inexorable burdens of successive winters. Virginia Hansen and Al Funderbunk, *The Fabulous Past of Cooke City*, 11. It was named for Jay Cooke, Jr. in hope that he would bring a railroad to end its isolation.

8. The West was filled with old-timers who "remembered" Bridger, Wild Bill Hickok, Billy the Kid, and others.

9. A photograph of Koerner at the glacier appeared in

Our Boys, the Curtis house organ for their 35,000 "boy salesmen," 2/1926. The grasshoppers crumbled on exposure to the air.

10. "I packed into Cooke City [c. 1933] from the Wyoming side for the annual fish fry. I was a kid trailing along with four ranch cowboys who intended to ride some bucking horses at the celebration in Cooke City. Three of them got too much fire water and were arrested and handcuffed to a wagon wheel before the bronc riding got started. They spent three months in jail in Livingston, Montana, and I remember the stirrups flopping on their empty saddles as the one remaining adult and I trailed their horses along with the pack outfit back to the Wyoming ranch country." Chuck King to Ruth Koerner Oliver, 6/25/1974.

11. A painting of Cooke City by Koerner still was extant there as late as 1941, Koerner Papers. Shaw's chaps today are owned by his daughter in Great Falls, Montana.

12. They came out of Cooke City by Cooke Pass, shown as Colter Pass today, and Cody, Wyoming, thence across South Dakota to Chicago and home.

13. Mott, *Magazines*, III, 490; IV, 363–93, 770; V, 136.

14. Dove returned to illustration from his pursuit of pure art during World War I.

15. Based upon Fred Lewis Pattee, *The New American Literature, 1890–1930*, 465.

16. F. L. Paxson, *When the West Is Gone*, 98.

17. In one of Tom Mix's films during this period, the cry of geese overhead caused his eyes to blaze with a yellow, feral light to the great excitement of his youthful audience.

18. Vance requested one of the paintings for himself and Koerner graciously complied. Dodd, Mead used two of the paintings for the dust wrapper and frontispiece of the book version and used these same paintings, matted onto board 20-3/4 × 27 inches, for window displays by book stores. Lillian Koerner is authority for the statement that colored reproductions suitable for framing of Koerner's "Wild Geese" illustrations were made for commercial sale. (*Saturday Evening Post* would not permit such use of illustrations done for it.) If so, his records do not reveal which they were or remuneration therefor.

Vance, who had paid Koerner $4,000 for his illustrations, wrote him (1/13/1926) that the John Anderson Publishing Co. of Chicago had purchased second serial rights to "Wild Geese" and that he believed Koerner could get at least $750 for permitting their use of his illustrations. If he did, no evidence of remuneration appears in his records. These outward signs of his success were hard won, as his widow remembered it.

19. It ranked sixth on the best-seller list for 1927, which was topped by Sinclair Lewis's *Elmer Gantry*. Whether Mrs. Rinehart found her model for "Lost Ecstasy" in the marital accident that marred the Koerners' summer is beside the point that such happenstances were commonplace when feminine East met cowboy West amidst dude-ranch surroundings. And certainly Mrs. Rinehart had had ample opportunity to observe this chemistry in action ever since she began her acquaintance with the West by taking a summer trip through Glacier Park with Howard Eaton in 1915, which produced a book, *Through Glacier Park*, the following year. Her visits West thereafter had been annual ones and produced a steady stream of both factual and fictional treatments of her experiences; at least twenty-two

such being of record between 4/1/1916–10/2/1926 in *Saturday Evening Post, Collier's*, and *Cosmopolitan*.

20. Rinehart's and Koerner's names were the only ones on this issue's cover, which was by Norman Rockwell. The serial's appearance coincided with that year's dude season.

21. Three brothers—Howard, Willis, and Alden Eaton—are regarded as the founding fathers of the dude ranch. In 1904 they moved from the Custer Trail Ranch in the Little Missouri country of the Dakotas to Wolf Creek, west of Sheridan, and expanded tourist operations.

22. He found, too, a family that symbolized the changes on the northern ranges, from the days of unfenced grass to the cattle-*cum*-dude rancher of the post-war years. Phil was one of the four children of Willis M. Spear, who had come to Montana from Missouri in 1875 as a boy of thirteen. His father's start in the cow business began in earnest with the terrible winter—the Big Die—of 1886–87, when he forehandedly had 250 tons of alfalfa hay and could buy racks-of-bones at $1.00 a head or less to consume it. At the peak of his operations, 1900–10, the Spear Cattle Company grazed 50,000 head along the Powder River and its tributaries in Montana and Wyoming, and he made annual trips to Texas and Chihuahua to buy trainloads of steers to fatten on the blue-stem grass with which the range abounded.

That Willis Spear was not alone in raising hay before the "Big Die" struck is borne out in Leland E. Stuart's unpublished dissertation "Men and Cattle on the Northern Plains, 1860–1887."

Whether "cow" or "cattle" is the proper appellation has been known to produce heated argument among semanticists. "Cow" is the word used by the people who raise "cattle."

23. Spear-O had been his brand; it was carried on by his younger son, Willis B. "Junior" Spear.

24. A United Press International dispatch, 12/12/1974, related that the Crow would receive the "highest coal royalties paid in America today" by a contract approved by the Secretary of Interior between the Crow and Westmoreland Resources. The mining was to be done on lands in the Sarpy Creek drainage.

25. William Curry Holden, *The Espuela Land and Cattle Company*, 136–37. Other data on Binion were derived from newspaper clippings in the Koerner Papers.

26. Among the younger riders at Phil Spear's ranch was Frank Goe, who had a peculiarity all his own. He carried his saddle gun under his left leg, stock back and the lever-action up. Koerner so depicted him and his rifle in an illustration and received numerous letters of criticism for the way in which the rifle was carried in the saddle scabbard. As with discussions of art versus illustration, the different ways in which different men handle their horse hardware is a field that should be barred to dogmatists.

27. Koerner and his family were the "very first" dudes at the Spears's ranch, later dubbed Rimrocks Ranch, as their dude business increased.

28. Koerner Papers.

29. She went to a dance that night with Phil and Jessie and did not return until six the next morning, because "the roads were muddy."

30. One descent into Black Canyon was known as "The Toboggan" among the timorous, who dismounted and held

onto their horse's tail to make the passage.

31. An installment of Zane Grey's "Drift Fence."

32. A. S. Mercer, *The Banditti of the Plains.* Koerner was starting on the illustrations for Evarts's "Shortgrass" at this time.

33. She combined a visit home with soliciting dudes for next summer's business.

34. "Reps" means riders from other outfits, whose cattle ranged with the Spears's, that joined the Spear work to cut out and trail home their respective outfit's stock. There still were not too many fences on the lands Spear and others leased from the Crow.

35. Wyola was a wide spot on the railroad, south of Lodge Grass.

36. Bill, Jr. was the model for the young warrior on this *Post* cover, 10/24/1931.

37. Struthers Burt, "Dude Wrangler," one of a projected series on the breed.

38. By this time, the Spears could accommodate ten dudes at a time. Many of their visitors were members of the *Post's* staff, who had heard Koerner talk about its appeal. Herbert Johnson once stayed a month with them.

39. Diligent digging by Michael Harrison makes it probable that Pease was a descendant of Fellows D. Pease, a trader along the Yellowstone in latter 1860s, and agent for the Crow 1871–73.

40. Koerner Papers, excerpted and arranged for continuity by W.H.H.

41. Koerner bought all of this first lot except the parfleche trunks. Mable Morrow, *Indian Rawhide, An American Folk Art,* is excellent on the manufacture and decoration of these "trunks," which were folding wallets of some size in actuality.

42. "Of course the regalia was not worn on raids and war trails. It was snugly packed against a time of need, but when the party met a hostile force and there was no chance for a surprise attack or ambush, time was taken out to put the war paint on both horse and rider, and the war bonnets were donned." Francis D. Haines to W.H.H., 9/1/1972.

43. There is no explanation in the Koerner Papers to explain the lag between completion and appearance of this painting.

Chapter X
"WHEN EARTH'S LAST PICTURE IS PAINTED"

Nineteen twenty-nine was a fateful year for "Big Bill" Koerner and the world in which he had lived and worked so long. One harbinger of change was the advertisement by a still embryonic airline that "The giant, tri-motor Coast-to-Coast Limited is ready for its cool 31½ hour sky-journey to the Pacific Coast" from Newark, New Jersey, airport, with only two changes of planes en route. On a more personal level, this was the last year that he did illustrations for any magazine other than *Saturday Evening Post*. This narrowed field of assignments was his own choice, albeit it removed him from the ken of other editors who needed illustrations for their wares.

He knew the *kind* of stories he *wanted* to illustrate and the *Post* sent them to him in such quantity that he appeared in more than half of its issues for four of the next six years, averaging sixty-three illustrations in each of these four years. His daughter remembers him telling the art editor in Philadelphia that he could not accept a new story and meet the required deadline because he already had all that he could handle in the way that he wanted to handle it. Wesley Stout, now Lorimer's editorial right hand, wrote a long article, "Yes, We Read the Story" (6/25/1932), that was devoted to the artists who illustrated for the *Post* and their methods. It contained photographs of Koerner, J. C. Leyendecker, and Arthur William Brown, with a drawing by each of them, and Koerner's photograph appeared again (7/7/1934) above the notation that his illustrations would appear in Evart's new serial, "Wolf Dog," which would begin "Next Week."

Most of his work in these years was for the post–"Covered Wagon" western stories discussed in Chapter VIII. What Lorimer had begun as an antidote to post–World War I disillusionment with his country and its meaning, he continued as an anodyne to the traumatic effects of the Great Depression.[1] Many of Koerner's illustrations in these years enhanced Steward Edward White's continuing episodes in the saga of "Andy Burnet" and they brought him a letter (4/20/1932) from the author:

I've had it on the tip of my typewriter for over a year to tell you how much I like your end of the work we have been doing together. It has been a constant delight to me, as I know it has been to the many readers of the Post. *Not only in its wonderful artistic merit; but also in its sense of movement and life, and in its accuracy of detail. These latest color reproductions [4/9/1932] are the final touch that makes me feel how remiss I have been in not expressing my pleasure before. . . . My hat is off: I clap heem the hand; I also thank heem from the heart, for while nothing is more delightful to an author [than] to be well illustrated, nothing is more depressing than the opposite. Sir: I salute you!*

Story versatility long had been one of Koerner's strengths and his work for a non-western action serial, brought him this undated letter from its author:

When Mrs. [Ben Ames] Williams and I were in Philadelphia a week or so ago, we admired your illustrations for "The Son of Anak," and now Mr. Costain writes that you're going to be kind enough to send us one of those canvasses. This is just to express my appreciation in advance.

Your portrait of Judd, in "Miching Mallecho,"[2] hangs before me just now, and I have always been reminded by the way the lantern light in that picture is broken into segments of [Robert Louis] Stevenson's description of the firelight in [his] "A Lodging for the Night." We particularly liked the "Son of Anak" canvas which showed the girl standing in the farmhouse door, light streaming across her figure, with her father and the two youngsters outside. I know no man who handles the combination of darkness and lamplight as well as you. The portrait of the smaller boy seemed to me particularly to express those qualities which I tried to suggest in his character.

The partnership which has so often been formed between you and me has always seemed to be a happy one. Your illustrations have a way of adding immeasurably to the effect of a story, even in my eyes. And I don't recall that I ever remarked in one of them those minor divergences from the text into which many illustrators are so apt to fall. I hope we may some day supplement this partnership by a personal acquaintance.[3]

J. P. Marquand began his real rise to literary eminence, as well as popular acceptance, with his first story in the *Post* for which he received $500, its standard fee to first-time authors, and for which Koerner received $300 for its two illustrations. After 1929, Koerner illustrated many short stories by Marquand, at least seven of which were sea stories, and one north-woods lumberjack serial. He also illustrated three exotic-adventure serials by C. E. Scoggins;[4] one was laid in the islands of the Caribbean, one in Mexico during its post-Porfirio Díaz turbulence, and one on the pampas of Argentina. He completed this display of versatility by illustrating two of the famous serials by Nordhoff and Hall, "Pitcairn's Island" and "The Hurricane," that followed in the wake of the book success of *Mutiny on the Bounty*.

March 17, 1929, marked the thirtieth anniversary of Lorimer's assumption of the *Post's* editorship and it was marked by an appropriate gift devised by the magazine's staff. On his desk awaiting his arrival that morning was a book of more than two hundred individual letters, each carefully mounted on parchment, from President Herbert Hoover, former Presidents Coolidge and Taft, Admiral Richard E. (South Pole) Byrd, and other luminaries and dignitaries beyond enumeration. Also, and more perhaps to the *Post's* point, were letters from artists and authors, Koerner among them,[5] who had contributed to what Lorimer had made it—one of the most significant and successful magazines in the history of American publishing and letters; a magazine that brought good art to millions of readers weekly. He had done this by making it and keeping it what he advertised it to be, "It is first, last and all the time an American periodical, convinced of the essential integrity of American principles and intentions."[6]

In 1929, it generated advertising revenues exceeding $84,000,000, and paid dividends of nearly $20,000,000. Its net paid circulation exceeded 3,000,000 copies weekly of a nickel magazine that averaged more than two hundred pages per issue, each containing two to three serial installments, eight to ten short stories, and the same number of articles. On December 7, 1929, it published the largest issue in its history, 270 pages, that consumed 3,000 tons of paper, sixty tons of ink, and three weeks of press time to produce.[7] By the time of the famous "Bank Holiday" in 1933, it was down to eighty pages and less per issue—one serial installment, four to five short stories, and the same number of articles.[8] Its circulation had not dropped substantially—where else during the Depression could so much wholesome, family entertainment and information be procured for five cents—but its advertising revenues had declined precipitously. Lorimer was confident that he could meet its bills when the banks re-opened and he did. One means to this end was a request that the *Post's* artists and authors take a substantial reduction in their remuneration, although the fee at which artists had begun work for a serial story would continue at that level until its completion. Another reduction in these fees brought the total decrease to 25 per cent by the end of 1933.[9]

Perhaps more important to both artists and authors was the reduction in the number of fiction and fact pieces used per *Post* issue, a pattern common throughout the magazine field in this time of travail, as well as the *Post's* increased use of photographs with feature articles. The competition for markets increased dramatically and among the authors who had not appeared in the *Post* previously were such as James Warner Bellah, Paul Gallico, Nunnally Johnson, Frank Wead,[10] A. R. "Dick" Wetjen, and Ben Hecht. Illustrators who were newcomers to the *Post* in this period included Gilbert Bundy, Corinne Boyd Dillon, Tempest Inman, Henrietta McCaig Starrett, Matt and Benton Clark, Donald Teague, Adolph Triedler, Albin Henning, and Robert W. Crowther. Lynn Bogue Hunt illustrated Hal Evart's continuing flow of wildlife articles, and Captain John W. Thomason, Jr.'s self-illustrated pieces did for the Marine Corps what the writings of General Charles King had done for the Regular Army in the post–Civil War years. In light of this competition, Koerner's consistent appearance in the *Post* speaks for itself.

Wall Street's resounding crash in 1929 affected the Koerners immediately but not catastrophically. The securities they had bought on margin went aft a'gley, never to return; their General Motors bought at 170 had risen above 220 before sliding steadily to 7 5/8. Given the margin requirements of those times, this basically was a loss of paper profits, not a crippling blow to their financial well-being. The aftermath of the crash was more serious in its cumulative effect. They had spent a brief skiing vacation in 1928 at a new resort-and-residential development called Lucerne-in-Maine. The developers commissioned a landscape of it, for which they paid him $1,900, and featured the fact in their monthly promotional publication that he was buying property there (thirteen lots) on which to build a summer residence.[11] This account made much of his earlier summers spent in Maine and what these summers had contributed to his illustrations for Maine stories by Ben Ames Williams and Mary E. Wilkins Freeman. Plans for the house had been drawn and Lillian had purchased its draperies and some of its furniture when the development collapsed without salvage, although Koerner's fee for the aforementioned painting was a partial offset to their loss.

More serious in its relation to their unforeseen future was the loss of income-producing real estate near Deal, New Jersey, which Lillian was purchasing as a long-term investment, after the manner of her successful acquisitions and renovations of Interlaken properties. They did retain much of what she invested at the urging of Frank Stick, who had ceased illustration about 1928 to investigate other things in life that interested him.[12] One of these had been the speculative appreciation inherent in a tract of sandy, low-lying dunes along the North Carolina coast, which contained the spot where Orville and Wilbur Wright had made their epochal flight at Kitty Hawk. After joining with the Sticks in donating several hundred acres of the tract to the government as the site for a memorial to the flying brothers,[13] there was enough left to provide some income for Lillian when she needed it the most. Despite Koerner's humorous protestations down the years that he did not approve of widows grown rich from collecting life insurance, he had continued what he had begun in Chicago to such a point that he once regarded himself as life-insurance poor. He paid these premiums, regardless of what other demands were made upon his purse, throughout the deepest years of the Great Depression.

The full impact of the depression smote the Koerner family in 1933, when the *Post*'s reductions in fees dropped his income by more than 60 per cent to its lowest level since 1924. The Interlaken residence required extensive repairs and a new "Daylight" lamp for his studio was as necessary as paints and brushes and canvasses. Far more important than these external drains upon his purse were the responsibilities he had expressed succinctly twenty-five years earlier upon being asked to make one of the Naaman's-on-Delaware group: "In considering plans for future years, we would like you to realize that these two—children and mothers—are always provided for. 'Tis the safest and best way."

His mother was still alive and so was his mother-in-law; their support was still his charge.[14] So was his children's education. Bill, Jr. was bound for the Art Students League as soon as he completed his secondary schooling at The Principia, a boarding school in St. Louis, whence Ruth Ann already had graduated. Eschewing college, she was acquiring professional secretarial and business training in New York. These continuing responsibilities, plus the necessity of continuing to provide for the future, had to be met from a drastically reduced income and Koerner worried. He could not have been the sensitive, imaginative, creative person that he was and failed to do so.

He had another worry, too. Bess Riddell, whom he had shepherded up to Grasshopper Glacier in 1925, retired as art editor of the *Post* in 1931, and was replaced by W. Thornton "Pete" Martin. Riddell had been more than just an art editor to Koerner and his family—friend, confidante, staunch supporter of the art of illustration as Koerner practiced it. Martin was new to the job, perhaps the most prestigious in the field, necessarily ambitious to do well in it, and his tastes in art ran along completely different lines. This shift added anxieties to the existing economic uncertainties.

Blessed with robust health, a tremendous asset to his consistent productivity, vigorously active in all that he did, Koerner's only addiction was to Lucky Strike cigarettes and Prince Albert pipe tobacco. Many of the cigarettes immolated themselves in the ashtrays with which his studio abounded or on the edges of his palette and easel frame. His first intimation of mankind's common mortality came shortly after his 1933 stay on Phil Spear's ranch. This was a painful attack in the lower right jaw of what was diagnosed as neuritis.[15] He visited a specialist in New York, who advised an operation. Koerner refused because a friend had had a similar operation which left the affected side of his face sagging and flabby. Given Koerner's acute sensitivity to physical deformities, his reaction is understandable. The acute neuritis passed and was succeeded by mid-1934 by an even more traumatic ailment with deleterious physical and psychological effects. Koerner began to experience difficulty in making his hands do what his eye and mind demanded that they do. Diagnosed as arthritis, it became increasingly worse, and it appears that this was kept within the family as a closely guarded secret.

It increased in severity to the point that he would write his son (4/22/1935) that a "big" picture had required seven to eight weeks to complete. Herbert Johnson, who still was doing the editorial cartoons for the *Post*, said that it was one of the best paintings Koerner ever had done. Its significance rests in a comparison of the time he took to complete it with the work he did in 1931 for Eugene Manlove Rhodes's "The Trusty Knaves," for which Rhodes received $7,500 for three installments and Koer-

ner $2,800 for its seven illustrations. Rhodes mailed the manuscript from his New Mexico residence on February 11, 1931; Koerner received the galley proofs of the first installment on February 22 and delivered the first three paintings on March 10.[16]

On September 9, 1935, he received a letter from the Pontiac (Michigan) *Daily Press* offering him $650 to do a full-size painting of Pontiac, the great Ottawa leader who had set the frontier aflame in 1763. This painting was being underwritten jointly by the newspaper and the Pontiac Motor Company, and Koerner had been recommended to them by the *Post*. His refusal to do the painting brought him another letter (9/12/1935) raising the ante to $1,000, which received another polite refusal. When he washed his brushes and cleaned his palette two days before Christmas, after completing the last of twelve paintings for "Hurricane," he had taken his last step on the ladder "Dick" and "Boy" had set out to climb together more than thirty years before.

The next three years were not easy ones, as Koerner's malady, whatever it may have been, slowly but inexorably made him a bed-bound invalid. They were made more bearable by occasional visits from old friends—Interlaken truly was out-of-the-way for most of them—and the manner in which Koerner bore his affliction is well described in a letter from Henry J. Soulen, after a visit in December, 1937.[17]

I can't tell you Bill how glad I was to see you. I've been thinking of you so much this week and wish I lived a little closer so I could run in to talk over old times. You know I've been worrying a lot the past six years, and then after I saw the fine courage with which you face life, I felt so ashamed of my own petty troubles. Mrs. Soulen and I have always admired your work so much, and now we have something even finer to admire. There is so much I would like to say but I don't know how to say it. I can only hope that because we are both a little older and understand things a little better, that words are not so necessary to express our feelings.

There were letters, too, from Phil Spear which were careful not to give any hint that he knew of Bill's condition, which Lillian had conveyed to his wife.

Bill, we haven't had any rain since you cut out from us. Receiving 600 cattle latter part of May [1938]. Better come out and help trail them home. Then we will help the Indians roundup their buffalo, and I believe we could have a lot of fun all summer. Really Bill we would love to have you with us as our guest all summer, so if you can come don't hesitate. Love to Lillian and Ruth-Ann.

A series of minor strokes culminated in a massive cerebral hemorrhage on August 11, 1938, three months short of his fifty-ninth birthday. Funeral services were held three days later in his Interlaken studio, where the casket was surrounded by paintings that he and she had prized together. A minister of Lillian's choosing conducted the services and a brief but heartfelt eulogy was delivered by Herbert Johnson, whose Quaker faith added an ecumenical note to the proceedings. Johnson also delivered the benediction at graveside, where, in the words of the old cow-country song, there were "roses to deaden the clods as they fall." It was fitting that Johnson do these things for his long time friend. As art editor of the *Post*, he had given Koerner his first assignment from that magazine and his presence symbolized the long association between Koerner and the creation of George Horace Lorimer.[18]

Lorimer had retired from the *Post* during Koerner's illness and succumbed several months thereafter to an inoperable cancer.[19] In the context of their productive years, it is appropriate that Koerner and Lorimer went when they did. Neither would have adjusted comfortably, if at all, to the changed tenor of the nation that the Great Depression wrought. The land that they had known and loved was no more. It now was an alien land bound on a foreign voyage to an unknown port, which it has not yet reached, as these lines are written.

For Koerner, it was well that his end came when it did. Even as such other Pyle students as Stanley M. Arthurs and Frank E. Schoonover, he had his roots in the traditions of American realistic art and had divorced himself from the mainstream of the emergent "new" art of the twentieth century,[20] an art being re-shaped by the influences of Alfred Steiglitz and Robert Henri. It was fortunate, too, that he did not live to see the popular image of the American man-on-horseback, an image given personal substance by the riders he had come to know and thus respect, change from that of the country's own Theseus-in-leather-leggin's to the nation's foremost anti-hero, whose pistol was the phallic symbol of an unbridled lust and whose scabbarded saddle-gun was the definitive expression of his country's foreign policy.

Shortly after his death, the Asbury Park Society of the Fine Arts held a memorial showing of his work at the Berkeley-Carteret Hotel Galleries in that city. When the fifty-two canvasses were returned to the studio where he had created them, they joined the others there to gather dust under lock and key until Lillian's death a quarter-century later. The first major showing of his by now forgotten work came in 1968 at the Los Angeles County Museum of History, followed by one in 1969 at the Amon Carter Museum of Western Art, Fort Worth, Texas.[21] These began his restoration to the recognition he had earned so long before, and have been followed by continuing appearances of his work in major galleries and museums West and East.

It is this belated but growing re-recognition that prompts the following summary of the work of W.H.D. Koerner: As all *great* illustrators must, otherwise they are not great illustrators, he early made his peace with the hard fact that his emotion, his private vision, had to be tempered by the techniques that he must learn to become an illustrator. Then, in the years after World War I, he found his private vision heightened by his personal awareness of and experiences with the land and the light and the people of the West. He fused this heightened vision with the technical virtuosity that already was his hallmark to produce the paintings that mark the zenith of his art and craft. His work was not marred by a long back-slope, such as ended his corporeal existence. Like the sheer eastern escarpment of the true High Sierra Nevada, the Range of Light, his work stands today as it was upthrust by his creative force, and time has not eroded it.

Publisher's Note: On June 17, 1978, Mr. Koerner's re-constructed studio was dedicated as an integral and permanent part of the Whitney Gallery of Western Art, itself a part of the famous Buffalo Bill Historical Center, Cody, Wyoming.

1. These were the years of *Anthony Adverse, The Good Earth, Lost Horizon,* and *Gone with the Wind.*

2. An earlier story by Williams.

3. This did not materialize, so far as is known.

4. Born in Mazatlán, Sinaloa, Scoggins knew whereof he wrote. A ship's surgeon in s/s *Matsonia* during the 1930s was wont to titivate the passengers by hinting coyly that "Scoggins" was his pen name, so great was this author's appeal to the *Post's* readers.

5. Very little of Koerner's outgoing correspondence has survived.

6. Tebbel, 218.

7. *Ibid.,* 236.

8. It was down to sixty pages for the Christmas issue of 1935. Three articles reflect the feature fare offered its readers in these years: "Insatiable Government" by Garet Garrett (6/25/1932); "The Red Flag—In Willow Pattern" by F. Britten Austin (5/24/1930); and Dorothy Parker's impressions of Germany, "Back to Blood and Iron" (5/6/1933).

9. Bobbs-Merrill auctioned off their collection of dust-wrapper paintings in 1934, and at least one painting by Koerner went for $10.00, that for Arthur Stringer's *Prairie Child.*

10. Wead is better remembered by film historians for his shooting scripts for such as *Dirigible, Air Mail, China Clipper,* and *Ceiling Zero,* many of which featured James Cagney and Pat O'Brien.

11. *Lucerne-in-Maine News,* 4/1929; copy in Koerner Papers.

12. He returned to illustration in the late 1940s.

13. Lillian and the children attended the dedication of this site in 1928; Koerner was too busy.

14. His mother died in 1934; his mother-in-law in 1935.

15. No medical history, as such is known today, exists for Koerner.

16. The *Post's* general policy was to use three illustrations for the first installment of a serial, which would make the "lead" piece in the issue in which it appeared, and two for each succeeding installment, which were moved progressively farther back in the magazine with each issue. If the readers had been "hooked" by the first installment, they would find its successors.

17. Soulen was one of the last to receive criticism and instruction from Howard Pyle in 1910. He was noted for the opulence of his "Chinoiserie" illustrations.

18. Koerner's last appearance in the *Post* was Arthur Stringer's "The Music Box," 4/17/1937, the illustrations having been completed on 3/13/1934. They were reproduced in four colors.

19. He was succeeded by Wesley Stout, 1/1/1937.

20. In his obituary notice, Peyton Boswell, editor of *Art Digest,* termed Koerner "One of America's most famous magazine and book illustrators."

21. A small but representative showing of his work was held at California State University, Chico, December, 1966.

Appendix A

CHECKLIST OF THE WORK OF W.H.D. KOERNER

No attempt has been made to list the individual stories and articles in *The Pilgrim* that he illustrated, nor has it been deemed necessary to list the appearances of his work in various anthologies and compendiums since his death. For these latter appearances, reference may be had to *Fifty Great Western Illustrators* (1975) by Jeff C. Dykes.

In preparing the roster of Koerner's appearances in magazines, the following abbreviations have been used for magazine titles not spelled out therein:

Amer.	*American Magazine*
Coll.	*Collier's Weekly*
Cosmo.	*Cosmopolitan* (combined with *Hearst's International Magazine*, 3/1925)
CG	*Country Gentleman* (a weekly until 1925, then monthly)
GH	*Good Housekeeping*
HM	*Harper's New Monthly Magazine*
HW	*Harper's Weekly*
LHJ	*Ladies Home Journal*
Metro.	*Metropolitan Magazine*
PR	*Pictorial Review*
RB	*Red Book Magazine*
SEP	*Saturday Evening Post*
WHC	*Woman's Home Companion*

MAGAZINE ILLUSTRATIONS

Anonymous (A War Bride)
    LHJ 5/1919. "At 7:30 I First Saw Him . . ."

Author Unknown
    Illustrated Sunday Magazine c. 5/27/1912. "Revenge."
    Illustrated Sunday Magazine c. 10/28/1912. "Like Another Wise Man."
    Illustrated Sunday Magazine c. 1/17/1913. "Wind in the Night."

Abdullah, Achmed
    HM 5/1917. "The Home-Coming."
    Coll. 12/8/1917. "Diplomacy." (*See:* Thomas H. Uzzell)
    Coll. 5/11/1918. "The Two-Handed Sword."

Alexander, Helen
    HM 9/1914. "Her Own Life Story."

Allen, Anne Story
    RB 10/1906. "Alex, Jr."

Altsheler, Joseph
    RB 4/1907. "The Empty Box."

Anderson, Jane
    HW 10/21/1911. "The Gift of the Hills."
    HW 1/13/1912. "The Spur of Courage."
    HW 7/13/1912. "The Red King."
    HW 2/8/1913. "The Forbidden Road."

Arbuckle, Mary
    WHC 12/1919. "One Day, A Story of the Western Plains."

Atherton, Gertrude
    McClure's 12/1917. "The White Morning."

Austin, F. Britten
    RB 9/1923. "The Drum."

Bacheller, Irving
    HM 10/1910. "Keeping up with Lizzie."
    HM 3/1911. "Socrates to the Rescue."
    HM 5/1912. "Marie and the Talk Trust."

Bagg, Helen Francis
    RB 10/1908. "What Happened on the Rigi."

Balmer, Edwin
    Amer. 3/1924. "The Song in the Dark."

Bartlett, Frederick Orin
    RB 10/1911. "The Furnace: The Story of a Trial By Fire."

Bechdolt, Frederick R.
    RB 3/1912. "The Romance of Lighthouse Tom."
    RB 4/1912. "An Adventure of Lighthouse Tom."
    RB 5/1912. "Red Larson's Account."
    RB 6/1912. "Sealed Orders."
    RB 7/1912. "The Piracy of Black Scotty."
    RB 8/1912. "An Epic of the Windjammers."
    RB 9/1912. "The Passing of Black Jack."
    RB 10/1912. "The Clubhauling of Monohan."
    RB 11/1912. "Tim Grappler."
    RB 12/1912. "The Keelhauling of Fat Dan."
    RB 1/1913. "Independent of Man."
    RB 2/1913. "Gold and Two Men."
    RB 3/1913. "A Bargain and a Woman."

Beer, Thomas
    SEP 7/1/1922. "Tact."
    SEP 11/4/1922. "Virtue Rewarded."
    SEP 12/9/1922. "Shock."
    SEP 11/13/1926. "Do and Dare."
    SEP 11/20/1926. "The Public Life."

Bell, Edward Price
    RB 7/1910. "In the Black Shadow: A Fight in De-
        fense of Honor."
    RB 2/1911. "Cyrus Aitken's Clear Call: The Judge-
        ment of the Storm."
    RB 4/1911. "Jack Halsey's Unmooring: He Swims
        the Johnstown Flood."

Bellah, James Warner
    SEP 6/16/1928. "The Cities of the World."

Bercovici, Konrad
    HM 4/1923. "Muzio."

Beymer, William Gilmore
    HM 2/1913. "Memory Plays us Tricks."

Biggers, Earl Derr
    SEP 6/26–7/31/1926. "The Chinese Parrot."

Blythe, Samuel G.
    SEP 2/22/1919. "War Wheezes."

Bonneau, Jean Xavier
    HW 12/30/1911. "The Magpie."

Botchkareva, Marie
    Metro., 11/1918–5/1919. "My Life."

Boyle, Jack
    RB 5/1918. "Miss Doris, Safe-Cracker."
    RB 6/1918. "Boston Blackie's Little Pal."
    RB 7/1918. "Alibi Ann."
    RB 10/1918. "The Poppy Girl's Husband."
    RB 12/1918. "A Problem in Grand Larceny."
    RB 1/1919. "An Answer in Grand Larceny."
    RB 2/1921. "The Heart of the Lily."
    RB 3/1921. "The Little Lord of All the Earth."
    RB 4/1921. "The Claws of the Tong."
    RB 6/1921. "A Mother of the Middle Kingdom."

RB 9/1921. "A Child of the Famine."

Brooks, Jonathan
    Coll. 2/9/1924. "Bug Grabs One for Sister."

Brown, Alice
    HM 10/1913. "A Homespun Wizardry."
    HM 10/1916. "Nicholas Woodman."
    HM 6/1917. "The Preaching Peony."

Brown, Royal
    Cosmo. 4/1921. "Priscilla Bags a Big One."

Burt, Maxwell Struthers
    SEP 6/11/1921. "Sweet Syllables."
    SEP 8/13/1921. "The Making of a Patriot."
    Hearst's Magazine 7/1923. "Man Who Grew a
        Beard."
    SEP 4/10/1934. "Dude Wrangler No. 1 — The Red-
        Haired Camp."
    SEP 10/12/1935. "Hidden Trails."

Byrd, Sigman
    SEP 8/31/1935. "October Corn."

Byrne, Donn
    Coll. 12/8/1923. "A Story Against Woman."

Cabell, J. Branch
    RB 7/1909. "A Fordyce of Westbrook."

Carpenter, Edmund C.
    RB 3/1907. "Ye Sign of Ye Flat Iron."

Carr, Catherine
    RB 2/1907. "Substitutes."

Casey, Patrick and Terence
    SEP 9/18/1920. "The Wedding of Quesada."

Chamberlain, George Agnew
    WHC 12/1918–1/1919. "White Man."
    WHC 12/1922–2/1923. "Lip Malvy's Wife."

Chamberlain, Lucia
    SEP 3/12/1921. "Corcoran."

Chase, Mary Ellen
    HM 11/1918. "A Return to Constancy."

Child, Richard Washburn
    SEP 6/19/1915. "The Phoenix — Her Negatives."
    SEP 9/4/1915. "The Phoenix — Very Truly Yours."
    SEP 2/26/1916. "On the Other Hand."
    SEP 3/18/1916. "One of the Chosen."
    McClure's 4/1919–6/1919. "The Cracking Knee."

Coe, Charles Francis
    SEP 12/29/1928–2/2/1929. "Hooch."

Colcord, Lincoln
    Amer. 6/1923. "Unmasked."

Collins, James H.
    SEP 2/1/1913. "The Business Side of the Church:
        Giving Value for Money."

SEP 3/1/1913. "The Business Side of the Church: Getting Money for Value."

SEP 3/22/1913. "The Business Side of the Church: Volunteer Choir."

SEP 4/5/1913. "The Business Side of the Church: The Country Church."

SEP 9/13/1913. "Letting a Sale Make Itself."

SEP 9/20/1913. "Selling That Concerns Everybody on the Payroll."

SEP 5/16/1914. "Cutting Down Some Staple Unnecessaries."

SEP 6/13/1914. "Cutting Down Some Staple Unnecessaries: Getting Rid of the Smoke From the Factory Chimney."

SEP 8/8/1914. "Cutting Down Some Staple Unnecessaries: The Imp of Darkness is the Oldest of Them All."

SEP 9/19/1914. "Cutting Down Some Staple Unnecessaries: The Three Costly Little Wastes of Dust, Noise and Vibration."

SEP 10/3/1914. "Turning Round on a Smaller Margin: The New Business Era Calls for Constructive Economy."

SEP 12/19/1914. "Turning Round on a Smaller Margin: How the Economy Man Helps by His Study of Materials."

SEP 1/2/1915. "Turning Round on a Smaller Margin: Bringing the Work Force Up to its True Capacity."

SEP 2/6/1915. "Turning Round on a Smaller Margin: The Chances for Saving in Selling and Management."

SEP 7/5/1919. "Sales Force Plus Trade Union."

Comfort, Will Levington
SEP 1/26/1924. "Soledad Steve."
SEP 4/3/1926. "Trouble in the Dust."
SEP 9/18/1926. "The Firebird."
SEP 3/5/1927. "Pelty."
SEP 10/20/1928. "Len Vittie, Descanso."

Cook, William Wallace
HW 8/5/1911. "Crenshaw of the Gold Mill."

Cooke, Grace MacGowan
The Home 10/1906. "The Wire Cutters."

Cooper, Courtney Rylay
Cosmo. 3/1921. "The Fiend."

Coppard, A. E.
Metro. 2/1922. "The Black Dog."

Cowdery, Alice
HM 2/1917. "Robert."
HM 11/1920. "The Tree."

Cram, Mildred
Amer. 5/1927–10/1927. "Scotch Valley."

Crissey, Forrest

SEP 9/28/1912. "Some Efficiency Secrets: An Apprentice Who Found a New Way."

SEP 10/12/1912. "Some Efficiency Secrets: Earning Fees as a Production Engineer."

SEP 11/2/1912. "The Selfmade Efficiency Expert: How to Solve Your Own Shop Problems."

SEP 9/12/1914. "Teaching the Retailer How to Fight."

SEP 3/6/1915. "Firing."

SEP 5/15/1915. "The Secrets of the Chain Store: Lessons in Efficiency for the Small Retailers."

Dalrymple, Leona
Metro. 4/1918. "Peter's Client."

Daly, Mark A.
RB 10/1909. "An Act of Providence."

Davies, Oma Almona
SEP 11/9/1929. "The Thin Edge of Truth."

Day, Holman F.
SEP 11/22/1913. "The Flareback of Old Ossian."
SEP 1/10/1914. "The Throne of Old Tantrybogus."
SEP 2/16/1918. "Stars and Wagons."

DeJeans, Elizabeth
LHJ 2/1920–9/1920. "The Moreton Mystery."

Deland, Edith Barnard
HM 12/1915. "The Gift of the Manger."

DeVoto, Bernard
SEP 6/2/1928. "Ranch Wondering."
SEP 1/10/1931. "You Jack O'Diamonds."

Dix, Gertrude
RB 6/1907. "Van Velsor's Apotheosis."

Downie, Vale
Success 7/1909. "The Autobiography of a Stolen Kiss."
HM 4/1914. "The Confidential Doll Insurance Co."

Downing, Marguerite
RB 6/1909. "The Intermediary."

Dwyer, James Francis
WHC 3/1921. "Cath."

Dyar, Muriel Campbell
HM 3/1916. "Ann Eliza Weatherby's Trip to Town."

Edmonds, Walter D.
SEP 4/22/1933. "The Trapper."
SEP 3/28/1936. "Indian Running."

Ellerbe, Alma and Paul
WHC 6/1924. "Mrs. Judge of Jackrabbit."

England, George Allan
SEP 7/21/1923. "The Nogg-Head."

Estabrook, William Chester
RB 2/1909. "The Second Chance."

Evarts, Hal G.
SEP 8/26–9/23/1922. "Tumbleweeds."
SEP 9/26–10/10/1925. "The Painted Stallion."
SEP 4/21–5/26/1928. "Fur Brigade."
SEP 11/3/1928. "Post Office at Dry Fork."
SEP 4/6–4/27/1929. "Tomahawk Rights."
SEP 5/25/1929. "Ride and Tie."
SEP 11/30/1929–1/4/1930. "Shaggy Legion."
SEP 5/21–7/2/1932. "Short Grass."
SEP 3/17/1934. "Detour."
SEP 7/14–8/18/1934. "Wolf Dog."

Faulkner, William
SEP 10/25/1930. "Red Leaves."

Fergusson, Harvey
WHC 3/1928. "All Signs Fail."

Finch, Lucine
HM 6/1913. "David."

Fitzpatrick, James William
Coll. 12/19/1914. "The Hospital Ticket."

Fletcher, Byers
Metro. 8/1918. "Chips."

Foote, John Taintor
SEP 12/14/1918. "The Last Shall Be First."
SEP 5/20–6/3/1922. "The Number One Boy."

Freeman, Mary E. Wilkins
HM 9/1912. "The Balking of Christopher."
HM 2/1914. "The Amethyst Comb."

Frost, Meigs O.
Coll. 6/28/1924. "The Mirror of Courage."

Garland, Robert
See: Kenneth L. Roberts.

Gelzer, Jay
Cosmo. 8/1921. "The Flower of the Flock."

Gerould, Gordon Hall
Scribner's 10/1914. "Pseudonymous."

Gerould, Katharine Fullerton
HM 11/1916. "Emma Blair."

Gerry, Margarita Spalding
HM 11/1914. "The Man Who Couldn't Miss."

Gibbon, Perceval
RB 4/1910. "The Thoroughbred: He Makes Good in Africa."
Cosmo. 2/1921. "When Gentlefolk Meet."

Gibbs, Sir Philip
SEP 11/6/1920. "The Return of a Rebel."
SEP 11/20/1920. "Venetian Lovers."

Gillmore, Inez Haynes

HM 5/1912. "The Frog in the Well."
HM 9/1912. "The Beautiful Young Man."

Glaspell, Susan
HM 4/1918. "Beloved Husband."
HM 3/1919. "Pollen."

Goodloe, Abbie Carter
WHC 6/1919. "The Ace's Story."

Grey, Zane
CG 5/4–7/20/1918. "The Desert of Wheat."
Amer. 4–10/1928. "Sunset Pass."
Amer. 4–10/1929. "The Drift Fence."

Hall, Herschel S.
SEP 3/6/1920. "The Yancona Yillies."
SEP 4/17/1920. "Bouillon."

Hall, James Norman
See: Charles Nordhoff

Hall, Wilbur
SEP 5/8/1915. "The Benevolent Exploitation."
SEP 4/14/1917. "A Matter of Blood Pressure."
SEP 9/22/1917. "The Maxim—Caveat Emptor."
SEP 6/12/1920. "Johnny Cucabod."

Hallet, Richard Matthews
SEP 10/22–12/3/1921. "The Canyon of Fools."
SEP 11/6–11/13/1926. "Beyond a Reasonable Doubt."
SEP 2/1/1930. "The Earthquake."
SEP 3/29/1930. "Zimbolaci's Daughter."
SEP 9/16/1933. "Bushed."
SEP 12/23/1933. "Cuba Libre."

Hamby, William H.
SEP 4/8/1916. "Rekindling the Fires."
SEP 12/2/1916. "Palms and Parasols."
SEP 5/10/1919. "The Bloom of the Peach."

Hampton, Edgar Lloyd
Metro. 3/1920. "The Return of Foo Chow."

Harriman, Karl Edwin
RB 10/1905. "Her Speech of Acceptance."

Harris, Corra
HM 8/1913. "On the Instalment Plan."

Harris, Frank Mann
SEP 11/5/1927. "Cryin' Johnny McElroy."

Harris, Kennett
SEP 9/20/1913. "Jacob Plays a Counterpart."
SEP 11/1/1913. "Pore Nance!"
SEP 2/7/1914. "The Follies of Mrs. Joe."
SEP 5/18/1918. "Tobermory."
SEP 10/1–10/15/1921. "According to His Lights."
SEP 11/28/1925. "The Pitcher and the Well."
SEP 3/26/1927. "Hindsight."
SEP 7/30/1927. "True as the Stars Above."
SEP 11/12/1927. "The Blowhard."

SEP 4/7/1928. "Smoothing the True-Love Trail."
SEP 12/8/1928. "Red Skies at Night."
SEP 1/5/1929. "In the Sweat of His Brow."
SEP 5/4/1929. "Often Woman Varies."

Harrison, Henry Sydnor
LHJ 7/1912. "The Everlasting Triangle."

Hartman, Lee Foster
HM 9/1922. "Out of the Air."
RB 5/1923. "The Transit of Venus."

Hendryx, James B.
McClure's 1/1919. "The Man from up the Creek."

Hergesheimer, Joseph
SEP 6/10/1916. "The Thrush in the Hedge."
SEP 7/30/1921. "Juju."
SEP 4/8/1922. "Traveler's Repose."

Hillman, Gordon Malherbe
Amer. 7/1926. "The Texas Queen."

Hilton-Turvey, C.
Coll. 5/2/1914. "The Lynching of the Night Marshal."

Hough, Emerson
SEP 7/5/1919. "Traveling the Old Trails: When Calico Was King."
SEP 8/2/1919. "Traveling the Old Trails: Once Upon a Time."
SEP 8/23/1919. "Traveling the Old Trails: The Road to Oregon."
SEP 9/13/1919. "Traveling the Old Trails: The Long Trail of the Cow Country."
SEP 4/1–5/20/1922. "The Covered Wagon."
SEP 4/7–5/26/1923. "North of 36."
McCall's 2–7/1924. "The Ship of Souls."

Howes, Benjamin A.
SEP 9/14/1912. "How to Beat the Building Game."

Hughes, Rupert
Hearst's 9–10/1917. "The Mobilizing of Johanna."

Hungerford, Edward
HW 9/9/1911. "The Honor of His Craft."
SEP 3/13/1915. "The Yardmaster's Job."

Hutchinson, Bruce
SEP 11/30/1935. "Park Avenue Logger."

Hutchinson, Elizabeth Dewing
HM 6/1916. "The Far Traveller."

Hyde, Henry M.
RB 9/1909. "Mr. DePeyster Intervenes."

Ingersoll, Will E.
HM 6/1918. "The Man Who Slept Till Noon."

Johnson, Fanny Kemble
RB 4/1909. "The Park Story."

Johnston, Calvin
SEP 10/16/1920. "Temple Dusk."

Johnston, William
GH 12/1914. "Limpy."
GH 1/1916. "Nothing to Tell."
GH 3/1916. "According to Code."
GH 6/1916. "His Heart's Desire."
GH 7/1916. "Cousin Jim."
GH 8/1916. "The 'Fraid Cat."
GH 11/1916. "Home."
GH 1/1917. "In a Strange Land."
GH 3/1917. "For Value Received."

Jones, Eugene
Amer. 6/1924. "Yeller as Deck Paint."

Jordan, Elizabeth
LHJ 4/1917. "What Everyone Else Knew: But Sidney Manson Had to Find Out."

Kahler, Hugh MacNair
SEP 1/22/1921. "Like a Tree."
SEP 9/9/1922. "The Tenth Law."
RB 12/1922. "The Mainspring."

Kelland, Clarence Budington
SEP 10/13/1917. "Scattergood Kicks up the Dust."
SEP 11/24/1917. "The Mountain Comes to Scattergood."

Kerr, Sophie
SEP 4/2/1921. "Wild Earth."

Kirk, Russell G.
Cosmo. 10/1921. "Friends of the Greyhound."
SEP 9/14/1929. "On the Square."
SEP 5/23/1931. "Cinder Dump."
SEP 6/10/1933. "Derrick."

Knibbs, H. H.
SEP 4/1/1933. "Why, Pericles!"

Kyne, Peter B.
SEP 7/12/1913. "The Blind Goddess: Tiberius Tinker Leads a Forlorn Hope."
RB 4/1914. "The Harbor Bar."

LaFarge, Oliver
SEP 12/30/1933. "Hard Winter."
SEP 3/31/1934. "Higher Education."
SEP 11/24/1934. "Women at Yellow Wells."

Lane, Rose Wilder
SEP 10/22–10/29/1932. "Let the Hurricane Roar."

Laughlin, Clara E.
RB 7/1908. "The House of Peace."

Laut, Agnes C.
SEP 11/23/1912. "Will Canada's Boom Last?"

Leary, Lewis Gaston

RB 4/1908. "A Postponed Proposal."

Lee, Jennette
LHJ 7/1917. "The Two Doctors."

Lee, Leonard
SEP 11/9/1935. "Conquest."

Leverage, Henry
SEP 4/13/1918. "The Silver Greyhound."

Luehrmann, Adele
McCall's, 11/1920. "The Lurania Mystery."

Lyman, Olin L.
RB 6/1908. "Man and Man."

Lynde, Francis
WHC 9/1920. "Bound for an Unknown Port."

McCall, Jessie Phillips
GH 7/1915. "The Passing of the Stork."

MacFarlane, Peter Clark
SEP 1/18/1919. "Cross and Double Cross."
SEP 12/13/1919. "Mad Hack Henderson."

McFee, William
HM 2/1924. "On the Malecon."

MacGrath, Harold
SEP 9/25–10/16/1920. "The Pagan Madonna."

McHarg, William
Cosmo. 12/1920. "The Wildcatter."
Cosmo. 1/1921. "The Rockhound."

McHenry, May
Coll. 10/10/1914. "A Serpent in Eden."

Manning, Marie
McClure's 5/1918. "The Third Generation."

Marcosson, Isaac F.
SEP 1/3/1914. "The Simple Life Among the Rich:
The Diet and the Method Behind Million Making."
SEP 1/17/1914. "Thrift Among the Rich."
SEP 4/25/1914. "The Wage-earner as an Investor:
How Employees' Organizations are Teaching
Thrift by Teamwork."

Marquand, John P.
SEP 7/23/1921. "The Right That Failed."
SEP 6/6/1925. "The Old Man."
SEP 7/20/1929. "The Powaw's Head."
SEP 8/10/1929. "The Best Must Always Go."
SEP 8/24/1929. "Captain Whetstone."
SEP 10/5/1929. "A Dog, A Woman."
SEP 11/16/1929. "The Ships Must Sail."
SEP 12/28/1929. "Jack's the Lad."
SEP 2/8/1930. "Bobby Shaftoe."
SEP 3/15/1930. "Leave Her, Johnny—Leave
Her."
SEP 4/12/30. "Slave Catcher."

SEP 7/5/1930. "Obligations."
SEP 8/2/1930. "The Same Things."
SEP 9/27/1930. "The Master of the House."
SEP 1/20/1934–2/17/1934. "Winner Take All."

Marquis, Don
SEP 3/15–3/22/1930. "King O'Meara and Queen
Guinevere."
SEP 6/21/1930. "O'Meara at Troy."

Marshal, Edison
Amer. 3/1920. "Count a Thousand—Slow—Between Each Drop."

Mason, Arthur
WHC 4/1924. "The Wreckmaster."

Mason, Elmer Brown
HW 2/22/1913. "The Blue Jay's Nest."
HW 3/15/1913. "The Beatitude of Jimmy
O'Meara."

Matteson, Herman Howard
Amer. 8/1919. "The Bag of Black Diamonds."

Mercein, Eleanor
SEP 11/30/1929. "The Diddikai."

Miller, Helen Topping
SEP 9/29/1928. "Barber, Barber, Shave a Pig."

Mitchell, Mary Esther
HM 11/1915. "A New England Pippa."
HM 5/1916. "The Dumb Peterses."
HM 9/1916. "The Asher Pride."
HM 3/1917. "The Smaller Craft."
HM 9/1917. "Then Came David."
HM 11/1917. "Miss Barcy's Waterloo."
HM 11/1917. "A Strike in the Mines."
HM 5/1918. "On Pinions Free."
HM 9/1918. "The Gifts of the Altar."
HM 10/1918. "The Fire Unquenchable."
HM 1/1919. "His Hour."

Mitchell, Ruth Comfort
WHC 9–10/1922. "Action."

Moravsky, Maria
HM 9/1919. "The Black City."

Morris, Gouverneur
RB 6/1911. "The Oldest Beginner: From Wire
Fences to Art."
McClure's 7/1918. "Behind the Door."

Mullett, Mary
LHJ 7/1909. "The Letter She Didn't Send."

Nason, Leonard H.
SEP 12/7/1929. "Itxas Gain."
SEP 5/20/1933. "The Mules and the Mascots."
SEP 3/24/1934. "The Little Maid of San Lucar."

Neidig, William J.

SEP 3/4/1916. "The Flight."
SEP 6/3/1916. "The Slipper Tongue."
SEP 7/31/1920. "The Brother Act."
SEP 4/2/1921. "The Wire Cutter."

Nordhoff, Charles B. & Hall, James Norman
SEP 9/22–11/3/1934. "Pitcairn's Island."
SEP 12/28/1935–2/1/1936. "The Hurricane."

Older, Mrs. Fremont
RB 12/1906. "Winston's Regrets."

Oppenheimer, James
RB 10/1910. "Steel: The Hot Heart of America."

O'Reilly, Edward S.
Coll. 9/29/1917. "Dead or Alive."

Osbourne, Lloyd
SEP 9/29/1923. "The City of Refuge."

Ostenso, Martha
PR 8–11/1925. "Wild Geese."

Oyen, Henry
CG 1/25–3/29/1919. "Big Flat."

Paine, Ralph D.
RB 11/1908. "The Freshman Full Back."

Pangborn, Georgia Wood
WHC 12/1920. "Orris Island."

Pattullo, George
SEP 6/5/1909. "The Gunfighter: Padden Meets His Match."
SEP 11/6/1915. "In Pursuit of Hicks."
SEP 11/27/1915. "Naughty Henree."
Am. Sunday Monthly Magazine 1/2/1916. "Five Hundred Reward."
SEP 1/22/1916. "Henree Tried."
SEP 4/29/1916. "The Cuckoo."
SEP 11/25/1916. "Leezie, The City Slicker."
SEP 4/14/1917. "Ways That Are Dark."
SEP 11/11/1922. "The Survival."
SEP 7/28/1923. "The Lease Hounds."
SEP 12/8/1923. "Shots in the Dark."

Payne, Will
SEP 3/30/1912. "The Downtrodden Automobile."
SEP 9/6–9/20/1913. "The Government Company."
SEP 8/22/1914. "More Government Wires."
SEP 8/29/1914. "Banking for Everybody."
SEP 6/12/1915. "A Dispensation."
SEP 10/16/1915. "The Blue-Sky Company."
SEP 10/30/1915. "The Blue-Sky Company: An International Affair."
SEP 11/27/1915. "The Blue-Sky Company: A Sentimental Adventure."
SEP 12/22/1915. "The Blue-Sky Company: On the Pirate Ship."
SEP 1/15/1916. "The Blue-Sky Company: In Strict Confidence."
SEP 1/22/1916. "The Blue-Sky Company: The Nick of Time."
SEP 11/10/1917. "The Crime at Pribbles."
SEP 3/2/1918. "The Iron Butcher."
RB 3/1920. "Lucky Mary."

Perry, Lawrence
RB 12/1920. "The Rocks of Avalon."

Pertwee, Roland
SEP 5/15/1920. "Elizabeth Anne."

Pickthall, M.L.C.
WHC 5/1920. "The Boy in the Corner."
Coll. 2/10/1923. "The Sleeping Faun."

Pierce, Frank Richardson
Amer. 2/1923. "In the Nick of Time: The Story of a Wise Old Dog."
Amer. 8/1923. "Settled Outside of Court: A Story of Revenge."

Post, Melville Davisson
SEP 3/4/1916. "The Sleuth of the Stars."
Amer. 9/1926. "The Forgotten Witness."
Amer. 10/1926. "The Survivor."
Amer. 12/1926. "The Invisible Client."
Amer. 2/1927. "The Heir at Law."
Amer. 6/1927. "The Leading Case."
Amer. 4/1928. "Colonel Braxton Chooses a Client."
Amer. 9/1928. "Colonel Braxton Hears the Silent Voices."
Amer. 2/1929. "The Vanished Man."
Amer. 4/1929. "The Mark on the Window."
Amer. 6/1929. "Dead Man's Shoes."
Amer. 8/1929. "The Mystery at the Mill."
Amer. 9/1929. "The Guilty Man."
Amer. 11/1929. "The Witness in the Metal Box."
Amer. 9/1930. "The White Patch."

Pottle, Emery
HM 9/1911. "Journey's End."

Pulver, Mary Brecht
SEP 6/29/1918. "Fuller Brothers."

Quick, Herbert
SEP 4/15/1916. "A Corn-Belt Pioneer."

Ransom, Joe H.
RB 5/1911. "The Long Way: When Love Was Lost and Won."

Reese, Lowell Otis
SEP 2/7/1920. "The Bachelor."
RB 3/1926. "The Furrow."
SEP 9/29/1927. "Man or a Mouse."

Rhodes, Eugene Manlove
SEP 9/11–10/2/1920. "Stepsons of Light."
SEP 4/11–4/25/1925. "Once in the Saddle."

SEP 2/20–2/27/1926. "Pasó Por Aquí."
SEP 8/16/1930. "Maid Most Dear."
SEP 4/18–5/2/1931. "The Trusty Knaves."
SEP 10/1–10/15/1932. "The Proud Sheriff."
SEP 5/26–6/9/1934. "Beyond the Desert."

Rhodes, Harrison
WHC 10/1918. "The Substitute."

Rice, Wallace
RB 9/1907. "Easily Satisfied."

Richmond, Grace S.
LHJ 6/1909. "Husband and Wife Sketches."
LHJ 11/1912–5/1913. "A Country Doctor: The Romance of a Patient of Red Pepper Burns."
WHC 6/1913. "The Red Head."

Richter, Conrad
LHJ 5/1917. "The Girl that 'Got' Colly: And the 'Mix-Up' His Partner Started Because of Her Picture."
SEP 4/7/1934. "Early Marriage."
SEP 9/14/1935. "As It Was in the Beginning."

Rideout, Henry Milnor
SEP 3/1/1919. "Runa's Holiday."
SEP 6/19/1920. "The Toad."
SEP 4/16–4/30/1921. "Fern Seed."

Rider, Fremont
HW 12/14/1912. "The Spirit of the Day."

Rinehart, Mary Roberts
SEP 11/18/1916. "Pirates of the Caribbean."
SEP 4/16–6/18/1927. "Lost Ecstasy."

Ritchie, Robert Welles
SEP 10/9–10/16/1915. "Lord of Many Peaks."
Coll. 7/28/1917. "Blue Bob Comes Home."

Roberts, Charles G. D.
Illustrated Sunday Magazine, c. 3/1913. Title unknown.

Roberts, Kenneth L. & Garland, Robert
SEP 8/30/1919. "The Brotherhood of Man."

Robins, Elizabeth
Metro. 9/1921. "Little Man Monday."

Roe, Vingie E.
LHJ 7/1919. "Blue Chap—A Dog That Knew."

Rowland, Henry C.
RB 6/1910. "Shamballah: The Lodge of the Great White Brotherhood."
SEP 11/25–12/30/1922. "The Return of Frank Clamart."

Russell, John
Coll. 8/18/1917. "The Lost God."
SEP 9/15/1917. "Jonah."
SEP 2/14/1925. "The Primitive."

SEP 6/17/1933. "The Dead Man's Chest."

Scoggins, C. E.
SEP 4/12/1924. "The Tumtum Tree."
SEP 11/15/1924. "The Proud Old Name."
SEP 4/24/1926. "Not So, Bolivia."
SEP 2/18/1928. "A Man Named Carrigan."
SEP 12/19/1931–1/23/1932. "Flame."
SEP 11/26–12/31/1932. "Tycoon."
SEP 7/13–8/17/1935. "Pampa Joe."

Sembower, Alta Brunt
HM 2/1911. "The Chaperon."
HM 5/1911. "Neighbors."

Shawe, Victor
SEP 5/3/1924. "Luck and the Red-Haired Lady."
SEP 5/17/1924. "Seattle Slim Meets Irish Olga."
SEP 6/7/1924. "The Faulted Ledge."

Singmaster, Elsie
HM 7/1913. "The Spite Fence."
GH 12/1913. "The Man Who Shot Given."

Smith, Wallace
SEP 12/12/1935. "Senor Henpeck."

Snyder, Carl
McClure's 3/1902. "Bordering the Mysteries of Life and Mind."

Somerville, A. W.
SEP 7/14/1928. "High Water."

Spofford, Harriet Prescott
HM 11/1914. "A Homely Sacrifice."

Stabler, Harry Snowden
SEP 3/22/1913. "The Story of a Live Wire: Plugging Up a Few Holes in the Banking Laws."

Steele, Rufus
SEP 7/18/1914. "New Rules for the Road."

Steele, Wilbur Daniel
HM 8/1919. "Luck."
HM 1/1920. "Both Judge and Jury."
PR 8/1924. "Marriage."
PR 12/1924. "The Thinker"
PR 3/1925. "Six Dollars."
HM 5/1925. "When Hell Froze."

Stevenson, Burton E.
McClure's 5–10/1917. "A King in Babylon."

Stringer, Arthur
SEP 2/21–3/28/1925. "Power."
SEP 9/20–10/25/1930. "The Squaw Woman."
SEP 4/17/1937. "The Music Box."

Taylor, Edith Mendall
RB 3/1910. "The Same Emotions: Estelle and the Cloak-Buyer."

Terhune, Albert Payson

SEP 1/25/1919. "Cash Wyble."
RB 5/1920. "The Devil's Doll."

Trayes, F. G.
McClure's, 10–12/1918. "Caught on a German Raider."

Trites, W. B.
McClure's 9/1918. "Tomorrow I Fly."

Turner, George Kibbe
SEP 6/10/1922. "Joan of Arc Smith."

Uzzell, Thomas H. with Abdullah, Achmed
Coll. 12/8/1917. "Diplomacy."

Van Campen, Helen
SEP 1/6/1917. "The Luck of a Sourdough."

Van Schaick, George
The Ladies' World 10/1917–1/1918. "The White Threshold."

Vorse, Mary Heaton
HM 2/1918. "Huntington's Credit."
HM 3/1919. "A Man's Son."
HM 10/1921. "The Halfway House."
HM 11/1922. "Twilight of the God."
HM 7/1923. "The Promise."

Walker, Elliot
The Home 11/1906. "The Left Guard's Pass."

Walker, Harry Wilson
SEP 3/7–4/18/1914. "The Trail of the Tammany Tiger."

Walker, Herbert C.
HW 12/16/1911. "The Lawyer's Christmas Socks."

Ward, Herbert D.
SEP 12/9/1916. "The Lion's Eyes."

Ware, Edmund
Amer. 1/1929. "On the Road to Jericho's."

Warner, Anne
RB 12/1908. "What the Buyer Bought."

Watauna, Onoto
RB 11/1909. "A Daughter of Two Lands."

White, Stewart Edward
SEP 7/29–9/16/1916. "The Leopard Woman."
SEP 1/1–2/12/1927. "Back of Beyond."
SEP 6/29/1929. "Tingra's Ghost Story."
SEP 7/5–7/12/1930. "The Long Rifle: The Grandmother."
SEP 2/7/1931. "The Long Rifle: The Mountain Man."
SEP 2/14/1931. "The Long Rifle: The Statesman."
SEP 2/21/1931. "The Long Rifle: The Trader."
SEP 2/28/1931. "The Long Rifle: The Buffalo."
SEP 3/7/1931. "The Long Rifle: Senorita."
SEP 3/14/1931. "The Long Rifle: Indian Country."
SEP 3/21/1931. "The Long Rifle: The White Buffalo."
SEP 3/28/1931. "The Long Rifle: Blackfeet."
SEP 4/4/1931. "The Long Rifle: Assiniboin."
SEP 7/11/1931. "Mountain Man: Council."
SEP 7/25/1931. "Mountain Man: The Surround."
SEP 8/8/1931. "Mountain Man: The Raiders."
SEP 8/22/1931. "Mountain Man: Wandering Foot."
SEP 9/5/1931. "Mountain Man: Rendezvous."
SEP 9/19/1931. "Mountain Man: Rendezvous II."
SEP 10/3/1931. "Mountain Man: Lowered Swords."
SEP 10/17/1931. "Mountain Man: The Battle."
SEP 1/30/1932. "Ranchero: The Lovely Land."
SEP 2/13/1932. "Ranchero: Valedor."
SEP 2/27/1932. "Ranchero: Reata."
SEP 3/12/1932. "Ranchero: Matanza."
SEP 3/26/1932. "Ranchero: Hacienda."
SEP 4/9/1932. "Ranchero: Fiesta."
SEP 4/23/1932. "Ranchero: Merienda."
SEP 5/7/1932. "Ranchero: Monterey."
SEP 5/21/1932. "Ranchero: El Politico."
SEP 6/4/1932. "Ranchero: Casamiento."
SEP 9/3/1932. "Folded Hills: Djo."
SEP 9/10/1932. "Folded Hills: I-Tam-Api."
SEP 9/17/1932. "Folded Hills: Rising Tide."
SEP 12/17/1932. "Wildman."
SEP 11/10–12/1/1934. "Foofaraw."
SEP 2/23–3/23/1935. "Stampede."
SEP 5/4/1935. "The Grampus and the Weasel."
SEP 7/6/1935. "Guest's Gold."

White, William Allen
SEP 7/11/1914. "How Kansas Boarded the Water Wagon."

Williams, Ben Ames
CG 1/26–2/23/1918. "A Charge to Keep."
SEP 6/28–7/12/1919. "Jubilo."
RB 11/1919–1/1920. "Black Pawl."
SEP 4/9–4/30/1921. "Miching Mallecho."
SEP 10/14/1922. "The Ax."
SEP 1/6–1/27/1923. "Pascal's Mill."
SEP 6/16–6/23/1923. "Fair and Softly."
SEP 8/4–8/11/1923. "The Bride's Light."
SEP 3/15–3/22/1924. "Partridge."
SEP 3/29–4/19/1924. "The Rational Hind."
SEP 7/19–8/9/1924. "The Silver Forest."
SEP 10/4/1924. "Thunderstroke."
SEP 12/13/1924. "Foreheads Villainous."
SEP 10/17–11/15/1925. "A Man of Plots."
SEP 11/7/1925. "Scapegoat."
SEP 1/2/1926. "Nerves."
SEP 1/30–2/27/1926. "No Thoroughfare."
SEP 4/24/1926. "The Glib and Oily Art."
SEP 5/22–6/19/1926. "The Dreadful Night."
SEP 8/14/1926. "The Uses of Adversity."

SEP 10/13–11/10/1928. "A Son of Anak."
SEP 4/13/1929. "Cinderella by Request."
SEP 5/18/1929. "A Matter of Business."
SEP 5/10–6/7/1930. "The Hermit of Three
   Buttes."
SEP 12/27/1930–1/24/1931. "Make-Believe."
SEP 5/2/1931. "Cash in Hand."
SEP 6/6/1931. "Witch-Trod Pond."
SEP 8/29–9/5/1931. "The Crutile."
SEP 10/24–11/7/1931. "Jephthah's Daughter."
SEP 7/1/1933. "Wampee."
SEP 2/24/1934. "Balance All."
SEP 3/16/1935. "The Old Men's Pool."

Williams, Michael
   RB 3/1909. "The Voice."

Wilson, Harry Leon
   SEP 7/6/1918. "Vendetta."

Wilson, Margaret Adelaide
   WHC 9/1921. "The Calling Doves."

Wood, Eugene
   GH 5/1914. "Decoration Day."
   GH 12/1915. "The Family Altar."
   GH 5/1916. "The Beautiful Moment."

Woolley, Edward Mott
   SEP 5/4/1912. "Inner Secrets of a Real-Estate
      Broker's Rise."
   SEP 6/29/1912. "The Rise of the Junior Partner."
   SEP 4/26/1913. "The Fighting Six: The Boy Who
      Stayed at Home."
   SEP 5/10/1913. "The Fighting Six: Easy Money."
   SEP 5/31/1913. "The Fighting Six: The Undis-
      covered Road."
   SEP 6/28/1913. "The Fighting Six: In Partner-
      ship."
   SEP 7/12/1913. "The Fighting Six: Fitting the
      Market."
   SEP 9/6/1913. "The Fighting Six: Rip Van Winkle
      in Business."
   SEP 12/6/1913. "At the Crisis: Builders of Appe-
      tites."

Wylie, I.A.R.
   Coll. 12/22/1917. "Candles for St. Nicholas."
   SEP 10/3/1931. "House That Jack Built."

Yates, L. B.
   SEP 8/30/1919. "Old King Baltimore."

MAGAZINE COVERS AND
RELATED MAGAZINE WORK

Blue Book: 2/1919, 3/1919, 4/1919.
Collier's: 1/9/1915, Automobile Section, full page.
Field and Stream: unidentified issue, c. 1910.
Fleming's Farm and Live Stock Almanac (Union

Stock Yards, Chicago), 1911.
Harper's Weekly: 2/26/1910; 8/6/1910; double-
   page, 6/4/1910; 9/3/1910; 10/1/1910; 12/3/
   1910; 1/7/1911; 2/4/1911; 4/1/1911; 10/14/
   1911; 11/4/1911; 6/1/1912.
The New Magazine (Chicago): 1/1911.
Outdoor America: 3/1924. (House organ of the Izaak
   Walton League of America)
People's Magazine: 8/1912.
The Pilgrim: 8/1903; 9/1903; 11/1903; 2/1904;
   3/1904; 4/1904; 5/1904; 7/1904; 8/1904; 9/
   1904; 10/1904; 11/1904; 12/1904; 1/1905; 2/
   1905; 4/1905; 9/1905; 11/1905; 2/1906.
The Popular Magazine: 3/1/1911; 9/?/1911; 5/7/
   1915; 7/23/1915.
Saturday Evening Post: 10/22/1921; 4/1/1922;
   10/6/1928; 10/24/1931; 5/27/1933; 3/3/1934;
   4/4/1936.
Top-Notch Magazine: 8/15/1915.

With the exception of the *Post* cover for 4/1/1922,
which was an illustration from "The Covered Wagon," all of the above were original works. With the
exception of his illustrations for Grape-Nuts, Postum,
and Post Toasties, Koerner did so little advertising
work that it has not been felt necessary to include it
here.

BOOKS

Bacheller, Irving, *Keeping Up with Lizzie* (Harper,
   N.Y. and London, 1911): 12 full-page plates, of
   which 4 were original work for this book.
——, *"Charge It"* (Harper, N.Y. and London):
   illus. mounted on front cover, frontis., and 5 illus.,
   all original work for this book.
Beach, Rex, *Flowing Gold* (Harper, N.Y. and London, 1922): d/w, frontis., and 3 illus., all original
   work for this book. (Dykes lists a Canadian edition
   this year by Musson Book Co., Toronto, with the
   frontis. by Koerner.)
Biggers, Earl Derr, *The Chinese Parrot* (Bobbs-Merrill, Indianapolis, 1926): d/w.
Bowman, Earl Wayland, *The Ramblin' Kid* (Bobbs-
   Merrill, Indianapolis, 1920): d/w(?), frontis., also
   5 illus. by J. Rumsey Micks. A later edition may
   have moved the frontis. by Koerner to face page
   106 (cf. Dykes, 191, who also notes a Grossett
   & Dunlap edition this year which used photographs
   from the film starring Hoot Gibson and a d/w in
   color by Koerner).
Boyle, Jack, *Boston Blackie* (H. K. Fly Co., N.Y.,
   1919): d/w, frontis., and 3 illus.
Chamberlain, George Agnew, *White Man* (Bobbs-
   Merrill, Indianapolis, 1919): d/w, frontis., and 7
   illus.
(Crockett), *The Life of Colonel David Crockett*, An

Autobiography (A. L. Burt & Co., N.Y., 1928): d/w, frontis., from the illustrations for H. G. Evarts's serial "Fur Brigade."

Dejeans, Elizabeth, *The Moreton Mystery* (Bobbs-Merrill, Indianapolis, 1920): d/w, frontis(?). (Dykes does not list frontis. for this ed., but the A. L. Burt & Co. ed. this year had a frontis.)

Deland, Margaret, *The Voice* (Harper, N.Y. and London, 1912): frontis. and 2 illus., all original work for this book.

———, *Around Old Chester* (Harper, N.Y. and London, 1915): 2 original illus. by Koerner; five other illustrations.

Evarts, Hal G., *Tumbleweeds* (Little, Brown and Co., Boston, 1923): d/w, frontis.

———, *The Painted Stallion* (Little, Brown, Boston, 1926): d/w, colored front cover.

———, *Fur Brigade* (Little, Brown, Boston, 1928): d/w, original work.

———, *Tomahawk Rights* (Little, Brown, Boston, 1929): d/w.

———, *Shortgrass* (Little, Brown, Boston, 1932): d/w.

Foote, John Taintor, *The Number One Boy* (D. Appleton & Co., N.Y., 1926): d/w.

Grey, Zane, *The Desert of Wheat* (Harper, N.Y. and London, 1919): d/w, frontis., and 3 illus.

———, *The Drift Fence* (Harper, N.Y., 1933): d/w.

———, *Sunset Pass* (Harper, N.Y., 1931): d/w.

Hallett, Richard Matthews, *The Canyon of the Fools* (Harper, N.Y. and London, 1922): d/w, frontis., and 3 illus.

Harriman, Karl Edwin, *The Girl and the Deal* (Geo. W. Jacobs & Co., Philadelphia, 1903): illus, mounted on front cover, frontis., and 11 full-page plates, all original work for this book.

Harris, Kennett, *Meet Mr. Stegg* (Holt, N.Y., 1920): d/w, frontis.

Hough, Emerson, *The Covered Wagon* (Appleton, N.Y. and London, 1922): d/w, frontis.

———, *North of 36* (Appleton, N.Y. and London, 1923): d/w, frontis., and 3 illus.

———, *The Ship of Souls* (Appleton, N.Y. and London, 1925): d/w, frontis.

Kimball, George Selwyn, *The Lackawannas at Moosehead* (Ball Publ. Co., Boston, 1908): frontis. and 2 illus., all original work for this book.

MacGrath, Harold, *The Luck of the Irish* (Harper, N.Y. and London, 1917): d/w, frontis. in color, both original work for this book.

———, *The Pagan Madonna* (Doubleday, Page & Co., Garden City, N.Y. and Toronto, 1921): d/w, frontis. in color.

Manning, Marie, *Judith of the Plains*, Tales of the Frontier Series (Harper, N.Y. and London, 1903):

frontis. by Koerner is from "The Forbidden Road" by Jane Anderson, *Harper's Weekly*, 2/8/1913, which indicates a later ed.

Ostenso, Martha, *Wild Geese* (Dodd, Mead and Co., N.Y., 1925): d/w, frontis.

Patten, William (selected and arranged by), *Stories of Today* (P. F. Collier & Son, N.Y., 1918, vol. 9, of 10): one illus. by Koerner (The Junior Classics).

Rhodes, Eugene Manlove, *The Proud Sheriff* (Houghton Mifflin and Co., Boston and N.Y., 1935): d/w.

———, *Stepsons of Light* (Houghton Mifflin, Boston and N.Y., 1921): d/w.

———, *The Trusty Knaves* (Houghton Mifflin, Boston and N.Y., 1933): d/w.

———, *Beyond the Desert* (Houghton Mifflin, Boston and N.Y., 1934): d/w.

Richmond, Grace S., *Mrs. Red Pepper* (Doubleday, Page and Co., N.Y., 1913, with an ed. by A. L. Burt & Co. this same year which had): d/w, frontis., and 3 illus.

Rinehart, Mary Roberts, *Lost Ecstasy* (George H. Doran Co., N.Y., 1927): Dykes, 194, shows as "illus. by K," but there are no illus. in the copy inscribed to Koerner by the author.

Sadlier, Anna Theresa, *Gerald Delacey's Daughter* (Kennedy & Co., N.Y., 1916): frontis. in color, original painting for this book.

Scoggins, C. E., *The Proud Old Name* (Bobbs-Merrill, Indianapolis, 1925): d/w(?), frontis.

———, *Pampa Joe* (Appleton-Century, N.Y., 1936): d/w.

Stevenson, Burton E., *A King in Babylon* (Small, Maynard & Co., N.Y., 1917): d/w, frontis. in color, and 4 illus.

Stringer, Arthur, *The Prairie Child* (Bobbs-Merrill, Indianapolis, 1922): d/w, original painting for this use.

———, *A Lady Quite Lost*, serialized as "The Squaw Woman" (Bobbs-Merrill, Indianapolis, 1931): d/w.

Turner, George Kibbe, *The Last Christian* (Hearst's International Library Co., N.Y., 1914): frontis., in color, original painting for this use.

Van Schaick, George, *The Peace of Roaring River*, serialized as "The White Threshold" (Small, Maynard & Co., N.Y., 1918): d/w(?), frontis., and 3 illus.

White, Stewart Edward, *The Leopard Woman* (Doubleday, Page, Garden City, N.Y., 1916): original d/w, frontis., and 7 illus.

———, *Ranchero* (Doubleday, Doran, Garden City, N.Y., 1933): d/w, title-page illus., back end-sheets.

Williams, Ben Ames, *The Silver Forest* (Dutton, N.Y., 1926): d/w.

Appendix B

PRODUCTIVITY AND INCOME OF W.H.D. KOERNER, 1905-1935

Year	Harper's		Good House-keeping		Ladies Home Journal		McCall's		Woman's Home Companion		Pictorial Review		American		Collier's		Cosmo-politan	
1905–1911 est.	19	67			2	4												
1912	9	37			6	18												
1913	10	46	2	7	2	4			1	1								
1914	3	15	2	7											4	8		
1915	3	6	3	11														
1916	7	13	7	20	1	2												
1917	8	15			2	4									5	15		
1918	8	16							3	13					1	3		
1919	3	6			4	14			4	8			2	4			1	3
1920	2	4			6	16	1	3	3	6							3	11
1921									2	5							7	24
1922	2	4							3	10			1	2			1	4
1923	3	5					4	8	1	2	3	8	3	6	3	8		
1924							9	18	2	2	1	2	1	2	2	6		
1925	1	2							1	2	4	15						
1926													4	10				
1927													8	18				
1928													10	24				
1929													10	37				
1930													1	2				
1931																		
1932																		
1933																		
1934																		
1935																		
Unallocated Misc.																		
TOTAL	78	236	14	45	23	62	14	29	20	49	8	25	40	105	15	40	12	42

THE FIRST COLUMN of figures under each magazine represents the number of individual stories, serial installments, or articles he illustrated during the year. The second column represents the total number of illustrations for such appearances. Both sets of figures are for the year in which Koerner produced the illustrations and was paid for them. No attempt has been made to compute the number of illustrations he produced during his tenure as art editor of *Pilgrim*. The number of illustrations does not include the many "spots" he contributed to stories and serials for which he made no charge.

McClure's		Metro-politan		Red Book		Saturday Evening Post		Country Gentleman		Misc.		Total Appearances	Total Illustrations	Income
				32	115	1	3					54	189	(Unknown)
				9	44	9	41					33	140	$ 5,020.00
				22	74			1	3			38	135	5,159.00
				1	5	20	73			1	7	31	115	4,555.00
						20	72			1	3	27	92	4,250.00
						19	73					34	108	5,663.00
6	19					7	26	5	15	6	10	39	104	6,725.00
7	10	8	31	6	24	9	27	13	17			55	141	8,950.00
3	3	6	19	5	19	12	35	7	14			47	125	10,325.00
				2	6	20	58					37	104	11,500.00
		1	3	4	12	24	55	1	2			39	101	11,455.00
				1	3	28	80					36	103	13,975.00
				1	2	17	51					35	90	12,275.00
				1	3	18	39					34	72	11,250.00
						23	50					29	69	14,700.00
						27	60					31	70	19,300.00
						19	40					27	58	17,750.00
						23	50					33	74	26,650.00
						26	53					36	90	30,300.00
						36	75					37	77	30,700.00
						35	76					35	76	23,050.00
						30	62					30	62	31,400.00
						18	39					18	39	11,975.00
						26	54					26	54	16,260.00
						22	45					22	45	14,250.00
										21	68	21	68	(incl. in above)
16	32	15	53	62	233	511	1311	27	51	29	88	884	2401	$347,437.00

Appendix C

THE MOTT LIST OF ILLUSTRATORS

| | The Taste-makers | | | The Women's Field | | | |
Artist	Century	Harper's	Scribner's	Good House-keeping	Ladies Home Journal	McCall's	Woman's Home Companion
Arthurs, S. M.	1	1 3	1		2		
Benda, W. T.	1		1	3	2 3	2 3	
Bransom, Paul	1			3			
Christy, H. C.	1	1 2		2	1		
Fischer, A. O.		1 2	2		2	2	
Fisher, Harrison	1		1	2 3	1 2		
Flagg, James M.		1 2	1	2 3		2 3	1 2 3
Frost, A. B.	1	1	1		1 2		
Gibson, Charles D.		1		3	1		2
Greene, Eliz. S.	1	1 2 3					
Hambidge, Jay	1	1 2	1		2		
Held, John, Jr.		3					
Herford, Oliver	1		1		3	2	
Kemble, E. W.	1	1 2		2	2		
Leyendecker, J. C.	1		1				
McCutcheon, John T.							
McMein, Neysa					3	2 3 4	
Newell, Peter		1 2 3		1 2	1 2	2	
O'Neill, Rose		1	1	1 2 3	1 3		2 3
Parrish, Maxfield	1		1		1 2		
Preston, May W.	1	1 2	1	1	1	2	2 3
Pyle, Howard (d. 1911)	1	1 2	1		1		
Remington, Frederic (d. 1909)	1 2	1	1				
Rockwell, Norman					3		
Stephens, Alice B.		1 2			1 2 3		2
Smith, Jessie W.	1	1	1	2 3	1 2		
Williams, Gluyas					2 3		
Wyeth, N. C.	1 2	1 2	1 2 3	3	1 3	1 4	3 4
Koerner, W.H.D.		1 2 3	2	2	1 2	2 3	2 3

In his *History of American Magazines,* Frank Luther Mott mentioned many illustrators *en passant.* As is unavoidable in any such monumental undertaking, a listing of those he mentioned is as notable for its omissions as for its inclusions. Koerner is shown in the listing below to enable a comparison of his place in the illustrators' pantheon with those Mott mentioned. Each illustrator's record of appearances was derived from the magazine files consulted in preparation of this volume. The numerals used indicate the decade in which their work appeared:

1 = 1901–1910
2 = 1911–1920
3 = 1921–1930
4 = 1931–1935

Appearances in *American* include those in *Frank Leslie's Popular Monthly* through October, 1906, and appearances in both *Harper's Monthly* and *Weekly* have been included under the heading of *Harper's.*

Mass-Circulation "Slicks"

Delineator	American	Collier's	Cosmopolitan	Everybody's	Hearst's Intern'tl.	McClure's	Metropolitan	Munsey's	Red Book	Saturday Evening Post
	1 2	1 2			2				2	1 2
2 3	1 2 3	1 2 3 4	3	1 2	2	1 2	2	1	2 3	2 4
3			2 4	2	2					1 2 4
1		1	1 2 3 4		2	1			3	
	2 3	2	2	2	2	2		2		1 2 3 4
	1	1	1 2 3 4	1	2	1	1			1 2
3	1 2 3	1 2 3 4	1 2 3 4	1 2	2	2			2 3	1 2
	2 3	1 2 3		1		1	1			1
	2	1 2	1 2 3		2	1				
										1
	1 2	1 2		1 2		1 2	1		1 2	1 2
		3 4	3 4			3			3	
	2	1 2	1 4	1		1 2				1
	1 2	1 2 3	1 2	1	2				1 3	1
1		1 2		1						1 2 3 4
	1 2	1 2	2 3	2	2	1				1 2
	2	3				2				2 3
2	1 2	1 2	1	1 2		1				1 2
	1 2		1 3			1 2				
		1 2 3	1	1		1 2				
	1 2	1 2	1	1 2		1	1			1 2 3 4
		1	1			1 2	1 2			
		1 2 4	1	1		1				1
	2 3									2 3 4
2	1	1 2	1			1				1
	1	1 2				1 2				
		2 3 4	3 4							
	1 2	1 2		2	2	1 2	1	1		1 2
	2 3	2 3	2 3		2 3	1 2	2 3		1 2 3	1 2 3 4

BIBLIOGRAPHY

As a general comment, it seems advisable to note that only those sources actually used are included in this bibliography. I see no merit in padding it simply to show my familiarity with the card catalogs of various repositories.

MANUSCRIPT AND PRIVATE COLLECTIONS

Koerner Papers. In custody of Mrs. F. L. (Ruth Koerner) Oliver, Santa Barbara, California. Contains family memorabilia, the artist's surviving correspondence, "Record of Work Produced," sketch books, preliminary compositions, hundreds of photographs, and most of his surviving original paintings and other illustrations. His widow's several drafts of her unpublished narrative of their life, together with materials pertaining to her family, are among these papers. The collection has been enhanced over the past dozen years by the correspondence initiated by Mrs. Oliver and by her patient accumulation of a virtually complete file of the magazines and books in which her father's work appeared.

Harrison Collection. A private collection of Western Americana maintained by Michael Harrison, Fair Oaks, California. Its cross-indexed files provided leads to materials pertaining to the artists and illustrators of the West.

UNPUBLISHED MATERIAL

Koerner, W.H.D., Jr. Typescript of address before the Potomac Corral of The Westerners, Cosmos Club, Washington, D.C., 5/20/1971.

Schwartz, Diane Koerner. Typescript analysis of her grandfather's use of color, 1972.

Shaul, Lowana Jean. "Treatment of the West in Selected Magazine Fiction, 1870–1900. An Annotated Bibliography." Unpublished M.A. thesis, University of Wyoming, 1954.

Stuart, Leland E. "Men and Cattle on the Northern Plains, 1860–1887." Unpublished doctoral dissertation, University of Oregon, 1971.

Interviews and Letters

Ayres, John O., California State University, Chico. Conversations, 1966–75.

Bodrero, James Spalding. Interview, San Francisco, 6/1/1970; letter, 1/26/1971.

Campbell, Lawrence, New York. Letters, 1970–74, concerning the Art Students League.

Clark, John R., M.D. Interview, Chico, California, 7/11/1975.

Coats, William H., M.D. Interview, Chico, California, 7/11/1975.

Coller, Ross H. Letters, 1970–71, concerning Koerner's Battle Creek years and *The Pilgrim*.

Dasburgh, Andrew, Taos, New Mexico. Telephone interview 5/7/1970, about his contact with Koerner at the Art Students League.

Dentzel, Carl. Interview, Southwest Museum, Los Angeles, 3/25/1970.

Ericson, Oscar Helmer. Interviews at his studio, Santa Barbara, California, 1970, 1972.

Evarts, Hal G., Jr. Interview at his home, La Jolla, California, 3/14/1970.

Griffen, Robert, Reno, Nevada. Letters concerning western story writers, 1970–74.

Haines, Francis D., Sun City, Arizona. Letter, 9/1/1972.

Hansen, A. A., Clinton, Iowa. Letters, 1970–71.

Harrison, Michael, Fair Oaks, California. Letters and conversations, 1970–75.

Hayne, F. Bourn, St. Helena, California. Letter, 6/

16/1971.

Hoffman, Father Emmett, Ashland, Montana. Telephone interviews with the staff of St. Labre Indian School, 6/28/1975; 7/7/1975.

Hughes, Rupert. Interview at his home, Los Angeles, 1/1953.

Kennedy, Lawton, San Francisco. Letter, 9/7/1972.

Kidd, ?.?., New York. Letter, 6/15/1970.

Koerner, W.H.D., Jr., Pittsburgh. Telephone conversation, 7/5/1975.

Krebs, Ward C., San Francisco. Letter, 8/22/1974, supplying formula for converting Koerner's income into 1974 equivalencies.

McCoy, Tim, Nogales, Arizona. Letter, 8/15/1975.

Moyers, William, Albuquerque, New Mexico. Letter, 3/27/1973.

Oliver, Ruth Koerner, Santa Barbara, California. Notes from conversations, 1966–75; also numerous letters.

Olker, Louis C., M.D. Interview, Chico, California, 7/11/1975.

Orkin, Frances L., New York City. Letters, 1974–75, transmitting data from the New York Public Library.

Pike, Donald G., Chico, California. Conversations, 1974–75, concerning the lay of the land between Wyoming's Sunlight Basin, Red Lodge, Montana, and Cooke City.

Ryan, Harold W., Takoma Park, Maryland. Letters, 1969–74, transmitting data from the Library of Congress.

Stick, David, Kitty Hawk, North Carolina. Letters, 6/24/1970, 9/?/1972.

Wheelwright, Mrs. M. C., Des Moines, Iowa. Letters, 1972, transmitting data on Clinton, Iowa.

Wylder, Delbert E., Marshall, Minnesota. Letter, 5/8/1970, anent Emerson Hough.

BOOKS, ARTICLES, AND
OTHER PRINTED MATERIALS

Anon. *Stanley Arthurs.* Wilmington, Del., The Wilmington Society of The Fine Arts, 1974.

———. *Years of Art, The Story of the Art Students League of New York.* Robert M. McBride & Co., 1940.

———. *Interlaken 50th Anniversary.* n.p., 1972.

———. *Norman Rockwell, Illustrator* (3rd. ed.). New York, Watson-Guptill Pubiications, 1970.

Abbott, Charles D. *Howard Pyle, A Chronicle.* New York and London, Harper and Brothers, 1925.

Abbott, Willis John. *Watching the World Go By.* Boston, Little, Brown & Co., 1933.

Allen, Douglas and Douglas Allen, Jr. *N. C. Wyeth.* New York, Crown Publishers, Inc., 1972.

Amaral, Anthony. *Will James, The Gilt-Edged Cowboy.* Los Angeles, Westernlore Press, 1967.

Apgar, John F., Jr. *Frank E. Schoonover, Painter-Illustrator: A Bibliography.* Morristown, N.J., 1969.

Ayer, N. W. & Sons. *Directory, Newspapers and Periodicals.* Philadelphia, various years.

Bigelow, Frederick S. *A Short History of the Saturday Evening Post.* Philadelphia, The Curtis Publishing Co., 1927.

Bland, David. *A History of Book Illustration.* Berkeley, University of California Press, 1969.

Boatright, Mody C. "The Formula in Cowboy Fiction and Drama," *Western Folklore,* 4/1969.

———. *Southwest Review,* Summer, 1951.

Bolton, Theodore. *American Book Illustrators.* New York, R.R. Bowker Co., 1938.

Boswell, Peyton. Obituary of Koerner, *Art Digest,* 9/1939.

Carr, Mary Jane. *Children of the Covered Wagon.* New York, Thos. Y. Crowell Co., 1934.

Culmsee, Carlton F. *Malign Nature and the Frontier.* Logan, Utah State University Press, 1959.

Curtis Publishing Co. "Who's Who and Why," *Saturday Evening Post,* 8/22/1925.

———. *Curtis Facts and Figures.* n.d. (c. 1927).

Davidson, Harold G. *Edward Borein: Cowboy Artist.* Garden City, Doubleday & Co., 1974.

Dresden, Donald. *The Marquis de Morès, Emperor of the Badlands.* Norman, University of Oklahoma Press, 1970.

Duggar, Ben. Untitled editorial comments, *Professional Art Magazine,* 2/1940.

Dykes, Jeff C. *Fifty Great Western Illustrators, A Bibliographic Checklist.* Flagstaff, Ariz., The Northland Press, 1975.

Easton, Robert. *Max Brand: The Big "Westerner."* Norman, University of Oklahoma Press, 1970.

Engen, Orrin A. *Writer of the Plains . . . B. M. Bower.* Culver City, The Pontine Press, 1973.

Etulain, Richard. "Origins of the Western," *Journal of Popular Culture,* Spring, 1972.

Everson, William K. *A Pictorial History of the Western Film.* New York, The Citadel Press, 1969.

Fenin, George F. and W. K. Everson. *The Western, from Silents to Cinerama.* New York, Bonanza Books, 1962.

Folsom, James K. *The American Western Novel.* New Haven, College and University Press Services Inc., 1966.

Frantz, Joe B. and Julian E. Choate. *The American Cowboy, The Myth and the Reality.* Norman, University of Oklahoma Press, 1955.

Furnas, J. C. *The Americans: A Social History of the United States 1587–1914.* New York, G. P. Putnam's Sons, 1969.

Galvin, John, et al. *The Etchings of Edward Borein,*

A Catalog of his Work. San Francisco, John Howell —Books, 1971.

Goulden, Joseph C. *The Curtis Caper*. New York, G. P. Putnam's Sons, c. 1965.

Goulart, Ron. *Cheap Thrills: The . . . History of Pulp Fiction*. New Rochelle, Arlington House, 1972.

Griffith, Richard and Arthur Mayer. *The Movies*. New York, Simon & Schuster, 1957.

Gruber, Frank. *Zane Grey*. Cleveland, World Publishers, 1970.

Hackett, Alice Payne. *Seventy Years of Best Sellers*. New York, R. R. Bowker, Co., 1967.

Haley, J. Evetts. *Life on the Texas Range*. Austin, University of Texas Press, 1952.

Hamilton, Sinclair. "Early American Illustrating," *Princeton University Library Chronicle*, 4/1945.

Hansen, Virginia and Al Funderbunk. *The Fabulous Past of Cooke City*. Billings, Mont., 1962.

Hart, Irving Harlow. "The Most Popular Authors of Fiction Between 1900 and 1925," *The Publisher's Weekly*, 1925, pp. 619–22.

———. "The Most Popular Authors of Fiction in the Post-War Period, 1919–1926," *The Publisher's Weekly*, 1925, pp. 1045–53.

Henderson, Harry B. III. *Versions of the Past: The Historical Imagination in American Fiction*. New York, Oxford University Press, 1974.

Hewes, Andrew M. *Wright Brothers National Memorial, An Administrative History*. Washington, National Park Service, 1967.

Holden, William C. *The Espuela Land & Cattle Company*. Austin, University of Texas Press, 1970.

Humphries, Rolfe and John Humphries (eds.) *Wolfville Yarns of Alfred Henry Lewis*. Kent State University Press, 1968.

Hutchinson, William H. "The 'Western' Story as Literature," *Western Humanities Review*, 1/1949.

———. "Virgins, Villains, and Varmints," *Huntington Library Quarterly*, 8/1953.

———. *A Bar Cross Man: The Life . . . of Eugene Manlove Rhodes*. Norman, University of Oklahoma Press, 1956.

———. *A Bar Cross Liar: A Bibliography of Eugene Manlove Rhodes . . .* Stillwater, Okla., The Redlands Press, 1958.

———. *The Rhodes Reader* (ed.). Norman, University of Oklahoma Press, rev. ed. 1975.

———. "The Mythic West of W.H.D. Koerner," *The American West*, Summer, 1967.

———. "Illustrator, Iconographer, and More" in *W. H.D. Koerner*. Los Angeles, Los Angeles County Museum of History, 1968.

———. "Illustrating the Western Myth" in *W.H.D. Koerner*. Fort Worth, Texas, Amon Carter Museum of Western Art, 1969.

———. "Packaging the Old West in Serial Form,"

Westways, 2/1973.

———. "The Cowboy in Literature." Cassette Lecture. Deland, Fla., Everett/Edwards, Inc., 1974.

Jackson, Carlton. *Zane Grey*. New York, Twayne Publishers, Inc., 1973.

Johnston, William A. "The Box Office Verdict," *Saturday Evening Post*, 11/10/1923.

Jones, Margaret Ann. "Cowboys and Ranching in Magazine Fiction, 1901–1910" in *Studies in Literature of the West*. Laramie, University of Wyoming Publications, 7/1956.

Koerner, Lillian Lusk. "W.H.D. Koerner," *Curtis Folks*, 1/1927.

Koerner, W.H.D. "Aim High—Work Hard—Stick To It," *Our Boys*, 2/1926.

Lehmann-Haupt, Hellmut. *The Book in America*. New York, R. R. Bowker Co., 1951.

Linn, James Weber. *James Keely: Newspaperman*. Indianapolis, Bobbs-Merrill Co., 1937.

Mahony, Bertha E., et al. (compilers). *Illustrators of Children's Books, 1744–1945*. Boston, The Horn Book, Inc., 1947.

Marovitz, Sanford E. "Romance or Realism? Western Periodical Literature: 1893–1902," *Western American Literature*, 5/1975.

McCracken, Harold. *The Frank Tenney Johnson Book*. Garden City, Doubleday & Co., 1974.

Morrow, Mable. *Indian Rawhide, An American Folk Art*. Norman, University of Oklahoma Press, 1975.

Mott, Frank Luther. *Golden Multitudes*. New York, Macmillan Co., 1947.

———. *American Journalism, A History: 1690–1960* (3rd. ed.). New York, Macmillan Co., 1962.

———. *A History of American Magazines*. Cambridge, Harvard University Press, 1966–68.

Nye, Russell. *The Unembarrassed Muse: The Popular Arts in America*. New York, The Dial Press, 1970.

Olson, Kenneth E. *Typography and Mechanics of the Newspaper*. New York, D. Appleton & Co., 1930.

Pattee, Fred Lewis. *The New American Literature, 1890–1930*. New York, Century Co., 1930.

Paxson, F. L. *When the West is Gone*. New York, 1930.

Pearson, Edmund Lester. *Books in Black or Red*. New York, Macmillan Co., 1923.

Pennell, Joseph. *The Graphic Arts*. Chicago, Chicago Art Institute, 1921.

Pitz, Henry C. *The Brandywine Tradition*. Boston, Houghton Mifflin Co., 1969.

Powell, Lawrence Clark. *Southwest Classics*. Los Angeles, Ward Ritchie Press, 1974.

Reed, Walt (compiler and ed.). *The Illustrator in America: 1900–1960s*. New York, Reinhold Publishing Corp., 1966.

Renner, Frederic G. *Charles M. Russell . . . A Descriptive Catalog.* Fort Worth, Amon Carter Museum of Western Art, 1966.

Reynolds, Quentin. *The Fiction Factory.* New York, Random House, Inc., 1955.

Rossi, Paul and David C. Hunt. *The Art of the Old West.* New York, Alfred A. Knopf, 1971.

Russell, Don. *The Lives and Legends of Buffalo Bill.* Norman, University of Oklahoma Press, 1960.

Schein, Harry. "The Olympian Cowboy," *The American Scholar,* Summer, 1955.

Schultz, James Willard. *Running Eagle.* Boston, Houghton Mifflin Co., 1919.

Smith, Henry Nash. *Virgin Land.* Cambridge, Harvard University Press, 1950.

Stick, Frank. *The Call of the Surf.* New York, Doubleday, Page & Co., 1920.

Tebbell, John W. *George Horace Lorimer and the Saturday Evening Post.* New York, Doubleday and Co., 1948.

Virgines, George E. "Colonel Tim McCoy—Westerner All-Star" in *The Westerners Brand Book.* Chicago, January, 1973.

Vorpahl, Ben M. *My Dear Wister—The Frederic Remington–Owen Wister Letters.* Palo Alto, American West Publishing Co., 1972.

Webb, Walter P. *The Great Plains.* Boston, Houghton Mifflin Co., 1936.

Wyeth, Newell Convers. *The Wyeths* (ed. Betsy James Wyeth). Boston, Gambit, 1971.

Wylder, Delbert E. "The Popular Western." Cassette lecture. Deland, Fla., Everett/Edwards, Inc., 1974.

NEWSPAPERS

New York *Herald:* 3/17/1923; 3/25/1923.
New York *Times:* 3/17/1923; 3/25/1923.
New York *Tribune:* 3/17/1923.

MAGAZINES: THE TASTE-MAKERS

Atlantic (no illustrations):
    1/1900–12/1910, 120 issues, *passim*
Century:
    11/1899–4/1911, 138 issues, *passim*
Harper's New Monthly:
    12/1899–5/1911, 126 issues
Harper's Weekly:
    2/26/1910–2/22/1913, 13 issues, *passim*
Lippincott's (*McBrides* as of 12/1914; no illustrations):
    1/1900–4/1916, 162 issues, *passim*
Scribner's:
    1/1900–12/1910, 132 issues

MAGAZINES: THE WOMEN'S FIELD

Good Housekeeping:
    1/1901–2/1905, 14 issues, *passim*
    3/1911–3/1917, 10 issues, *passim*
    2/1920–12/1930, 120 issues, *passim*
Ladies Home Journal:
    1/1900–12/1907, 84 issues, *passim*
    1/1910–12/1914, 57 issues, *passim*
    1/1916–12/1929, 116 issues, *passim*
McCall's:
    5/1904–11/1917, 24 issues, *passim*
    2/1924–9/1924, 5 issues, *passim*
    3/1931–11/1931, 4 issues, *passim*
Pictorial Review:
    2/1924–11/1925, 12 issues, *passim*
Woman's Home Companion:
    1/1903–12/1919, 16 issues, *passim*
    1/1924–12/1929, 72 issues, *passim*
Delineator:
    10/1902; 12/1916–12/1918, 25 issues
    1/1925–12/1926, 24 issues, *passim*

MAGAZINES: THE MASS-CIRCULATION "SLICKS"

American (*Frank Leslie's Popular Monthly* until 11/1906):
    11/1901–4/1905, 42 issues
    11/1906–4/1911, 54 issues
    1/1912–12/1920, 108 issues
Collier's:
    1/6/1900–9/26/1903, 188 issues, *passim*
    1/6/1906–12/26/1908, 142 issues, *passim*
    1/1/1910–12/28/1912, 156 issues, *passim*
    3/22/1913–9/8/1917, 182 issues, *passim*
    3/16/1918–12/25/1920, 83 issues, *passim*
    1/7/1922–12/30/1922, 43 issues, *passim*
    1/5/1924–12/27/1924, 52 issues
    1/2/1926–12/25/1926, 52 issues
    1/5/1929–12/28/1929, 52 issues
    1/2/1932–12/31/1932, 53 issues
    1/6/1934–12/29/1934, 52 issues
Cosmopolitan:
    5/1900–5/1911, 102 issues, *passim*
    12/1912–5/1918, 18 issues, *passim*
    6/1919–8/1930, 67 issues, *passim*
    11/1931–12/1934, 30 issues, *passim*
Everybody's:
    1/1900–12/1919, 179 issues, *passim*
    1/1920–12/1927, 60 issues, *passim*
Hearst's International:
    4/1912–12/1918, 77 issues, *passim*
Liberty:
    5/10/1924–5/2/1925, 35 issues, *passim*

McClure's:
    11/1900–4/1910, 82 issues, *passim*
    11/1910–4/1912, 18 issues, *passim*
    12/1912–8/1914, 6 issues, *passim*
    5/1917–12/1917, 6 issues, *passim*
    1/1919, 1 issue
Metropolitan:
    8/1900–8/1903, 13 issues, *passim*
    3/1906–10/1919, 23 issues, *passim*
    1/1922–6/1922, 6 issues
Munsey's:
    1/1900–11/1928, 199 issues, *passim*
Red Book:
    5/1903–4/1907, 16 issues, *passim*
    1/1909–12/1909, 12 issues
    2/1910–1/1930, 83 issues, *passim*
Saturday Evening Post:
    1/5/1901–12/31/1910, 440 issues, *passim*
    4/8/1911–10/27/1917, 144 issues, *passim*
    1/5/1918–10/28/1922, 241 issues, *passim*
    1/6/1923–10/31/1925, 121 issues, *passim*

    1/2/1926–10/27/1928, 115 issues, *passim*
    1/5/1929–11/30/1935, 236 issues, *passim*

MAGAZINES: MISCELLANEOUS

Country Gentleman:
    1/27/1917–12/27/1919, 145 issues, *passim*
Pilgrim:
    8/1903–2/1906, 18 issues, *passim*
Popular:
    1903–1912, twenty-two volumes checked for cover illustrators.
Blue Book, Hampton's, Pearson's:
    Scattered issues of each, 1901–1915.
Sunset:
    Little use was made of this magazine which used illustrators such as Maynard Dixon and Edward Borein, because its circulation was small and two-thirds of it was west of the Rockies, which is not where either popular or critical acclaim was earned during Koerner's lifetime.

INDEX

For Koerner-illustrated authors, stories, and books not covered in the text (and thus not in the index), see Appendix A, which contains a complete listing.